PRAISE FOR *THE RELENTLESS COURAGE OF A SCARED CHILD*

"Tana's book is a wonderful testament to the resilience of the human mind—and to how powerful hope and love can be."

—DR. CAROLINE LEAF, COMMUNICATION PATHOLOGIST AND NEUROSCIENTIST, NEW YORK TIMES BESTSELLING AUTHOR

"Tana Amen reveals how to manifest the empowering and life-sustaining gifts that the darkness can reveal."

—DAVID PERLMUTTER, MD, NEW YORK TIMES BESTSELLING AUTHOR OF GRAIN BRAIN AND BRAIN WASH

"By being so fearless in confronting her uncomfortable past, Tana Amen lets the rest of us know it's okay to be vulnerable."

—MARK HYMAN, MD, NEW YORK TIMES BESTSELLING AUTHOR OF FOOD FIX

"Tana Amen is living proof that no matter where you come from or how bad you've had it, you can rewrite your story with a new ending."

—DAVE ASPREY, FOUNDER OF BULLETPROOF COFFEE, NEW YORK TIMES BESTSELLING AUTHOR

"Tana's story will give you hope and courage to get unstuck from your past, learn to love yourself, and inspire you on your healing journey."

—SHARON MAY, PHD, FOUNDER AND PRESIDENT OF SAFE HAVEN RELATIONSHIP CENTER

the

RELENTLESS
COURAGE

of a

SCARED
CHILD

the

RELENTLESS
COURAGE

of a

SCARED
CHILD

HOW PERSISTENCE, GRIT, AND FAITH
CREATED A RELUCTANT HEALER

TANA AMEN

WITH BOB WELCH

NELSON
BOOKS

An Imprint of Thomas Nelson

Published in Nashville, Tennessee, by Nelson Books, an imprint of Thomas Nelson. Nelson Books and Thomas Nelson are registered trademarks of HarperCollins Christian Publishing, Inc.

Published in association with the literary agency of WordServe Literary Group, Ltd, www.wordserveliterary.com.

Thomas Nelson titles may be purchased in bulk for educational, business, fundraising, or sales promotional use. For information, please e-mail SpecialMarkets@ThomasNelson. com.

Any internet addresses, phone numbers, or company or product information printed in this book are offered as a resource and are not intended in any way to be or to imply an endorsement by Thomas Nelson, nor does Thomas Nelson vouch for the existence, content, or services of these sites, phone numbers, companies, or products beyond the life of this book.

ISBN 978-1-4002-2078-6 (audiobook)
ISBN 978-1-4002-2077-9 (eBook)
ISBN 978-1-4002-2076-2 (HC)

Library of Congress Control Number: 2020945132

Printed in the United States of America

21 22 23 24 25 LSC 10 9 8 7 6 5 4 3 2 1

For Chloe, Alize, and Amelie—the next generation.

CONTENTS

AUTHOR'S NOTE

This is not a religious book. It is a memoir. Yet my spiritual beliefs are a vital part of my story. For my readers who are Christian, parts of my story may sound critical, harsh, or even vulgar as I describe some of the more difficult parts of my journey. For this I apologize in advance. I've chosen not to omit some of the language, at least when I felt it was necessary to paint the picture of the extreme environment it was. Likewise, I've refrained from sharing some of the most troubling details where it wasn't helpful to the story or the people involved. For readers who find some content offensive or disturbing, I assure you, I have saved you from many of the harshest and most explicit details that were part of my life.

Amid our life struggles, the painful and the spiritual must coexist. If nothing else, I want my story to reflect the real me. That, I believe, is the least a reader deserves: the truth. In order to do that, I've chosen only those stories most relevant to my personal journey of healing from trauma, learning forgiveness, and overcoming my fear of forming relationships with certain family members. My greatest desire in telling these stories is to reach out to those who may be struggling to strengthen their faith and, despite the trauma and sorrow they may have endured, to build a bridge of hope.

In writing this book, I've relied mainly on my memory. To confirm certain details, especially of early years, I've involved family members and others. Some of the names and identifying details have been changed for the protection and anonymity of those involved.

CHAPTER 1

GOD PICKED THE WRONG PERSON

*If you win an argument with God, you lose. If
you lose an argument with God, you win.*

—MARK BATTERSON

Our tastes of heaven sometimes require a trip to hell—preferably
roundtrip. This wouldn't be the first time I'd been down this road, but
this particular journey would forever change me. Though some people lose
baggage while traveling, on this day, I would *find* it—baggage I didn't even
know I had.

On a clear afternoon in May, I drove along the Pacific Coast Highway
toward my destination. Sailboats rocked on the crystal-blue Pacific Ocean
glimpsed beyond palms that swayed to their own rhythm. But the beauty
around me only highlighted my growing distance from the safety of my
home—as if I wasn't already acutely aware of the enormous abyss between
me and the personal nightmare I was about to face.

The task? Speak to a couple hundred junkies at one of the largest inpatient chemical-addiction recovery centers in the country.

Bad fit, me and them. Not that I didn't have plenty of experience dealing with addicts. They had been prevalent in my past, and I avoided them in kind of the same way that cowboys avoid rattlesnakes. As far as I was concerned, you couldn't tame them, you couldn't trust them, and you'd better keep your distance if you didn't want to get bitten.

Each mile I drove lessened the safe space between my hard-won heaven and their self-inflicted hell. I could feel the demons closing in, the dream killers I'd banished as vigilantly as I'd banished some family members who threatened the serenity of the life I'd finally created. The safety I cherished. The home I would give my life to protect.

Stoplight after stoplight, the questions hounded me like an irritating backseat driver. Why had I agreed to do something that caused me to feel such anxiety and resentment? As my humanity grated against my faith, I wondered, *Will I still get brownie points in heaven if I'm this bitter about helping?*

I'd said yes to this speaking engagement because of Leslie. She was the director of this particular facility, a woman who, velvet hammer in hand, managed the nearly two hundred addicts there. Nearly all had criminal backgrounds. Most had been court-ordered to be there. All were high-risk "projects." And she loved every one of them—in a way I did not. *Could* not.

Leslie and I had met through my husband, Dr. Daniel Amen, a psychiatrist specializing in brain health. She had become fascinated by Daniel's research showing that good nutrition improves brain function and that a better brain leads to a better life. Even more enlightening to her was his research about how poor nutrition could lead to having a smaller brain and typically lower quality of life.

Her interest in Daniel's work had led her to me, because I had applied my nursing training and research in metabolic medicine and nutrition to help create the nutrition and lifestyle protocols for the patients we saw at Amen

Clinics. Because of my passion for helping others heal through food, I also taught twelve-week courses based on my book, *The Omni Diet*, that emphasized the power of food in decreasing inflammation, reversing illness and aging, and increasing focus and energy. Leslie had completed one of those courses and told me it changed her life. She'd lost nearly fifty pounds, her skin had cleared, her hot flashes had stopped, and her brain fog had cleared. She'd learned the impact of food on our bodies—that it could be either medicine or poison—and come to the startling realization that the food the rehab center served was inadvertently feeding the residents' illnesses. The toxic standard American diet—high sugar, low fiber, full of processed, genetically modified foodlike substances that lacked micronutrients—was making it harder for them to overcome their addictions and learn how to make good decisions.

Originally Leslie asked Daniel and me to help educate the residents and revamp the menu at the facility. Daniel agreed to help with the former, and I agreed to help with the latter. That was an easy yes for me. I would receive the reward of helping without the risk of dealing with addicts, a task Daniel was much better suited for.

But then Leslie wanted more, and when it came to these residents she loved, she could be quite persuasive. "Tana," she asked during one of my visits, "I'd really like you to come and help them personally with their nutrition, the way you helped me." Then she invited me to "get to know them" by attending a graduation ceremony that marked a major achievement for the residents who had completed the intensive program.

By then, I had come to appreciate the way the program worked. For twelve to twenty-four months, the residents lived in a cavernous industrial building transformed into a comfortable residence. The sofas, ping-pong tables, and donated art created an oddly pleasant ambience. They even had a quaint little chapel. But although it involved an all-expense-paid stay, the program was no vacation. It was purposeful. With all their physical needs met, the residents could focus on healing through therapy, acquiring job skills, and learning to live without relying on substances.

The nurse in me appreciated the structure, the mission, and even the stories of triumph. Another part of me—a wounded, cynical part, sneered,

What's the point? Most of them will be back within the year. Yet my perfect "why, of course" smile masked my inward groan as I thought, *I agreed to help with the menu, not the people.* But I agreed to go to the graduation if my husband would accompany me.

When Daniel and I arrived at the event, I immediately noticed the meticulous planning that had gone into it. The chef had prepared a delicious spread using recipes from my cookbooks, and the common room had been converted into a banquet hall complete with a dais and festive decorations. There was a buzz in the air as the graduates waited their turn to speak.

When the time for the ceremony arrived, I sat next to Daniel and listened, searching my heart for a thread of empathy for their pain. And I almost found it—until, that is, I could no longer ignore their repeated refrain about how drugs had ruined their lives and the lives of those they loved. Their stories brought back painful memories from my own past. (Exit empathy, enter judgment.) I *wanted* to be encouraged by their successes, but I felt myself numbing to what I perceived as an endless loop of stupidity, entitlement, and total disregard for others. I tried to laugh at the humorous comments when everyone else did, but my laughter felt hollow and disingenuous. None of it was remotely funny to me. These people weren't discussing harmless traffic violations; some had done time for burglary, rape, even manslaughter.

I thought, *What is wrong with you? Why can't you just follow the rules put in place to keep everyone safe, the same rules the rest of us follow?*

I hated my judgmental musings even as I mentally defended them with indignation. My heart pounded. Instinctively I clutched my purse closer and began scanning the room. I was forty-three years old, a black belt in both Taekwondo and Kenpo Karate, and a trauma-unit nurse. I'd overcome difficult life experiences in excess. When I spent time "at the range," I was *not* hitting golf balls.

In other words, I liked to believe I was a card-carrying bada**. I was also a big fan of order and predictability, and I liked the concept of taking responsibility. So why were fear, apprehension, and resentment the only noticeable reactions I could muster in this moment?

By the time the evening ended, I was nearly overcome with emotion. But only when Daniel and I were safely ensconced in our car did I let it out. I'm not a crier by nature, so the sight of my mascara-stained tears startled him.

"Did something happen?" he asked with his usual gentle concern.

"I don't think I can come back here." My voice quivered. "I can't do this."

"Why not?"

The ugly honesty spilled out. "I don't have the compassion I need to help these people, Daniel. I think most of them are full of crap and only here because they have to be. I hate drugs, and I don't much like the people who use them. They scare me. How can I help someone I don't feel compassion for?"

My words hung in the silence of the car like a pall.

"God picked the wrong person this time," I muttered dejectedly.

With a smile I think only husbands and psychiatrists can produce, a smile that was as irritating as it was warm and reassuring, he took my hand.

"Honey, God picked the perfect person. You just have to tell them your story. You have to tell them the truth."

Daniel was as confident as I was not. He thought my background would be a blessing, while I saw it as a barrier. He thought our involvement with a rehab center was a great idea, and not simply because we had helped to educate the residents and make their menu more nutritious.

Unlike me, Daniel *loved* people's stories. It's why he'd become a psychiatrist. He liked the "walkie talkies"— people who preferred to talk about their experiences so that they could heal.

Not me. What he called history, I called excuses. As a former trauma-unit nurse, I was the person you'd call if your skull had split open when you did a flip off the high dive while drunk and missed the water. I preferred dealing with patients who were sedated and intubated.

Daniel was the guy you'd call for the years of PTSD that followed a traumatic episode. He listened to people's stories. I didn't want to hear excuses.

His motto was: It's easy to call people bad, harder to ask why.

My motto was: Stop sniveling and take responsibility. Do whatever it takes to get the job done. Meanwhile, don't whine like a little twit. No one promised you that life would be fair. Fair is a place with bad food and farm animals.

Clearly, I was the wrong person to meet face-to-face with a bunch of people who'd made choices I despised.

So why in the world had I said yes when Leslie asked me back to speak to "her people"? I honestly had no idea. I just knew I was going to do it.

———

Standing in the main room, listening to Leslie introduce me before my talk, I looked down at my freshly painted toes, peeking out of my heels. The perfect red nail polish looked as out of place as I felt. As a health expert, I usually dressed to show my level of fitness—it was my calling card. I could only assume that my mostly male audience would be sporting an array of tattered sweatshirts, threadbare jeans, and an occasional T-shirt spouting Socrates-level wisdom like "A day without beer is like . . . just kidding. I have no idea."

As the butterflies churned in my stomach, I appealed to God with half a dozen fleeting thoughts. I usually wasn't this nervous before a talk.

As I climbed the steps of the platform stage, it's hard to say who was shouldering the biggest chip, me or my audience. I could feel their eyes on me before I looked at them. It was a well-honed survival instinct I'd developed as a child, one that told me I was being watched. A blink—that's how long it took for me to know the intent behind a look: lust, admiration, envy, jealousy, disgust, or just plain boredom. Every such look elicited a visceral feeling, warning me when anything around me was wrong, dangerous, or suspicious.

My "Spidey sense" had saved my life more than once, so I never ignored it. And what I sensed in the room that day was resentment. Distrust. And, frankly, the feeling was mutual. I knew the men and the sprinkling of women in the audience were perusing my physique and assessing the quality of my clothes. I was being judged by a jury of two hundred recovering addicts who were at varying levels of withdrawal or sobriety. The obvious verdict, of course, was that I was shallower than low-tide backwash.

My confidence ebbed. Gone was the strong, successful businesswoman and health professional I usually displayed to the world. Instead I felt like the knock-kneed girl in the school cafeteria trapped in a game of "mean girls"—as if it was only a matter of time before someone threw the Monday mystery meat at me. I felt defenseless . . . and defensive. *Am I a healer or a hostage?*

I tried to break the ice with some light comments, but my audience was less animated than the presidents on Rushmore, which made me all the more annoyed. *Why do any of you have the right to judge me for being healthy, for looking successful, for not being a law-breaking addict . . . for not being like you?*

I scanned the room and saw a sea of bored, empty eyes and an occasional look of mild curiosity. People whose arms were crossed and bodies were slouched. A few had already checked out, open-mouthed and dead to the world, their drowsiness triggered by the need for drugs and the effects of detox.

I highly doubted that anyone in this crowd cared about the evils of sugar and gluten. Most of them were still jonesing for a pipe or a needle with a tequila chaser. If they were willing to risk jail, losing their children and even their lives to follow their addictions, why would they care about the effects of leaky gut or insulin resistance? We were on opposite shores of a vast ocean, speaking different languages, and I had no idea how to cross over—not that I really wanted to.

I'd just begun my speech when my hands started shaking and my heart started racing. I was doing something I never did—panicking. I thought I'd left all the memories behind, buried them deep. Now they were stalking me like some horror-flick zombie popping up to kill again.

Stop it, Tana, I told myself. *Get your act together! Toughen up!*

But then something deep within me whispered a reply that stopped me in my tracks. *Tough isn't what this group needs. They just need you . . . being real.*

I wasn't sure I could trust the voice that was nudging me to drop my guard, but I decided to listen. That voice was telling me that I needed to level with them. Needed them to see beyond the facade created by the designer shoes and the well-coifed hair and the never-let-'em-see-you-sweat disposition. In short, I needed my audience to see that, although substances hadn't been my addiction, I might have more in common with them than they assumed.

And then it happened. As if it were a time-release pill that wouldn't work unless I surrendered my pride and narrow-mindedness, the quick prayer I'd said before my speech finally took hold:

God, please help me set aside my own needs, my pride, and my fear and focus on the purpose You have for me. Use me as an instrument; speak through me. If one person out there needs to hear Your message, open their ears. I am broken and angry, but You have promised that You can use anyone for Your purpose. So, here I am. Prove it. This is not about me. This is about the people in front of me. Finally, please give me patience with these people—like right now! Amen.

I stopped and scanned the room, taking time to look beyond the doubting looks and shabby clothes. "I know what a lot of you are going through," I said. "I know—"

A woman in my field of vision twisted her body with an exaggerated "harrumph" that few could ignore.

"Yes?" I asked, thinking a question from her would ignite some buy-in from the audience.

"How would you know?" she asked.

"I'm sorry?"

"How would you know what I'm going through? Look at you. Your life is perfect. You can't know what I'm going through."

With a flick of her wrist she dismissed me, the way one might shoo a pesky fly. In that moment I went from concern to anger to total deflation. The words I'd hoped would break the ice had brought me a frigid slap in the face.

The group perked up, waiting for my response. I half expected to hear them chant, *"Fight, fight! Hit her back!"* like kids jeering and egging on an after-school brawl. My first thought was to snap, *How could you judge me? You don't know me!* Then, as quickly as I'd had that thought, I was haunted by another one: *How can I blame her?*

In a sense she *did* know me. I was standing on a stage, literally looking down at her, projecting exactly what I'd wanted them to see. Since adolescence I had engineered the perfect mask, designed to prevent all but the most persistent eyes from seeing beneath the surface. I had felt protected behind my shield of meticulously applied makeup and carefully chosen clothes—until she saw through it. No doubt they all had.

Lord, why am I here?

As quickly as the question flashed in my mind, the answer came in the words Daniel had said in the car: *God picked the perfect person. You just have to tell them your story. You have to tell them the truth.*

I exhaled.

"So," I said with a blend of defiance and candor, keeping my tears in check, "how many of you are judging me right now?"

As if I'd pulled a fire alarm, I suddenly had their attention. A couple of them rolled their eyes or furrowed their brows. Two or three crossed their arms. A few snickered. Though briefly encouraged, I didn't see anybody raise a hand.

"Really?" I asked. "That's interesting—because *I'm* certainly judging *you*."

The room quieted, as if my honesty had shattered their own protective armor. In that screaming silence I thought, *What are you doing, Tana?* I tend to crave security, and what I was doing felt anything but secure. This was raw and wildly unpredictable. Instead of seeking shelter behind my protective walls, however, I decided to forge ahead.

"Let's be honest, shall we?" I said. "We're judging each other."

I raised my hand. "Seriously, how many are judging me?"

After an awkward pause, one hand in the third row went up, then another in the back. I simply nodded, more than willing to wait for the truth to touch other hearts. Another hand here. Another hand there. Soon hands were popping up throughout the audience as we confessed to passing judgment without even knowing one another—without knowing our histories, our deeper selves.

In that moment I saw truth. And, as the "truth shall set you free" Bible verse suggests, I could already feel it diluting the presumptions I'd made about my audience. For the first time since I'd walked in that room, I didn't see addicts or junkies. Instead, I saw wounded children. And I saw *me*—the me I thought I'd left behind many years before.

Each person in front of me was dealing with adult problems and adult consequences, but the common thread that superseded our diverse backgrounds was childhood pain. As their hands went up and my pride faded away, my purpose for being there was suddenly crystal clear: If I could help just one person in this room, there would be one less scared child in the world. One less scared little girl who felt like an afterthought. One less scared little boy who had tried to go unseen because "invisible" felt safer. One less scared child who would go on to become a scared adult in need of healing and forgiveness.

But the payoff wouldn't end there. With one less scared little girl or boy in the world, with more of us choosing differently at the proverbial fork in the road, the carryover would benefit not only this generation but the one to come and perhaps the ones to follow. I could help change the world, one scared child at a time.

Maybe I could even change me.

I took a deep breath, peeled back what remained of my mask, and looked at my audience. I was about to meld my mind with people whose lives, I realized, had been no messier than my own. In that moment I wasn't healer or hostage. I was just another beggar looking for a piece of bread.

When I first took to that podium, the gap between me and my audience had made the Grand Canyon seem like a sidewalk crack. But as we began letting down our guards, the gap became a mirror. We weren't nearly as different as I'd imagined. We all were—or at least had once been—in the same boat: the *Titanic*. Just like them, I knew what it was like to find myself alone in cold, treacherous water, wondering if anyone was going to come and throw out a life vest. The only difference was that I'd made it safely to shore while they were still flailing in the choppy sea.

Beyond that, something else was suddenly crystal clear: the stage did not belong to a warrior, a black belt, or even a skilled trauma nurse. On this day the stage belonged to the vulnerable part of me I had worked so hard to leave behind. And yet the very thing I'd been so afraid to do—deal with my past— was the very thing that, when revealed, would make this perhaps the most powerful talk I would ever give.

In the next hour, in the next weeks, in the next months, these men and women and I would build an amazing bridge between us—a bridge built of bricks only God could provide, mortared with the pain of everyone in the room—my own not only included, but the most conspicuous. It would be as if the "open their ears" part of my prespeech prayer had been for my own ears, the ones most in need of hearing.

It wasn't my first come-to-Jesus moment, nor would it be my last. But the experience would teach me a powerful lesson: *sometimes God calls us to help those we don't want to help so He can provide healing for the broken parts of us.* In other words, the help was for them, but the healing was for me—and for the rest of us willing to enter the fray, even if it means facing the past and exposing a terrifying vulnerability.

"Okay," I said, completely going off script, "let me tell you a story." The room stilled with what seemed like a new sense of genuine curiosity, perhaps even a side dish of respect. "It's a story about a scared little girl. Her name is Tana."

CHAPTER 2

MURDER, PSYCHICS, AND SAVED BY A DOG

The monsters that rose from the dead, they are
nothing compared to the ones we carry in our heart.

—MAX BROOKS

The musty smell of orange shag carpet and peeling yellow paint—those were my first memories. I woke with my cheek pressed against the carpet and one eyeball staring at the wall. I couldn't move. While I slept I had somehow wrapped myself in the blanket and was now trapped between the bed and the wall.

I started yelling. Nobody came.

"Mommy!" I cried again. No answer.

Why wasn't anyone answering? Managing to wiggle free, I toddled to the window to look for my mommy. Maybe she was in the pool.

Nope. Terror set in. I started screaming. Shaking.

I wondered if I could find Mommy on that funny thing she talked to people on. I picked up the part she held to her ear and started turning the dial like I had seen her do. Nothing. I kept turning.

"How can I help you?" I heard a woman ask.

"Where is Mommy?" I choked through broken sobs.

I don't remember the details of that call, only a voice on the other end telling me not to put the phone down. She kept asking me questions, things I didn't know how to answer. Except about my dog! How did she know I had a dog?

"Is the dog big or small?"

"He's big. Oso not here."

She told me not to go outside or near the pool. When she asked my age, I told her I would be "free" on my next birthday. Then I dropped the phone and ran outside to the chain-link fence, clung to it, and cried. Soon I saw Mommy coming down the street in the car.

I learned much later that Mom had left me with yet another babysitter while she went to do errands for work. The babysitter claimed she hadn't seen me in my bed napping and so had left the house. But Mom had had a premonition of me crying and decided to come home early. I was probably alone for no more than fifteen minutes. I'm not sure. But a toddler has no concept of time.

Not long after that event, my mom, Oso, and I went to my mom's oldest brother's apartment. While Mom and Uncle Ray talked, I slipped away unnoticed to play by his pool. The next thing I remember, I was underwater. Everything was strange and distant. I reached for the side of the pool and heard the water-muffled sound of Oso barking wildly. A murky figure reached a hand down, grabbed me, and pulled me out of the water. Though Oso rarely allowed strangers near me, that day he had summoned one to rescue me. I emerged coughing and sputtering but safe, my life saved by the most consistent, protective, loyal male in my life.

My father had disappeared soon after I was born. Mom had married him when she was only eighteen, two years after she dropped out of high school and ran away from home. She'd left to get away from the chaos of her family in Wasco, California, and made it 137 miles to Los Angeles before she ran out of money.

That grueling journey became part of our family story, told and retold. After narrowly escaping a rape attempt while hitchhiking, she'd splurged for a Greyhound bus ticket. Once in LA, she'd slept in the bathroom stall of the bus depot for a few nights, then upgraded to an old storage trailer because it had a locking door and a battered sofa. Her only food for the entire trip had been a can of beans and one all-you-can-eat budget buffet dinner.

Eventually Mom smooth-talked her way into a series of low-paying jobs, using a fake name and staying on the move to avoid being discovered. Then she met my dad, David, who was handsome, clean cut, and a safe choice—or so she thought. She married him only a few months later.

The marriage was rocky right from the start as one might expect of two teenagers with little life experience. Dad's infidelity and penchant for partying, coupled with Mom's fiery temper, became a recipe for disaster. But Mom was determined to make it work—until she couldn't. They separated two months after I was born.

After Mom's divorce her mother—my grandmother—lived with us off and on. Grandma Alba had been born in Hardin, Lebanon, in 1910, during a period of national tragedy and unrest. As a young girl she'd wanted to be a nun, but her parents had wanted her to marry and have a family. She was devoutly Christian, but she was also intensely superstitious. I remember the curse of her "evil eye" and the chanting she would do for hours in Arabic if anyone dared cross her.

Grandma adored her sons, but she had never bonded well with her daughter. As a child, Mom told me, she would be wakened by Grandma raging in the middle of the night and ordered to scrub the floors or wash windows. And even after Mom was an adult, Grandma remained harshly disapproving of her, no matter how hard Mom tried to please her. She frequently told Mom that her red hair was going to get her killed.

But Mom always loved Grandma, even when Grandma yelled at her in her thick Arabic accent as she waved her fists: "I not stay home babyseet so you go wid de bad mans. De mans are son-a-ma-beeks," she'd say.

"Mom, I need to go to work, not with the son-a-ma-beeks," Mom would say, stifling a giggle. She never seemed to get angry at her mother, no matter how mean or disapproving Grandma could be. Grandma was just "different." In spite of their difficult childhood memories, none of her children doubted her deep love for them.

"You have baby. You need man to marry so you stay home," she'd say. "Sin to be out wid de son-a-ma-beek!"

Eventually Uncle Bob, my mom's youngest brother, also came to live with us. So instead of having a dad at home, I had an uncle who prowled our hallways like a zombie. Sometimes he would look at me as if his eyes could see right through me, as if I were a ghost, and then stumble on by.

I was nearly four when we all moved into the first house I remember living in together. It was a rental—they were always rentals during my early years—a haunted-looking old Victorian in the San Fernando Valley, north of LA. It looked like the mansion in those scary-funny Addams Family movies, only this house wasn't scary-funny. It was scary, period, like no place you wanted to be, particularly if you were a little girl whose mom was always away at work. I called it the Creepy House, and I never liked living there. But Mom was proud she'd found a place she could afford that was big enough for the four of us.

I didn't have any friends in my new neighborhood yet, so I spent a lot of time alone. I'd sit on the cracked step out back, in a shady spot under the thick tangle of shade trees that canopied the patio. The interlacing branches above me swayed with the whispering breeze, as if they were telling secrets about people who'd lived there before. I wondered what they would whisper about us.

Uncle Bob and his freaky friends were often around, but they weren't much company for me. Mom called them hippies, and they melded with that old house and its dark hallways and shadow-dimmed corners and doors. They never tried to hurt me. They were just weird—and even as a little girl I knew they weren't normal. Some of their arms had bruises and pinprick holes, and Mom warned me never to touch their "toys" because, apparently, they played with needles and other dangerous things.

Bob and his friends came and went like motel guests. A few even tried to steal stuff from the house—not that we had much to steal. But mostly

I remember the long, greasy hair and the red, lifeless eyes. They often lit incense and smoked weird stuff that was not like Mom's cigarettes. They draped heavy blankets over all the windows and kept the rooms completely dark as they listened to music amid a bunch of bad-smelling odors. Their music gave me shivers. Even now, more than forty years later, I feel agitated and unsettled, like hearing nails on a chalkboard, when I hear the Doors' "Riders on the Storm," with its lyrics about killers on the loose and toads squished in the road. The music that I heard my uncle and his friends listening to elicits feelings of a time when life was scary, unpredictable, and out of control. Nearly everything about that decade was scary for me, but the music was the worst because it beckoned the nightmares.

Only years later did I learn that Uncle Bob was a full-blown heroin addict who had already overdosed once. He lived with us because Mom felt responsible for him. She had helped raise him following my grandmother's mental breakdown and hospitalization when he was an infant. But when Mom left home at sixteen, she'd had to leave him behind. Bob had eventually joined the navy during the Vietnam War, serving as a medic. After leaving the navy, he worked in a pharmacy, which is where he became addicted to morphine. The heroin was a natural progression.

For a brief period, my generally absent father resurfaced to join the party. He came to live in our house not as a husband, a provider, or a father, but as a roommate and a paid babysitter—not that he actually did much to take care of me.

One of my earliest memories of my dad was of him spanking me when I was about four. Dad was supposedly babysitting, but he'd disappeared with my uncle into the "scary room" in the back of the Creepy House. I was doing my best to take care of some kittens I'd found. They were so tiny their eyes weren't even open, and Mom had said we might not be able to save them. But I was trying, feeding them with a bottle the way Mom had shown me.

I spilled the formula and got them all sticky, so I took them out to my inflatable pool in the backyard to give them a bath. And the next thing I knew, Dad was bolting toward me, screaming in anger. He took the kittens from me and used a belt on my backside to teach me a lesson—about *what* I'm still not sure. I remember thinking, *What did I do wrong? I was taking care of my kittens. You were supposed to be watching me. You were the one doing something bad.*

When Dad wasn't "babysitting" for me or partying with Bob—or both—he was working for Mom in one or another of her many business ventures. Since my mother couldn't turn away anyone in need, no matter how much they had hurt her, this ragtag team of family members and an ex-husband doubled as her employees. Uncle Bob supposedly worked for her, too, but he was usually high when he showed up to work or family gatherings, if he showed up at all.

Though Mom hired other babysitters, most of them were not any more responsible than Uncle Bob and his friends. One sitter got her jollies when she made me smoke cigarettes and kiss the little boy she was also babysitting, then threatened to lie and tell my mom I tried to start a fire with matches if I didn't comply. Another babysitter let me bake a cake with no supervision when I was six, and then, when I burned it, made me sit at the table and eat the entire charred mess, threatening to take a leather belt to me if I refused.

One night while I was watching TV with a babysitter, we heard a noise out front. The sitter opened the front door, and there in our driveway sat a hearse. The engine had stopped, and all was quiet. Slowly the door opened, and in the dim light I could make out the silhouette of the driver. He stood and closed the door, and as he slowly began walking toward us, we could make out frizzy shoulder-length hair and a bushy beard that looked like a black lion's mane.

The babysitter squeezed my hand and let out a bloodcurdling scream that shattered the quiet. When he started waving his arms, she squeezed my hand harder and kept on shrieking. But I wasn't scared. Not in the least.

"It's okay," I said and wrestled out of her grip. I ran and jumped into his arms. I gave him a big hug and pulled on his beard. "Uncle Ray!"

The babysitter, who wasn't used to such entrances by my eccentric uncle, nearly fainted. I didn't understand what her problem was. Didn't everyone have an uncle who drove a hearse?

Despite having a master's degree and being a licensed speech therapist, Ray was a seventies hippie personified. Most of the time he lived with a bunch of people in a cabin in Big Sur, passionately protesting the Vietnam War and "capitalistic materialism"—that is, until he reached the point that he couldn't survive any longer without a job. Then he'd move back to Los Angeles to make a little money before disappearing for several more months.

During one of Uncle Ray's "will work for food" missions, he temporarily worked for my mother in the commercial janitorial business she had started. He and Mom spent most of that time fighting. I didn't understand their political and lifestyle differences, but Mom said their "heated arguments" were due to the fact that they didn't agree about basic life values, like having jobs and being responsible adults.

"You're too uptight," Uncle Ray would say to my mother. "You're a capitalist, a conservative, and an antiseptic broad. I'm doing my own thing. I'm independent. I'm a free thinker."

"No, you're not!" she'd respond. "You're doing everyone else's thing. You just moved out of a commune. The very word suggests communism—like sharing everything and doing everything everyone else is doing. There's nothing independent about you. You look like every one of your long-haired hippie friends. Meanwhile I'm actually working and contributing. I'm doing something worthwhile. And oh, by the way, you now *work for me.*"

This cycle of Ray appearing, working for Mom and arguing with her, then disappearing again continued until one day Mom told me he had finally "pulled his head out of his rear" and would be moving back to civilization permanently, to live like a responsible adult. I had no idea what civilization was, but I figured it must be a good thing if I would see Uncle Ray's fuzzy face more often. I assumed he was going to join us and live in the Creepy House. But then, on Mother's Day that year, life changed forever. I was four years old.

I was up in my room when I heard the first screams coming from my mother. I pattered down the steps, heart pounding. That's when I heard more screams, these coming from my grandmother and much louder. The two women were shrieking and wailing in anguish, and Uncle Bob had tears running down his face.

Two police officers stood awkwardly in the doorway, trying to look calm amid the chaos.

"Mommy, what's wrong? What's wrong?" I tried to wrap my arms around her leg, but she pushed me away and sternly told me to go into the other room. I felt scared, confused, and rejected. The two anchors of my life, my mother and my grandmother, were crumbling right before my eyes, and I had no idea why.

Then I heard the police officers telling my mom that Uncle Ray was never coming home again. *But he just came back to civilization*, I thought. *Why would he leave again already?* My grandmother kept wailing, "God, please take me. Please take me." Nothing made sense. *Why did Uncle Ray leave, and where does Grandma want God to take her?*

I tried to ask questions, and Mom finally responded, "Honey, he went to live with Jesus. Now please go in the other room. I'll be in soon."

I went to the stairwell to get away from the screaming. It didn't work. I could still hear it, so I ran up to my room and did what I always did when I was scared and felt alone in the world: I built a little fort next to my bed out of all the blankets and pillows I could find, then burrowed into it as deeply as I could. I had spent hours quietly playing in such pillow forts—hidden away, where I imagined no one could find me. And on that day I sat in my fort and tried to figure out why Uncle Ray would want to leave us and go with a guy he didn't know.

I had heard stories about Jesus, who lived somewhere in the sky in a place called heaven. From the pictures I'd seen, this Jesus had a beard that looked a lot like Ray's. Maybe Ray had gone there because Jesus liked beards.

Days later the uncle who had driven a hearse was taken to the cemetery in another hearse—a dramatic effect for his final act.

Gradually, over time, I learned what had happened to Uncle Ray. Some of the details remain sketchy and unclear to me even as an adult, but the basic facts were simple. Ray had planned to visit Grandma for Mother's Day and inform her of his upcoming move. He never got there, though, because he went to meet Uncle Bob at a friend's house first.

Bob was about to get on his motorcycle, inebriated, to sell two ounces of heroin. Ray, being a good brother, decided to do it for him so Bob wouldn't kill himself or someone else.

There is speculation that Ray was working as an informant, but no one knows for sure. The only thing we know for certain is that Ray was murdered. He was hit over the head, held down, and given an intentional overdose by members of a transient motorcycle gang who stole the heroin he was there to sell. His body was found by a "friend," who dumped it in front of a hospital to avoid being connected to the crime. The most bizarre part of the story was the way the police came to find the house where the killer had given Ray the overdose.

They found it because Mom had a vision.

I was well accustomed to my mother's "visions" and "feelings" by then. Sometimes random people would show up at our house offering to pay her if she'd "read their future." She always refused, claiming her "gift" didn't work like that. Mom was adamant that she wasn't psychic, and she believed her premonitions were from God, but she never capitalized on her abilities. In fact, she'd spent most of her life concealing or downplaying her gift. Her copper-red hair drew enough unwanted attention already, and because Grandma had had a mental breakdown when Mom was a young girl, she was afraid people would believe she was also "crazy" if they knew.

When Mom was nine, she had inadvertently revealed she'd seen the spirit of a childhood friend and believed that he had died, not moved away, as all the children had been told to shield them from the truth. When her words proved to be true, Ray had called Mom a witch, confirming her fear.

So Mom had mostly kept quiet about her gift—until Ray's murder, when she was anything but quiet. She claimed to have seen the entire event in vivid color while holding Ray's hand in the funeral home. She described it right down to the location and description of where it happened.

Uncle Harold, Mom's middle brother, thought Mom might be having a nervous breakdown and wanted her to take ten milligrams of Valium (an old prescription Mom had) to calm her nerves. But when Uncle Bob arrived at the funeral home and heard about the vision, he immediately confirmed the truth that only he and Ray had known. She had given a detailed description of the house where Bob frequently made drug deals, right down to the type of fencing around the house, the floor plan, and the name on the street sign.

The realization devastated Bob. He was the one who was supposed to make that deal, so he should have been the one to die. In his mind, he was responsible for killing his brother. But instead of using Ray's death as a reason to stop doing drugs and turn his life around, he used it as an excuse to sink deeper into his addiction.

Unable to handle the grief and guilt, Bob decided to end his life the same way Ray's had been taken, with an intentional overdose of heroin, and he nearly succeeded. Fortunately a friend found him unconscious with a needle still in his arm. His lips were blue and he was barely breathing, but he was alive and Bob was saved. My grandmother narrowly missed losing two sons to heroin overdoses within months of each other.

The police confirmed the location of the house and told Mom it was under surveillance but refused to give her more information. The motorcycle gang, believed to be drug dealers from Northern California, were in the wind. The police seemed to be aware of their identities, but they had no evidence—psychic visions didn't count—and no idea how to find the suspects.

Mom became so frustrated that she took Oso and went to the drug house herself, hoping that being in the place where Ray had been murdered would trigger a vision that might help lead to an arrest. But the vision didn't come. Both Mom and Grandma were overcome with grief. Adding to Bob's grief and guilt was the fact that Grandma never really recovered. Any time Ray's name was mentioned she would break down and wail. Grandma's already frail health further deteriorated as she became a shell of herself. After Ray's death, Bob commented that it was as if a quarter of her life disappeared the day Ray died. She desperately held on to the other three-quarters—her three living children.

Within two weeks of Uncle Ray's death, I was in the hospital for an endoscopy to help explain my persistent gastrointestinal issues. Though my regular diet of cereal and chocolate milk probably didn't help, the doctors suspected my issues were more likely to be physical manifestations of the stress I was experiencing. Soon I was having other symptoms as well. I started having high fevers on a fairly regular basis. I seemed to always be sick. I became an emergency-room frequent flyer, earning miles the hard way. I'd get a battery of tests, and Mom would pick up my latest prescription for antibiotics along with the bill.

My mother didn't have much of a support system at that time. My father's absence meant that she had nobody to help shoulder the burden of raising a sick child. She tried to be both mother and father, but she was overwhelmed by financial obligations and life in general. She was working several jobs to pay our rent, food, and utilities. She also tried to help Uncle Bob, who eventually started to rebuild his life, courtesy of intense drug counseling, controlled methadone treatments, and an extended vacation to the LA County Men's Central Jail.

It wasn't as if Mom had had great role models while she was growing up, either. Her mother never finished elementary school—in her culture a privilege reserved for boys or the eldest girl in a family. In spite of being college educated—and later owning his own business—my grandfather struggled financially as a result of my grandmother's mental health issues, a subsequent divorce, and his own stress. Her mother had become emotionally abusive and mentally unstable, and her father had started drinking after her mother was hospitalized for what was then called a nervous breakdown. He'd used a belt on the four kids regularly, the boys getting the worst of it, until a terrible automobile accident left him a quadriplegic. Mom had taken care of him shortly after she was married, until he needed more care than she could provide and had to go into a nursing home.

Essentially Mom had grown up surrounded by screaming, mental illness, physical fights, severe physical discipline, and constant chaos. To her credit, she never blamed her parents or doubted their love for her. But she did develop a fierce determination to make my life better than hers had been. In Mom's mind that meant getting out of poverty, even if she had to work ungodly hours doing unladylike jobs and leaving me to basically raise myself in the process.

In hindsight, I realize that my mom was desperate and only doing her best to try to save me from the same life she was still struggling to be free of. At the time, however, the word that would have described me was *scared*.

CHAPTER 3

A GIRL'S BEST FRIEND

When it's too hard to look back and you're too afraid
to look ahead, look right beside you. I'll be there.

—Unknown

I was four when Mom claims I had my first "vision." It's not a memory for me, though I've heard Mom tell the story so many times, I can recall it as though it were my own.

Perched on the side of a mustard-colored porcelain tub, I watched Mom carefully apply makeup as she got ready for work. Pointing to the center of my forehead, I said, "Mommy, in my mind's eye I see a piece of blank paper, and it makes me sad because it reminds me that my daddy never writes to me."

Mom paused awkwardly. "Honey, Daddy sent you a gift for your birthday."

With a perceptive frown I replied, "Hmmm, okay."

She decided that day that it was time to stop lying to protect me and to help me start protecting myself. She would no longer buy presents and say they were from my daddy or tell me he didn't call on my birthday because he was working. She gently and lovingly started telling me the truth.

"I'm sorry, Tana. I don't know where your daddy is or whether he's coming back," she said. "But I love you more than anything in the whole world. And I know your daddy loves you, too, even though he acts silly sometimes. When you both grow up a little, you might be able to visit him for summer vacation."

"What's summer vacation?" I asked.

"It's a time for families to go to fun, exciting places together," she said. "But right now I want to talk about your 'mind's eye.' Do you see other things, like the blank paper?" Mom was looking at me intently. "I started seeing things like that when I was your age. Things that other people couldn't see."

"I'm not sure," I said, kicking the tub with my heels. "But sometimes I get feelings about people."

Mom nodded. "I always want you to trust your feelings. And talk to me, all right?" she said.

"Okay, Mommy," I said.

She lifted me from my perch on the side of the tub and gave me a quick squeeze before leaving me with the sitter. I don't remember seeing anything in my mind's eye again, but I didn't have the heart to tell Mom that I didn't have her gift.

I was sad about being abandoned by my father, but even more so, I was filled with anxiety and fear over the thought of losing my mother. Sometimes I'd hide in the hallway when I was supposed to be asleep and overhear my mom and uncles talk about my mom's "close calls" while at work; then they'd discuss ways she could protect herself. A beautiful woman working alone in industrial areas in the middle of the night was not safe. But it never stopped her. Mom always carried a gun to her night jobs, and she started taking Oso for protection.

The little ball of fur I'd seen in photos with me as a baby had grown into an enormous shepherd who had been trained to protect Mom and me. I wasn't scared of Oso, and I didn't really understand when I heard neighbors make comments about him being scary. He was my pet, and he followed me everywhere. Mom made me take him outside with me to play, and said he was better than any babysitter.

Once, after she'd arrived at the General Telephone building after work hours to begin her cleaning work, she got out of the car to open the gate and noticed three intoxicated men had stopped their truck on the road behind her. They got out, and even through their slurred words, she understood their intentions. She pressed the button for the security guard to open the gate, and they came closer. They either didn't see or didn't care about the open door to her El Camino where Oso sat. When the hair on his neck went up in a protective reflex, he looked like a demon-possessed wolf, and in a blur, he flew out of the car then positioned himself in front of my mother. Teeth bared, frothing at the mouth, Oso must've been a frightening sight because the men scrambled back to their truck. Later, while talking about it with her brothers, Mom said Oso's training had paid off. Uncle Harold had laughed and said, "They got off easy," referring to the .38-caliber revolver my mom had hidden under her bulky poncho. Years later, when I asked my mother if she'd had a permit to carry that gun, she'd just shrugged and said, "Rather be judged by twelve than carried by six."

I didn't know Harold, Mom's middle brother, as well as I knew Bob and Ray, but I was always fascinated by the larger-than-life stories I'd heard about him, and I liked our occasional visits. Harold was the "cool" brother. He had chosen to stay close to his hometown of Wasco, settling in the neighboring town of Bakersfield. And why not? He had lots of friends in the area. Mom said he'd been the popular one since childhood, despite the trouble he tended to attract.

When I was a kid, Harold was slowly working his way through college to become a teacher, but his studies never seemed to be a top priority. His reputation for drinking, carousing, and fighting in high school preceded him. When we visited I was told not to look at the magazines he had in his bathroom—so of course I did. I was embarrassed, yet captivated, when I saw photos of beautiful women without their clothes, and I wondered how Harold usually seemed to have a pretty girl with him—pretty like the ones in the magazine, and almost never the *same* girl.

But no girls were allowed when Harold went hunting, which was often. The first time I saw a dead deer staring at me from the back of his truck, I cried, and sometimes, when my mother left for work, I'd think of that dead deer. Then I'd think of the movie *Bambi* and worry about how scared Bambi must have felt when his mom went to sleep and never woke up.

When I heard Mom and her other brothers talk about Harold's "epic" parties, I imagined that meant lots of balloons and games, like the awesome birthday party my best friend, Mia, had just had. After it ended I ran home, burst through the front door, and announced, "I want a stuffed papata for *my* birthday!"

"A what?" Mom asked. "Slow down."

"You know, a papata, stuffed with candy. You spin and spin and try to hit it, until candy flies everywhere."

Mom laughed. "You mean a piñata."

Meeting Mia and her little sister, Isabel, was the best part of the summer we lived in the Creepy House. They lived down the street, and I loved going there, because Mia's house always felt happy. Even though her parents mostly spoke Spanish, I could usually figure out what they were trying to say. Mom would praise me for being able to understand people just by watching their faces. I did the same with Grandma, who didn't speak much English either.

Under the giant willow tree in Mia's backyard, we would play house and tell secrets. It was our favorite thing to do—until one day I told a "bad secret."

My mom asked, "Tana, did you tell Mia where babies come from?"

Figuring I was in trouble, I ran to my room and threw myself on the bed. Mom followed me.

"I had to." I sobbed with a hitch in my breath. "She said that some stupid bird brings babies and drops them off on the front porch!"

"Honey, Mia's mommy is very upset. What did you say?"

"What you told me. Babies come from mommies' tummies. She didn't believe me. She asked how a baby could get out of the mommy's tummy, and I pointed—*down there*. Then she asked how the baby got *into* the mommy's tummy. I told her it takes a daddy, too, and somehow when he loves the mommy, *he* makes the baby go in there. Is that wrong, Mommy?"

"No, sweetheart, it's the truth," Mom said, gently stroking my hair. "Some parents tell stories like that one about the bird because it's easier. I told you I would never lie to you, and I won't, but you probably shouldn't tell your friends things we talk about, or some parents won't want them to play with you."

Mom was right. Mia's parents never let her play with me again, and I still didn't understand what I had done wrong.

When that summer ended, Mom took me to Kmart because, she said, I was starting kindergarten and would need some clothes.

"What's kindergarten?" I said.

"It's your first year of school. You're a big girl now," Mom replied.

"*Finally!*" I was so proud of the plaid pinafore dress, white knee socks, and shiny black patent-leather Mary Janes we bought. The night before school started, I set my windup Minnie Mouse alarm clock, climbed in bed, and counted the ticks as the second hand made circles around Minnie, imagining how my life would be different as a big girl. I wouldn't need a babysitter, probably. Only babies needed those.

The next thing I remember, Mom, not Minnie, was waking me up. I felt happy, wondering if going to school meant Mom would be there every morning. That first day wasn't as magical as I'd imagined, though. A boy named Billy pulled my hair. Some of the other girls were dressed like me, so I didn't really feel special in my new dress. However, I liked being like everyone else, but by lunchtime the excitement was gone. After school a babysitter was waiting for me as usual.

On the following days, Mom didn't pick out cute outfits for me to wear, and she woke me with little time to spare before we rushed out the door. During school I had trouble focusing on what the teacher was saying, so I rarely answered the questions correctly when the teacher called on me.

When summer arrived, I wasn't disappointed to learn that we were moving again. I was happy to leave the Creepy House. And I was giddy when the little girl who lived next door to our new house came over and asked if I wanted to be friends. We were the same age and went to the same school, and I thought I'd really grown up when Mom decided I could walk to school with Vicki—just the two of us, like big girls. Then she agreed that I could stay home after school without a babysitter as long as I locked the door and called her as soon as I walked in the door. I was convinced my life was the best it had ever been.

One morning I arrived late at the new school. I was sent to the auditorium where all the late kids, including me, were lined up on the black squares of the black-and-white checked floor. The principal stared sternly at each of us as he walked up and down the line holding up a large wooden paddle.

"This is your only warning. Anyone who is late again will get a swat. The second time you get two. Go home and tell your parents you were late and have them sign this paper so they know the rules also," he said gruffly.

I was way more afraid of telling Mom I'd gotten in trouble than I was of the mean, paddle-wielding principal—not because I thought she'd punish me, but because I hated disappointing her. But instead of being mad at me, Mom was furious with the principal. She marched into the principal's office with me the next morning—late again, without an appointment—and shouted, "If you *ever* touch my child, you'll regret the day you laid eyes on me." Eyes blazing, she waved the crumpled form in the air and added, "I am the only person who is going to discipline my child! You call *me* if there's a problem. Nod if you understand!"

I don't remember if he nodded. But I do remember that I was never paddled in that school, even when I was late.

Socially I was a dork. Skinny. The awkward kid with crooked teeth and mismatched clothes. I still cringe at the thought of my secondhand denim jacket and matching "flood" jeans that were too short and covered in a ridiculous strawberry pattern. And bed-head tangles that suggested June Cleaver wasn't standing by in the morning with a brush and fresh ribbons. I'd see Suzie with her perfect, mirror-image pigtails, and longingly wonder, *What's it like to have your mom around to fix your hair every day?* I'd have settled for a hot breakfast instead of my regular Pop-Tart on the run. But if someone were judging by the perfect hair showcased in yearly school photos, I would have passed with flying colors. Mom always wanted to be sure I had cute pictures to look back on, to pass on to my kids—as though the annual effort frozen in time would erase all the uncute stuff of our lives.

I didn't even get the consolation prize of being a good student, largely because I was the youngest kid in the class and a little behind developmentally. My birthday had fallen on the *last* day to be able to start school. School administrators had suggested I wait another year, but Mom had insisted we couldn't afford to keep paying babysitters when I could be in school. And going to school early might not have been a problem if I'd had someone around to read to me at night, practice flash cards, and make sure I was keeping up. But Mom was always working, so I was more or less left to my own devices.

Essentially I was learning that being a big girl wasn't so much fun. I'd walk home from school, lock myself in the house, call Mom, and then watch TV until she got home, which was usually after dark. Whenever I got scared, I'd resort to my tried-and-true practice of gathering blankets and pillows from my bed to build a fort just big enough for Oso and me to hide in.

Things got worse when Mom started dating more. It bothered both me and Oso, but Oso even more than me. He loved us, but he *hated* men.

"I swear that dog thinks he's the man of the house," Mom would say whenever Oso would growl and conveniently nestle between male visitors and us.

One of Mom's dates thought he would playfully pick me up and spin me. Quick as a snap, Oso had the guy's arm in his mouth. He didn't break the skin, but he tore the guy's jacket.

"Why do you keep that vicious beast?" he said.

"Mostly because he's a great judge of character," Mom responded dryly. I don't remember seeing that guy again.

When Oso wasn't with Mom at work, he went with me when I went out to play. He was also around Vicki and her brother at times. Once I started running down the street, screaming playfully as Vicki's brother rode his skateboard behind me. Before we realized what was happening, Oso had knocked the boy off the skateboard, clamped the board in his jaws, and dragged it to our yard. He wouldn't let anyone have it until Mom came home. Vicki's parents were furious.

Life in that house had just settled into a rhythm when Dad showed up again. It was the morning of Christmas Eve, and he'd brought his pretty new wife, Kathy. I had a December birthday and was used to getting combination

Christmas-birthday presents—Mom said combo presents were better because they were extra special—and I thought Dad showing up was definitely extra special.

In the two years since we had seen Dad, he'd apparently had some kind of miracle makeover. He said he'd cleaned up his life, stopped doing drugs, and—of all things—become a minister. But his disposition hadn't changed much, and he still held a deep contempt for Mom. It wasn't long before they were arguing. Dad yelled Bible stuff and threats at Mom.

"I will take Tana away from you for good, you whore!" he said in front of the house while neighbors watched. "Jezebel!"

I didn't know what a whore was or who Jezebel was, but I figured they must've been bad because Mom leapt onto him, one fist primed, ready to beat the snot out of him. If the fight turned physical, my money was definitely on Mom. Uncle Bob heard Dad yelling and ran out, grabbed Mom around the waist, and pulled her off of Dad. She only got one punch in, not enough to leave any obvious marks.

After everyone had cooled down a little, Kathy apologized for Dad's behavior and then asked if I could go with them to her mother's house in Santa Paula. She promised to take care of me if I went. As this all unfolded, I sat on the porch with Oso, who never took his eyes off Dad.

Eventually Mom agreed to let me go. On the drive, the awkward silence in the car was only occasionally disturbed by Dad's mumbling about Mom—until Kathy put me on her lap and started singing, "This little light of mine, I'm gonna let it shine . . ." The warmth and joy in her voice quickly dissipated my shyness, and for the rest of the trip, Kathy taught me hymns. Even Dad couldn't stay mad.

Finally we pulled up to an old house surrounded by agricultural fields. Kathy's mom, Grandma Jane, ran outside to meet us. She was a louder, bigger version of Kathy. As I got out of the car, she surprised me with a big hug and said, "Don't worry, all Slavs are this way." To which Dad replied, "So are drunks."

Christmas at Grandma Jane's was madness—very loud, with much cooking, singing, and Grandma Jane playing the accordion. Oh, and alcohol—a lot of alcohol. Kathy's brother, Anthony, and her sister, Diane, danced with me, and we played games all weekend. Then, best of all, Santa showed up.

After Uncle Ray died, my faith in Santa had waned. But that evening I heard him on the roof at Grandma Jane's, and I *saw him* carrying a big bag just before I heard a big thud on the porch. When I ran outside he was gone, but my belief in the jolly man had been restored.

The next day at Christmas dinner, everyone except Dad was laughing when Kathy's brother hobbled in, limping.

"Christmas is about Jesus, not Santa," Dad said disapprovingly.

"Ah, lighten up, ya big guzy," said Grandma Jane, shooing dad with a flip of her wrist. I would later learn she was calling Dad an a**hole.

After dinner Dad asked me if I knew what Christmas meant.

"Presents?" I asked.

"No, honey," Dad picked me up and took me to the one quiet spot we could find in the house. Sitting on the steps of the dimly lit staircase, above the ornate Christmas tree, I watched the lights twinkle on and off as Dad told me the story of baby Jesus in the manger—the story of Christmas. At that moment I felt safe and happy with Dad. At other times during that visit, though, he read from the Bible loudly, as though shouting would help me understand better. It didn't.

The next summer, Mom allowed me to fly alone to see Dad in New Mexico, where he was now pastoring a small Baptist church. When I arrived at the shabby cinderblock house where he and Kathy lived, I was reminded of places in the dreary old Westerns I'd seen, places where someone usually dies and no one was around to find the body. It was a ten-minute walk to the nearest neighbor's house. I bit back tears, wondering when six weeks would end.

But my time there didn't turn out that bad. Dad spent most of his days at the church, so I stayed at the little house with Kathy, who cooked and sang with me. But the best days were Sundays. I didn't like sitting still and listening to Dad shout about heaven and hell, but I liked Sunday school and being around other kids.

When I visited two summers later, when I was eight, I noticed something different about Dad and Kathy in the airport. Kathy gave me a big hug and blurted, "You're going to have a little sister. By next summer!"

Laughing, I said, "Oh, you're *pregnant!* I thought you were getting chubby."

I was excited about the new baby, hopeful that we'd feel more like a family. While I no longer dreaded my summer visits, I still felt like a visitor when I was there. Maybe everyone would be happier if there was a baby around. But instead of being happier, Dad and Kathy started arguing more that summer. About money. About church business. About Grandma Jane being a crazy drunk. "She's got the devil in her," Dad would say. Dad and Mom had also been arguing more about child support and visitation schedules—like I was a package being shipped back and forth.

During that summer, Kathy and I had spent one day preparing gnocchi, and at the dinner table that evening I waited impatiently for Dad to finish grace so I could dig into them. But he'd barely uttered an amen before he started yelling at Kathy about how much money she had spent that week.

"I work and contribute," Kathy said. "I should be able to buy something for the house."

"You will submit, woman!" he barked. "I'm the man of the house."

"You could have fooled me," Kathy snapped back.

Then, with a stunning crack, Dad slapped her across the face.

I gasped, waiting for Kathy to pounce—Mom would have smashed his face in with her dinner plate. But instead she burst into tears, threw her fork, flipped her chair, and stormed out of the house.

"Her histrionic tantrums are unacceptable," Dad said to me. "That's not how a pastor's wife should behave."

I wondered if pastors were supposed to behave by slapping their wives.

I ran to my room, too terrified and angry to say anything. Kathy walked for hours, a pregnant woman in the dark on those dusty roads, Dad making no effort to find her and apologize. I'd already been disappointed by Dad many times, but that night my respect for him dipped to an all-time low.

I knew Kathy wasn't perfect. She had her trauma too. There were multiple suicides in her family, and her mother had become a severe alcoholic after her father's death during her teen years. But Kathy had been a good stepmother to me, and I had a soft spot in my heart for her.

Not surprisingly, my dad's example didn't make it easy for me to understand the God he talked about or the vague bedtime stories he'd tried to tell me about who Jesus was. How was a little kid supposed to be inspired by some "heavenly Father" she couldn't see if the father who was supposed to protect her and tuck her in at night had abandoned her and then suddenly showed up and hurt the people around him? Especially when he was also trying to sell her on the idea of some Savior in white robes.

All I wanted was for my actual dad to show up when I needed him. If God was like my dad, I assumed, then He couldn't be trusted.

When that summer visit came to an end, I arrived back at Mom's to find that she had given Oso away.

"He finally got the mailman," she said. "Someone left the front door open, and he nipped his fingers trying to grab the mail." Wiping tears from her cheek she said, "I gave him to a lady who owns a ranch, before Animal Control could take him."

I cried and wasn't sure I'd ever feel safe again without Oso.

———

The following summer, when I visited Dad and Kathy, I met my new half sister, Tamara Faith, and I also discovered that the family was moving to Oregon. The large moving truck was just pulling away from the little house as we were pulling up. Two days later the four of us loaded into Dad's old pickup truck and drove from New Mexico to Drain, Oregon, where Dad became the pastor of a small church.

Kathy was busier now that Tamara had joined the family and she had a new home to settle, so I did a lot of babysitting. I'd pass the afternoons pushing Tamara in her stroller down the dirt road that ran alongside a little creek, grateful there were no rattlesnakes to worry about. Tamara babbled as I filled a bucket with wild blackberries, feeding her berries along the way to keep her quiet. Kathy would giggle when she saw the bright purple stains on our faces and clothes.

When I returned to California at the end of that particular summer, I felt a lonely void. I really missed Oso. And though I didn't get along well with Dad, I did like the feeling of having a family in Oregon. Compared to that, our house in California felt dark and empty.

The times I felt happy at home were when Mom came home from work, scooped me up, and let me snuggle in bed with her. For those couple of hours before the sun came up, I felt safe, secure, warm—ways that I rarely felt.

Once when I was nine, the insurance agency where Mom worked part-time awarded her a couple of Disneyland tickets for exceeding her sales goal. Mom was so proud to be able to spoil me, and I was ecstatic to spend the day with her. We headed off to Anaheim in high spirits, but by midmorning I was beginning to feel sick. Of all the days to get a fever, this wouldn't be the one to choose, but by midafternoon I was sure I had one. I was no stranger to high fevers and the accompanying chills.

I said nothing about how terrible I felt because there was no way I was leaving the park. It was my first time at Disneyland, and I was with Mom—I was certain there wouldn't be many days like that. Mom only figured out how sick I was when I collapsed in the Swiss Family Robinson Treehouse. Because I had waited so long to let her know, she ended up carrying a lethargic, half-conscious kid all the way to the tram, then drove straight to the hospital where we were told my temperature was 104 degrees. It turned out I had mononucleosis, and it took several weeks for me to recover. A few months later I had a tonsillectomy. I missed so much school I nearly had to repeat fourth grade.

My fears of losing my mother only increased during that time. Once I woke up at nearly three in the morning and discovered Mom wasn't home from her evening bartending job. I started calling bars and restaurants to have her paged, and by the time she arrived home at five that morning I was hysterical. Sick. Throwing up. Having a full-on panic attack. The anxiety was so paralyzing that I had to stay home from school that day.

This happened two or three times—enough so that restaurants eventually refused to page Mom when I called. Mom explained that sometimes she went to breakfast with friends after finishing her shift so she could "unwind." She didn't want to call me and risk waking me. I guess she figured I'd get used to her not coming home and assume she was out with friends. I didn't. I couldn't sleep a wink until she was home, and the stress made me sick. I'd started having anxiety attacks and dreaded leaving the house. I also became something of a loner, which made me a target for teasing at school.

Once I was sent to the principal's office for threatening to beat up a boy who had pushed me on the playground and called me a "redheaded orangutan." When Mom showed up, Mr. Acosta, the principal, said, "I think you should see the boy Tana plans to fight." He opened the door to a darkened room where Jorge, the school bully, sat alone at a desk.

"Oh, my god," Mom exclaimed. "He's huge! He'd kill her!"

"Exactly. I've already called his parents. We're not tolerating his behavior, but we can't have Tana fighting either. She's never been in trouble before, so I'm just giving her a warning."

In a snap my fear of disappointing Mom evaporated. Looking from Mom to Mr. Acosta, I said, "I won't fight if he leaves me alone, but if he shoves me again, I'm gonna clean his clock."

Mom laughed. "Honey, you shouldn't fight with boys, especially ones double your size, but you *can* defend yourself." Then, turning to Mr. Acosta, she said, "I suggest you take care of your bullying problem, or Tana will be the least of your worries."

Jorge didn't bully me again.

Maybe because I needed a break from my worries about Mom, I was looking forward to going to Oregon that summer. Dad said Tamara was walking and getting into everything, and I had *another* new sister, Jenny, who was two months old.

When I arrived, Kathy was tired and cranky. Dad said she had the "baby blues." Kathy was relieved to have me there to "play with" the girls—which was code for "babysit"—and give her a break.

Adding more stress to the situation was the fact that Kathy's sister, Diane, had been diagnosed as schizophrenic and come to live with Kathy and Dad, staying in my room while I slept on the sofa. The woman who had once been full of life, who'd played and laughed with me, now stared through me with empty, lifeless eyes on the rare occasions when she came out of the darkened room. Kathy cried hysterically when Diane's hallucinations started and she danced on the kitchen table, screaming nonsensically at us until the town doctor could come to sedate her.

That summer was the last time I saw Diane. Several months later, she would commit suicide.

Dad and Kathy argued quite a bit that summer and, for the first time, I started arguing with Dad too. One day I showed a picture of my mother and uncles to some friends at church.

"Wow, who are the two hunks with her?" Michelle asked.

"My uncles."

"Great genes," Michelle's mom said.

Dad, who'd been talking to some folks behind me, perked up at the mention of Mom's name. He spun around, red-faced, and interrupted our conversation. "If I wanted pictures of my ex-wife shown to *my* congregation, I'd show them myself."

"You should have thought about that before she became *my mom*," I snapped back.

The venom in my voice shocked Dad. He wasn't used to me voicing anger. I marched out of the church to the parsonage next door and called home to tell Mom to get me on the next flight home—I was packing my bags.

And then, as if my extreme fears of losing Mom had manifested, I learned that Mom had nearly died. Following an emergency hysterectomy and after receiving five pints of blood for severe anemia, Mom had developed appendicitis, which was overlooked because of the previous surgery. By the time someone found her, her appendix had ruptured and she was barely conscious. Because of the resulting gangrenous infection, she had remained in the hospital for two weeks, then come home with drains in her abdomen for the green pus to continue to evacuate.

Worst of all, Dad refused to allow me to return home to help her. Mom agreed, saying she didn't want me to see her in that condition.

When I did finally get home, Mom was different. She wasn't as happy. She cried easily and seemed tired all the time. Though she continued to will herself to work, whatever savings she had quickly dwindled. For the first time ever my mother looked *fragile*, a word I never would have used to describe her prior to that time.

I'd always thought Mom was superhuman. Larger than life. My days and nights had been consumed with thoughts of her. Logically I knew we were two people, but emotionally I had never made the separation. I didn't know the term back then, but I lived the reality: we were *enmeshed*.

For as long as I could remember, Mom and I had played a game. When she called to say goodnight, to telephonically tuck me in, she'd always say, "I love you more than anything in the world."

"I love you more than anything in the universe," I'd always reply.

"I love you more than anything you can ever say."

And I'd be stumped.

Being stumped in the Who Loves Whom More game somehow made me feel like the winner. But after Mom's near brush with death, I stopped playing that game. I came up with a new game, one I played solo.

What's the worst thing that can happen? I'd ask myself. I would picture the most morbid thing possible and imagine every detail of what I would do to get through it. For example, when Mom didn't come home on time, I imagined what would happen if the police came to the door to tell me she'd died in an accident the way they'd told us about Uncle Ray. I visualized having to go to the morgue and see her body, the way she had done with her brother. I thought about whom I would call, where I would go. I had no idea where I would live, but imagining the details of living on the street gave me the illusion of control.

That's when I finally realized Mom and I were separate—and when I decided that the sooner I could take care of myself, the safer I would be.

CHAPTER 4

THE PAST HAUNTING
THE PRESENT

We repeat what we do not repair.

—CHRISTINE LANGLEY-OBAUGH

When I turned eleven, my grandmother came to live with us permanently. Her health had declined so much that she could no longer safely live on her own. She had type 2 diabetes and was legally blind. Since my mother wasn't home very often, she couldn't administer Grandma's insulin shots during the day, so that task fell to me.

My grandmother adored me, but we were never particularly close, in part because she had lived through intense trauma during her childhood in Lebanon (considered Greater Syria then). As a small child during World War I, she had watched the Ottoman Empire, which ruled her country, destroy more than half the forests for fuel, create mass starvation that killed more than two hundred thousand people, and set off a pattern of violence that lasted years. She'd nearly died when she had to run into the mountains to hide from the Turkish warriors riding through her town on horseback. She'd gotten lost and spent several days in the woods—alone, hungry, cold, and terrified of the wild animals. She'd found a creek to drink from but had gotten her long hair wet and muddy, which the chill night air tinged with frost. When she was finally found she was hypothermic, and her long hair had to be cut close to her scalp.

The trauma of those days stayed with Grandma all her life. Until the day she died, she kept her ration card on her dresser as a reminder of her suffering. When Mom was young, she had been mentally unstable and even emotionally abusive. When I knew her, she preferred isolating herself in her room, watching the news, and would cry and pray most of the day. She was devoutly religious and held deep faith in the Lord but had trouble creating a stable and loving environment for the children when they were young because of her untreated mental health. She'd often wave her fists, chanting and screaming for hours. Though the chronic chaos was one of the reasons Mom left home when she was sixteen—to protect her own mental health—she had empathy and love for her mother. Years later, she and my uncle Harold said that their deep faith in God came from seeing that their mother's faith never waned, in spite of her pain and challenges. Bob said that regardless of the chaos, he never doubted his mother's love for him.

I didn't have a warm relationship with this Lebanese grandmother. I felt sorry for her, but I didn't understand many of her ways, and I often resented the way she treated my mother. But because I spent most of my childhood with Grandma and my uncles, I still fully identified with being Lebanese. My blood may have been only 25 percent Lebanese, but my heart was fully so. It was the only culture I understood outside of my American upbringing. And I did know that Grandma loved me. She would make warm Syrian bread with honey, and she would let me sneak bites of kibby nayeh (a raw lamb dish) before anyone else got a bite.

Grandma's husband, Ercel, my grandfather, was descended from poor Irish immigrants, but he'd worked hard to attend college after serving in the navy. He earned a modest living by working in a tire shop until he was finally able to open his own business in Wasco, eventually expanding to three stores. He may have been more successful if life hadn't dealt such a cruel hand, but it did, and they struggled financially and emotionally. The kids frequently found bottles of whiskey he tried to hide. They knew he'd started drinking when things got ugly at home, but he didn't drink in front of them. Grandma had been hospitalized at Camarillo State Mental Hospital for a mental breakdown, though it was later suspected that she may have actually suffered from postpartum depression following Bob's birth and a hormonal imbalance following a hysterectomy shortly after. When Grandma suspected that Grandpa had an affair (a vicious rumor that was later discovered to be a lie), she filed for divorce and wouldn't listen to reason or apologies. The stress of the ugly divorce was terrible for the four children and for their father who lost the family home he had built, due to ongoing legal fees. Somehow he managed to keep all four children in private parochial school, but the financial burden was overwhelming, and they sacrificed in other areas. As the children became more unruly without regular supervision, their single father would crack down when he'd arrive home.

He physically "disciplined" his children with a belt, to a point some would consider excessive, the boys getting the worst of it. Yet, my mother and her two living brothers harbor no ill feelings for the man who worked so hard to provide for them. They now understand that he was doing the best he could for them and appreciate how hard he worked in the face of adversity. In spite of his tough exterior, they knew he loved them. But then, when he was fifty-five years old, Grandpa's car was T-boned by a train in the fog and he was left a quadriplegic. In the aftermath of the accident, he asked forgiveness of God for the chaos he'd heaped on his children and spent his days reading his Bible. Grandpa lived in a nursing home when I was a child. I met him only a few times and don't remember much about him except for his bright red hair and his motorized wheelchair, which I rode with him around the nursing home.

I didn't really know my father's parents, Loretta and Nate. Loretta was severely depressed and would chain-smoke and read romance novels all day, rarely speaking to me the handful of times I visited her. And I never actually knew Nate, a Russian-German Jew who had come to the US on vacation in 1918 from his home in Siberia and wasn't able to return when the Russian Revolution made it impossible.

Of all my grandparents, I'm told, Nate was the most "together"—charming, in fact, according to Mom, who had always loved him. He spoke five languages and was the son of wealthy merchants before the war. But Dad's parents divorced when he was barely a year old, so Dad rarely saw him and was mostly raised by his mother, who came from a long line of strict Southern Baptists. Then, when Dad was a young child, Loretta married a stern Southern Baptist Texan named Dave, who stepped in as a father figure. According to Dad, Dave took seriously the belief of "spare the rod, spoil the child," especially with him.

When my father became a Baptist minister many years later, he adopted the mindset of his Texas clan, believing the only way he could have a relationship with his Jewish father was if the man were to repent and "give his life to the Lord." Thus, I never knew my paternal family heritage well. Nor did I know my father had a half brother, Bill—from my grandfather Nate, until I was an adult. When we met we had so much in common, I secretly wished he had been my father.

Given their unusual and very different upbringings, it's not surprising that my parents were polar opposites. My mother was fierce and relentless; my father was fragile and depressed. While neither of them finished high school, Dad had very little sense of self-worth despite his obvious intelligence. For most of my life I perceived him as a guy who had never lived up to his potential and always had an excuse.

The man I *wanted* as my father was "Pa," played by Michael Landon on the TV show *Little House on the Prairie*. I had a serious "dad crush" on him. Unlike my own father, Pa was always around. *Always,* even when it snowed so hard that he had to tie ropes from the house to the barn so he could find his way back after feeding the stock. I dreamed of a father like Pa. Someone who would come for you, no matter how deep the snow.

Even at his best, my dad never came close to being a Pa.

Today, when I look back on the family stock from which I came, I could sniff and snivel that I didn't get the father I wanted, that I had grandparents who were traumatized and checked out, that one of my uncles was a junkie and another was murdered. But even if I didn't understand it at the time, I know it now: our history doesn't have to be our destiny.

My mother instinctively knew this. That's why she worked so hard to break the legacy of poverty and abuse she had been born into. Though she had no resources and was also living with wounds from her past, she did have a vision for finding something better—and the intelligence and perseverance to make it happen.

What my family heritage taught me is that our pasts can scar us, hold us back, and limit our chances for success, but they can also motivate us and help us carve out our place in history. My mother had her faults, but she always saw opportunity in chaos, and she was absolutely committed to finding a way for the two of us to make it in a world where she didn't get many breaks. Instead, she made her own breaks. Over the years I absorbed her stubborn determination.

Looking back now, I vividly remember a particular conversation I overheard.

Mom and I were visiting one of her friends, who was far more interested in partying and trying to snag a rich husband than working. Suddenly, right in front of me, the woman lit up a joint. Mom asked me to go outside and play. Under the open kitchen window, I heard the friend offer the joint to Mom.

"No thanks," my mother said. "I don't smoke pot."

"Ah, come on," said the friend. "Light up, girl. Enjoy."

"I have to work. I can't get high all day, and I don't like it."

"Hell, why not smarten up and go on welfare instead of working your life away? At least then you could spend more time with your kid."

Yeah, Mom, I wanted to say, *why don't you go on welfare?* I had no idea what welfare was, but I figured it must be a good thing if it meant Mom could spend more time with me.

"Are you kidding me?" Mom asked.

"Hell, no, I'm not kidding. You're working yourself to death, Mary. And for what?"

"I'll never go on welfare. *Never.*"

"You can't even afford to put food on your table half the time. If you had half a brain, you'd work the system."

"I've got brains enough to know that if you let the government pay your way, then they own you—*forever!* I have more faith in my ability to work hard. My daughter is going through the hard times with me now, but she will go through the good times with me later. Welfare will hold me down. Besides, I couldn't own property if I was on welfare."

"You're dreaming, girl. You're *never* going to own property."

"I already do! And I'm saving to buy another piece of investment property right now."

Mom's friend had made the mistake so many others had—underestimating her. Only later would I understand just how much.

On the surface, we were dirt poor. We seldom got to splurge on anything. Only later would I learn that we *lived poor* in part because she was squirreling away her paychecks. To a kid, though, living poor and being poor are the same. But now I know that there's a big difference. The difference is *hope.*

Mom had been designing her "get out of poverty ASAP" plan long before she had two nickels to rub together. And the first step had been learning how to invest in property. She studied to become a real-estate agent and started working real estate on the side, which gave her the opportunity to scout the market for distressed property she could buy cheap. Having the real-estate license also meant she would not have to pay an agent fee when purchasing property for herself. But she hit a wall when she actually tried to purchase her first home because the seller didn't want to sell to a single woman, even if the woman was an agent.

Undaunted, Mom hired an attorney to write a letter to the seller. The letter was a "gentle reminder" of the several hundred lawsuits that had recently been filed on behalf of the Women's Rights Project (WRP). Thanks in part to Ruth Bader Ginsburg, the future Supreme Court justice who had cofounded the WRP, my mom was able to buy her first shabby rental house in a low-income neighborhood. Then she squirreled away the small profit she made on that property until she had enough money to buy another one. And so on and so on.

When I matured enough into my tweens to realize what Mom was doing, I became frustrated that she wouldn't just sell all her houses and upgrade the house we *lived in*. The idea of owning a bunch of rental houses made no sense to me, especially since she could combine the money from them for a better house—maybe with a pool—for us. But Mom wanted property that brought her income. And she had a rule to never sell property unless it was unavoidable, because paying taxes on the sale of investment property didn't fit her plan. Instead she figured out how to defer the taxes.

As Mom had already learned, sexism still ran strong in the 1970s, making it nearly impossible for an unmarried woman—at least where we lived—to get financing for a loan. Mom also already knew that without a college degree, it was extremely difficult to work enough hours to get ahead in the jobs that were available. (Women weren't even allowed to work overtime in many industries.) And sexual harassment was considered normal in many work environments. That's why she decided to start her own business ventures over the years, including a commercial cleaning company, obtaining a commercial driver's license so she could drive big rigs and then owning and later operating a pet store. But doing business as a single woman was difficult, too, so she started a corporation under two names: Mary Grossman (her married name) and Jo Harris (a combination of her middle name, Josephine, and her maiden name, Harris). Not only could she secure fairer service fees this way, but the ploy helped eliminate the sexual harassment she often experienced on the job. She had a "boss," Jo Harris, to hide behind when men got too friendly. And no one suspected that Mary Josephine Harris Grossman was, in fact, both people.

Mom's corporate ploy worked a lot of the time. When it didn't, she hired a lawyer. Ultimately she got what she wanted, and her career as a business owner and landlord was born.

The first house Mom bought was located in Granada Hills—not likely to be confused with Beverly Hills. We lived there for several years before it became one of her rentals. Once, shortly after we'd moved in, someone burglarized the house. Mom was surprised to see the man in her bedroom, but not as surprised as he was when she quickly ducked and grabbed her gun from under the bed, firing two bullets into the wall behind him. He dove headfirst out the window. When the police came, gunshots were never mentioned, so Mom didn't acknowledge it.

A short time later we surprised *another* burglar as we came home from the movies. We returned home to find our furniture upended and my parakeet's cage knocked over, and Mom put her hand up to prevent me from going beyond the front threshold. Then she carefully reached into the front coat closet and grabbed her shotgun just as a man emerged from my room. When he saw her, he ran toward the backdoor. Mom chased after him, and he screamed when he heard the sound of Mom racking her .12-gauge close behind him. I have no doubt she would have shot him if he hadn't made the wise decision to exit our home.

That was vintage Mom. Possessive and fiercely protective—particularly of me—she was the closest thing I knew to three other TV idols of mine—*Charlie's Angels*. Kelly, Sabrina, and Kris were smart, beautiful, and successful, and they didn't need men to solve their problems—in fact, quite the opposite. They were cool and in control. And I grew up not only hoping there were women in the world like the *Angels* but wondering how I might become one myself. Now I realize I actually grew up with one.

I might have been raised on junk food and junk TV, but I had a hustler for a mom. She never shied away from hard work and usually had simultaneous ventures. She cleaned carpets and offices, served drinks, drove eighteen-wheelers, sold insurance and real estate, owned a pet store—whatever she could do to make a buck. She was seemingly always working.

Mom's response to my frequent complaining about her absence was, "I'm working hard to keep you out of the projects—to give you a chance I didn't have." And with all the memories I have of Mom *not* being present, I still remember her managing to sing "Happy Birthday" before running out the door to work or sliding into the school auditorium just in time to see me make a fool of myself at the talent show before slipping out to her next job. Somehow she pulled it off.

Mom was—and is—intense, colorful, and a touch eccentric. Think Lucille Ball with a touch of Looney Tunes' Tasmanian Devil. She was pretty and loved hot pants, the very short shorts that were popular at the time. Occasionally she'd take me out with her, dressed to match in plaid skirts with high boots or bell-bottoms and halter tops, as if we were the Stevie Nicks twins. But Mom was a tomboy at heart and preferred guns and horses—she was excellent at handling both—to fancy clothes and restaurants.

My favorite childhood memory of Mom comes from when I was nine. We rented horses and went horseback riding in the mountains. I had Mom to myself for almost an entire, glorious day. We stopped near a creek to eat lunch, and an odd contentment washed over me as I watched Mom dismount the chestnut gelding, her familiar holstered pistol peeking out from under her leather jacket. She was fiercely beautiful, and I felt a rare peace just watching her. I wished I could freeze time that day.

Time didn't stop, of course, but watching Mom paid off. Her grit became my grit, a fact I first became aware of in third grade when I realized I was tired of being the worst student in the class. Tired of being the kid in the back of the class with the tutor helping her. Tired of feeling that everybody "knew the secret" but me. I don't recall being made fun of for my supposed stupidity, probably because I was too insignificant in the eyes of others for them to bother with me. But I still felt the stigma, and it hurt.

In hindsight, I clearly understand the source of my feelings of insignificance: I lacked any power to make a difference in my world. I thought of myself as small and weak, and I hated being that way with a vengeance. So I decided to take control and change it.

I went to the school library one Friday afternoon, checked out the thickest Laura Ingalls Wilder book I could find, and spent the entire weekend forcing myself to read. I read when I arrived home. Read during dinner. Read instead of watching TV. Read late into the night. Read over my Frosted Flakes on Saturday morning. Read the rest of that day and the next. And by Monday morning I was a reader.

It was as close to a literary born-again experience as you could have, and it stuck. All the way through high school, the only thing I would consistently get in trouble for was reading (usually novels) in class.

I was so relieved to realize that I wasn't dumb or "slow"; I was actually quite intelligent. My problem had been the classic tale of kids living in poverty. By starting school so early (to save on babysitting money), I'd been thrown in with a "fast heat," scrambling to keep up, unable to understand. I had no one at home to nurture and teach me, to encourage me, to reinforce positive messages. I ate crappy food and slept poorly, forever worried about when Mom would get home.

Year after year, this unending loop left me behind and convinced me I was dumb. But once I convinced myself otherwise, there was no stopping me. After that I wasn't the outcast any longer—at least academically.

As I grew up, I began to realize that in many respects I didn't want to be like the family generations that preceded me. But in other ways I wanted to be *just* like them—especially Mom.

The world kept telling her that she couldn't be anybody. That she didn't matter. That she was a nobody. And she turned those messages into the fuel that fired her desire to prove the world wrong.

I started to wonder if I could do the same thing.

CHAPTER 5

WITCH IN THE MIRROR

The trust of the innocent is the liar's most useful tool.

—STEPHEN KING

I entered my teen years in the midst of the Valley Girl phenomenon, which, like me, had been born in California's San Fernando Valley. It was the early eighties, the movement was reaching its zenith, and my friends were committed to playing the part to perfection. We even decided we would only date the wannabe bad-boy punk rockers, who were basically jocks in leather jackets and Doc Martens. We talked the talk, like, perfectly.

But the truth was, I was a wannabe too—a Valley Girl wannabe. I didn't qualify as the real deal for at least three reasons. First, my mom and I weren't exactly upper-middle class. Second, my life wasn't exactly wrapped up in the trivialities of malls, parties, and conspicuous consumption. Third, I didn't live in a prestigious neighborhood in Encino.

Sometimes I'd fudge and say I lived in Downey, figuring that was close enough because it beat the truth, which was that I currently lived in South Gate, Downey's bordering city—a distinctly *non*prestigious locale.

I had spent my childhood years bouncing around the Valley while Mom figured out what low-rent apartment we could afford month-to-month until she could scrounge enough cash to provide a more permanent spot. But we'd rarely stayed long enough in one place to think of it as home. For me, home had always been wherever Mom was. And now home was in South Gate. And though I remember that rental being less rundown than the others, South Gate was statistically one of the most dangerous cities in California.

We'd moved out of the house Mom owned in Granada Hills when the forced busing initiative of the late seventies passed. "I didn't bust my a** to move you to a decent school district for some a**hole bureaucrat to decide to bus you right back to where we came from," Mom had said.

Mom's political rant was lost on me, but the two times I'd taken the hour-long bus ride to a new school while Mom was figuring out where to move, I'd gotten motion sickness and thrown up on the bus. After that Mom had rented out our house, and we'd bounced around to numerous other rentals that were not in forced-busing districts, finally landing in South Gate and becoming a Valley Girl wannabe.

Over the years I'd gotten used to coming home to a quiet house with only the television for company, but this wasn't something I bragged about with friends who were deep into discussions about, like, you know, who has, like, the most bitchin' tan. I wasn't a Valley Girl, though I pretended to be. I was a scared little girl looking for a protector.

Occasionally Mom brought home a new loser. In my mind, all her boyfriends were losers because none of them made our lives better and some made my life worse—much worse. If God created red hair as a warning signal, then He made my mom's beacon extra bright. Her hair matched her fiery personality, and the woman chose men the way Custer chose fights.

Mom married her second husband, Dale, after dating him for only a couple of months. He'd convinced her the quick marriage was necessary for tax purposes. She'd met him shortly after the hysterectomy and following appendectomy that had nearly killed her. She'd been depressed and vulnerable, was busy with her newest business venture, a pet store, and her fragile health left little time for dating. But Dale had pursued her with stories of love and promises of an easier life until Mom gave in. We moved into Dale's house, which was nicer than ours but still the size of some of my friends' garages. "Personal space" was rich-people talk, not our reality.

In those weeks before Mom and Dale were married, he'd come home from work, barely acknowledge me, pour himself a drink or three, and watch TV before falling asleep. After they got back from their honeymoon, however, he changed in a hair-raising sort of way. When Mom was around, Dale still didn't look at me or talk to me. But when Mom was out of earshot, he greeted me with a saccharine-sweet voice and a creepy smile. I wasn't sure why he had changed, but I knew there was a serious slime factor behind his plastic smile. I resorted to flying under the radar and staying in my room to avoid being seen. But a girl has to eat now and then.

The first time *it* happened, Dale grabbed my wrist and yanked me onto his lap. When I instinctively tried to wriggle free, he restrained my arms and whispered, "It's fine. Just relax, Tana. When do I get to teach you how to kiss?" I didn't need experience or knowledge to know that what I felt happening *down there* with him wasn't right, not with a child. My "Spidey sense" was going berserk.

"Never!" I struggled to get free, feeling like a fly trapped in a web.

"This is normal. All dads teach their daughters how to kiss. You wouldn't know that since you haven't had a dad. But I want to do that for you now."

The smell of alcohol on his breath was making me nauseous. I didn't know much, but I was certain this wasn't what a dad did to show his daughter affection.

When he leaned in for the kiss, I yelled, "Get away from me!" and twisted my body out of his grip, breaking free and retreating to my room, where I put a chair in front of my door.

For the next week the two of us eyed each other warily. His glare suggested that by resisting him I'd done something wrong, but my heart suggested I'd done something right. I knew I had been lucky to get away, yet the whole experience had been so bizarre that eventually I began to wonder if I'd imagined it.

Did that really happen?

Did I misread his intentions?

He couldn't be dumb enough to do that with my mom down the hall, could he?

Yeah, I probably read him wrong.

Meanwhile I struggled with whether to tell Mom. And I needed to be sure before I did. She seemed so happy to finally be married, to not be carrying the whole load alone. I didn't want to spoil her newfound peace.

Looking back now, I realize Mom and I likely fit the classic "easy prey" setup for a predator on the hunt. Desperate woman struggling to keep her head above water falls for a slick guy who tells her what she wants to hear—stories of love and an easier life. Guy rationalizes that "what's hers is mine"—in this case the woman's daughter—and makes his move, knowing there's nobody around to stop him. With no witnesses, guy knows that if it comes down to his word against the daughter's, who is going to believe a kid?

I didn't know any of that then, of course. I just knew something wasn't right. So I said nothing and decided to be more cautious around him. I stayed in my room for even longer periods of time, praying that what had happened was a one-and-done event.

No such luck. The next time was nearly identical to the last, except he was much more aggressive. When I tried to get away, he restrained me and tried to kiss my ear. I almost didn't break free.

At least now I had a clear answer. It was not my imagination. I just had to figure out when and how to tell Mom. But tell Mom *what*? He hadn't *exactly* touched me in private places, had he? With my limited experience, I couldn't put words to what actually *had* happened. Maybe it wasn't all that bad. And even if I found the words, I knew he would deny it and say nothing had happened.

But I had heard an expression—"hard-on"—from a bunch of giggling boys talking at school. And when I learned its meaning, I knew that's what had happened to Dale when I was on his lap. There was also the fact that he had restrained me. *That* was a big deal. *Does making me sit in his lap when he has a hard-on qualify as touching?* Those unanswered questions occupied my every waking moment.

One Saturday morning after Mom had left early for work, I was sleeping soundly when something shattered my slumber: my new stepfather was in my bed, kissing my ear and sliding his hand up my T-shirt. I screamed and pushed him away. He smiled and cooed that I should relax, that he wouldn't hurt me. I managed to wedge my foot between my body and his and, pressing my back against the wall, kicked as hard as I could. He landed with a thud on the floor beside my bed, then got up and left with a huff of four-letter words. I left the house in my pajamas and ran to a friend's house, where I stayed until Mom came home.

I had no more time to wait or to figure out what to say. I was certain the next time I wouldn't be so lucky. So that night after my mom went to sleep, I went to her room and woke her. I leaned over to whisper in her ear but changed the subject at the last minute.

"Mom, Mom, can we go out in the kitchen so you can get me some water?"

No response. Maybe it was a mother's intuition. Maybe it was the fact that my request was so odd. But from a dead sleep she suddenly sat up with lightning-bolt speed.

"Why? Tana, tell me why."

"I'm not exactly sure, Mom, but I'm scared."

With a half-crazed look in her eye, she tried to keep her voice calm.

"Just tell me what happened."

But she already *knew.*

"I know what it was, and I believe you," she said. "I need you to trust me and tell me everything."

Feeling safe and secure for the first time in weeks, I told my mother what had happened. My red-hot cheeks burned as tears streamed down my face. I felt so ashamed.

She cradled me in her arms.

"Tana, you did nothing wrong. I am so, so proud of you. I believe you, and I am going to take care of this."

"But he'll call me a liar."

"Then we will make sure he doesn't. Do you trust me?"

"I think so," I said with as much apprehension as confusion. *Trust her to do what?*

"I'm going to set this up so he can't say you're lying. We're going to catch him in the act. You're going to need to go out there one more time, but this time I'll be watching."

I looked at my mother, a tad fuzzy about her plan, but fairly certain that it was going to involve me as bait.

"At exactly eight tomorrow tonight," she told me, "I want you to go out there just like you have in the past. Go out to the kitchen to get a drink of water."

"Mom, no. Please, no, don't make me do that. What if you fall asleep and something happens?"

"Trust me, Tana, I will *not* be sleeping."

I was terrified, but I had seen my mother in action before.

"He won't get away with anything. If he makes a move for you, I'll be all over him."

I exhaled. "Okay," I said, "but don't fall asleep. Please, please, *please.*"

Her icy grin and determined eyes were all the confirmation I needed.

As was her routine at that point in our lives, Mom went to bed early the next night. Her plan was to prearrange a mirror kitty-corner down the hall, so she had a perfect vantage point into the living room. A test run confirmed that, with her room dark, she would be able to see him from the bedroom, but he wouldn't be able to see her. When he grabbed me she would arrive, I suspected, like the FBI on TV making a drug bust.

I was petrified. What eleven-year-old has to be put in this kind of situation? Then again, what eleven-year-old should be the victim of a predator? Worries kept running through my mind. *What if Mom falls asleep? What if he hurts me before she can ride to the rescue? What if he hurts Mom?*

I waited in my room until eight that night, my heart pounding, my fingers fidgeting, my mind racing. By now Dale would have had enough time to down a few drinks and assume my mom was asleep.

I peeked down the hall to make sure her door was cracked open before walking out.

Check.

As soon as I tried to walk past him toward the kitchen, he grabbed me and pulled me onto his lap once again, restraining me in the fashion I expected. I yelped. He tried kissing my ear, and I glanced at the cockeyed mirror, seeing Mom's faint silhouette in the background.

Suddenly there was a blaze of red hair and a black nightgown flying from the shadows like a crazed witch. I gasped. Stunned, he released his grip.

"Tana, go to your room *now*!" Mom yelled.

Relieved when Dale released his grip, I jumped up and started walking away.

She pounced on him like a mama bear protecting her cub—flailing her arms, scratching with her nails, scorching him with eyes ablaze in anger. The screeching of her voice suggested she was reaching the level of psychotic rage.

"You evil son of a b*tch! I will kill you!"

Looking at her, I almost believed the words.

Dale broke free and pointed a finger at me. "She's lying!" he said, an odd accusation given that I hadn't said a word.

"Tana, stay in your room and block the door," said Mom.

I obeyed. Beyond my closed bedroom door, I heard scuffling and angry words exchanged. Then the front door opened and shut, and the house got quiet for a moment. Fearful that Mom had been hurt, I raced out to the porch. Dale was standing on the lawn, unsuccessfully trying to quiet Mom, who was now running up and down the street in her nightgown, unleashing an expletive-peppered burst of fury into the night air, ensuring that the neighbors got the message that Dale was a child molester. Over and over she screamed until her voice all but gave out. Finally, she dropped to her knees in the middle of the dark street, shaking and crying.

"What the hell's going on out here?" a neighbor yelled just as Dale was driving away.

As I watched through the window I thought, *Great, Tana, now the entire* neighborhood knows your deepest secret, that your new stepdad has been "molesting" you. *Molesting*—yet another word to add to my growing vocabulary.

In terms of putting an end to a daughter getting sexually attacked, I'm not sure Mom's "bait, bust, and embarrass" ploy would have passed muster with Child Protective Services, though her heart was certainly in the right place. And legally at least, it didn't get us anywhere.

When my mother tried to prosecute, a lawyer told her that because there'd been no "penetration," she'd most likely be fighting a losing battle in the courts. In other words, it would be difficult to seek justice for me as a child because I hadn't been traumatized badly enough. *Really?*

"And meanwhile your daughter is going to get dragged through the mud and teased for years," he said. "The defense will paint Tana out to be someone she's not, which could be psychologically damaging."

So Mom gave up on legal remedies and took matters into her own hands. She "suggested" to Dale that he might want to take a really long vacation on an isolated piece of farmland he owned in Canada. Phrases like "statute of limitations" and "or else" were tossed around. While I didn't understand all of it, the result was that Dale agreed to leave the state and have the marriage annulled. Mom had made him believe she wasn't afraid to do whatever was necessary to protect me.

"And one more thing," she told him. "You're going to pay us ten thousand dollars for a new start and the counseling my daughter is going to probably need to get over the trauma you created."

Dale reluctantly accepted that part of Mom's "sentence" too. But I remember seeing a therapist only once, though Mom says it was more. It was Mom I remember going to see "the doctor" regularly, though at the time I didn't know the doctor was a psychiatrist she had started seeing for anger and depression.

For me, the most important takeaway from the whole situation was that Mom had taken a stand for me. She'd believed me, and I felt validated. Even though Dale hadn't gotten what he deserved, under the circumstances, Mom had done a pretty good job as detective, prosecutor, judge, and jury.

A few weeks later I was working the front counter at the pet store when the phone rang. I answered it.

"Hi, Tana. How ya doin'?"

I was stunned at hearing Dale, particularly because he had the *nerve* to speak to me in that slimy-sweet voice as though nothing had happened. I felt as if I'd been sucker punched. Every fiber in my body recoiled.

"Are you fricking kidding me?" was all I could manage. Seething, I slammed the phone onto a nearby metal rabbit cage.

Mom rushed over and asked what was going on.

"The *a**hole* is on the phone for you," I shouted, intending for him to hear. Mom looked as shocked by the use of my new vocabulary as by the intensity behind it.

"Tana!" she hissed. "Be polite."

"*Be polite?* He tries to rape me, and you think I'm supposed to be *polite* to him?"

"Don't. Be. Rude," Mom said with clenched teeth, her staccato warning making me reconsider her view of the bad guy in this scenario.

I just blinked. I felt totally justified in being rude, and I wasn't sorry in the least. My fury raged internally at my mother for thinking I should be polite to a predator, and that black seed of anger turned into a dark root of resentment that I wouldn't fully recognize for years. My mother and I would still be close, but that unfinished conversation would linger in our relational background like thunderclouds threatening to burst.

It would be decades before I understood—if not agreed with—Mom's side of the story. She had been as frightened by my rage as by Dale's predatory behavior. When she had scolded me for being rude, she had been scrambling to regain control. I'd lost my temper in our place of business, which I'd failed to see as important under the circumstances. Plus, it turned out that he was calling to arrange a payment, one he had never been legally obligated to make, and my tantrum had threatened to screw that up.

What I also didn't know at the time was how much my stepfather had hurt my mother. When he molested me, he'd violated her trust. She believed she'd failed as a mother, as a protector, and as a woman, and she was having a lot of trouble getting over that. The worst part for Mom was knowing that Dale was likely to victimize another young girl and she felt helpless to prevent it.

As a young girl who had barely escaped the bogeyman, I couldn't comprehend any of that. Overcome with my own pain, I felt misunderstood, isolated, and angry. God knows my mom was doing her best. But her sudden backtracking that day in the store nearly undid whatever affirmation I'd originally felt when she'd fought for me.

It would take years of perspective and intense therapy to find out how this incident had affected me, but I ultimately got it. After protecting me and telling me I could always be honest, my mother had unwittingly taken away my voice with three words: "Tana, be polite." I would spend the next twenty years trying to find my voice again. And when I did, I would wield it as a double-edged sword.

On one edge it contained the truth I needed to advocate for myself.

On the other, it held the power to destroy anyone who tried to hurt me.

Unconsciously I'd claim a new motto: *If you think you're in danger, fight. Be a b*tch if you have to, and if you're wrong, apologize later. But never, ever let anyone take away your voice.*

CHAPTER 6

FROM SEXY B*TCH
TO SCARY B*TCH

One's dignity may be assaulted, vandalized,
and cruelly mocked, but it can never be
taken away unless it is surrendered.

—MICHAEL J. FOX

At West Middle School in Downey, there were only so many ways you could gain social status, and chief among them was making the cheerleading squad. As spontaneously as I'd decided to learn to read, I decided that's what I must do—become a cheerleader.

I admit that was an unlikely quest for me. I'd finally overcome my academic awkwardness. But socially, well, that was another story. I was tired of feeling like an outcast. I wanted to fit in, and for the first time in my life I was determined to make it happen.

How to make the cheerleading squad was the big question. The competition was fierce. I didn't have a dance background or friends I could practice with. In fact, I didn't have many friends at all. Mom and I didn't have money for the expensive dance classes the other girls attended. But my mother had already taught me another important life lesson: First you commit to getting something done. Resolve to do it. Because if you want the "what" bad enough, you'll figure out the "how."

This may sound small, shallow, and conniving, but remember the context: seventh grade. Realizing that my biggest obstacle was being a bookworm, a nerd, I began to study how I could be more like the others—how I could dress, talk, and act like them. I resolved to transform myself as I watched them slyly from behind a book during every break, to avoid being accused of stalking. Then I took action.

Mom was able to afford less expensive dance lessons at the YMCA, and I attended every class possible. Every night for hours I practiced cheerleading moves in front of our mirror. Every morning I practiced using makeup and a curling iron. Then, finally, tryouts arrived, and no one was more shocked than I was when I made the squad.

It took a few months for the other girls to accept me and for me to fit in after spending my first seven academic years as an outcast, but eventually we melded and I started eighth grade as a popular cheerleader. Something I had once thought impossible. Those middle school years turned into good ones. Sporting my new curls, Keds, and bubble gum lip gloss, my past experience of feeling like a scrawny victim didn't fit the new identity I was going for. So I left it behind. Wardrobe malfunctions and figuring out how to get the newest Journey cassette were about the biggest problems I was willing to take on. I felt happy about who I was. I had confidence for the first time, reinforced by all the hard work that had ultimately paid off. Best of all, I had a group of girls who were like sisters to me, something I had never felt.

That close-knit group of friends helped to make up for the loneliness of my nights. Mom's pet store kept her working so much every day that she was usually too tired to make the hour-long drive home. She bought a rundown motor home, parked it in the alley behind the store, and began living there about half the week. The only person providing supervision for me when

Mom was gone was my grandma, who rarely came out of her room other than to get food.

Grandma was there primarily so we could take care of her. She had become a hoarder and a recluse and was morbidly obese. She always had sweets hidden in her room, which she sometimes offered me in exchange for company, but I was usually too busy with my blossoming new social life to hang out. Her room was packed with boxes, trinkets, and recycled margarine tubs that she was afraid to throw out, in case of another war. She watched the news all day, looking for signs of doom, though with her limited English she often confused the news with daytime television dramas and sometimes recited events from the latest episode of *Days of Our Lives* as if Ted cheating on Myrna was actual headline news. My heart broke for her, but secretly I was glad she stayed in her room when my friends came over. I'm not sure which was worse: my being embarrassed by Grandma or the sadness and anger I felt when people made fun of her.

It was about this time that Mom met Joe. At zero for I-lost-count, her stats in the boyfriend department already stank. But Grandma and I agreed that Joe had all the makings of another strikeout. He wasn't good enough for Mom—none of them were as far as I was concerned—and he was seventeen years older than she was. He was crude and frequently told racist jokes, which no one thought were funny, yet he kept telling them. I was sure he did it to shock people. When Grandma vowed to make Joe's life miserable, she and I formed a bond with the unspoken mutual goal of getting rid of him.

Joe's presence was intimidating at best, despite his fifty-two years of hard living—or maybe because of it. He was six foot four and gruff, not the kind of guy you'd want to meet in a dark alley. He had been in the Special Forces and flown jets in Vietnam and had told us that once his plane had been shot down and he'd hit his head on the canopy as he ejected. After a rough landing in the rice paddies, he had lain unconscious for a day. The result was a metal plate in his head and multiple partial gold crowns over his front teeth.

Joe's quick, gold-toothed smile added a chill to his already menacing appearance, but I'd already come face-to-face with things that go bump in the night. After Dale I was fed up, angry, and looking for a reason to fight with Joe. I even secretly hoped he might cross the line and lay a hand on me, knowing *that* was one thing that would buy him a one-way ticket out of town, courtesy of Mom.

Joe pursued my mother relentlessly and soon moved in with us. But something felt wrong to me—something that went beyond my tendency to distrust any man in Mom's life. His "business" trips didn't add up, and I told Mom as much. Maybe if I could reveal whatever he was up to, the discovery would deep-six this blossoming relationship.

"Something's going on, Mom," I said. "He's not being honest with you."

Not like anyone was listening to an angry adolescent who was obviously hell-bent on banishing her mom's love interests to the back forty. However, Mom must have had her own suspicions because she hired a private investigator and discovered that Joe had a house about a mile from ours—where he lived with his *wife and daughter,* who was about my age. We drove by once and saw them in the front yard.

After Mom confronted Joe, their fights were hellacious, but the end result wasn't what I'd hoped for. Joe convinced Mom that he was actually separated and only living in the same house with his family for financial reasons after their house had gone into foreclosure. He then divorced his wife and moved in with us permanently. Just my luck. What's more, Mom paid off his debts, bought the house that had been in foreclosure, and let Joe's wife and daughter live there rent-free for years.

My intervention had backfired big-time. Now Joe was always around, even when Mom wasn't. Despite being a chemical engineer, he wasn't employed, so Mom put him to work chauffeuring me around. I was embarrassed for my friends to meet Joe when we all piled into the back of his battered pickup truck. But my friends were fascinated by him.

————

Despite Dale and Joe, my middle-school years were fun and fulfilling, but high school brought an entirely different set of challenges. I had erroneously believed the acceptance I'd found in middle school would be mine to keep forever. But two concurring events changed everything and left me chasing the elusive acceptance like a fickle, fair-weather friend.

The summer between eighth and ninth grade, I had a "glow up." I got my braces off, learned a thing or two about makeup, and gained a few pounds in an, um, critical area of my anatomy.

I'm not talking training-bra-sized boobies, the kind moms giggle over and say, "Ah, how cute!" My breasts emerged that summer as if in time-lapse photography. And believe me, people *noticed*—especially male people. Kids who'd once called me "carrot top," "bird legs," and "freckle-faced dork" now teased me for being "stacked." I couldn't walk anywhere without catcalls from the guys driving by. Older boys I didn't know were asking me out. One senior I'd never met gossiped that he'd *slept* with me.

I still had my girlfriends for support, at least for a while. But I looked much older than they did, and because of that I drew far more attention—usually derisive, and not limited to boys. It became overwhelming. The changes confused me about who I was and how I was valued.

Joe did nothing to deter this dark side of my life. He would look me up and down with a leer, sometimes saying "Nice a**" as I walked by or "You're one sexy b*tch." In some twisted way, I could tell that he meant it as a compliment, as if being a "sexy b*tch" was some sort of superpower. But I hated it, and I really couldn't stand him.

It's not like I just took it. I also had a nickname for him: Di**head. He'd just laugh when I said it, even though I wasn't trying to be the least bit funny.

Unlike Dale, Joe wasn't sneaky. He made his blatantly vulgar comments in front of family and friends. But talking that way about me was a right he reserved for himself alone—God help anyone else who did the same. Joe threatened to kill more than a few people for making similar comments to me. And he wasn't beyond violence in the name of protecting people he cared about, which weirdly included me.

This point was first made patently clear to me one afternoon after he'd picked me up from a cheerleading competition. I was still in my uniform when we stopped at a 7-Eleven for a Slurpee, a hot dog, and a Ding Dong, one of my favorite dinners. While we stood in the checkout line, a slovenly drunk came up behind us. He reeked of alcohol and struggled to stand up. But he was sober enough to say, quite vividly, what he wanted to do to my body—starting with the f-word and ending with a vivid word for my backside.

Joe didn't say a word. He simply took a step back and, with his foot planted on top of the guy's foot, slammed his elbow into the guy's solar plexus. The besotted fool dropped to the floor without a sound. I was still trying to figure out what had happened to the guy, who writhed on the ground, gasping for air, when Joe dropped a ten-dollar bill on the counter to pay for our food and walked out to the car without waiting for change. I followed obediently as the kid behind the counter stifled his laughter.

Still in shock, I got into the car with my food and heard Joe say, "You need to learn to protect yourself."

"Like what do you mean?"

"Like learn to fight. Karate. Judo. Learn to hit soft targets, like the balls," he said. Making a fist and a twisting motion, he added, "Grab and rip, and I promise their hearts and minds will follow."

"Seriously?" I rolled my eyes. "For just a moment I thought you were a decent human."

That was it—the deepest conversation we ever had. But I realized something about Joe in that moment. He was unequivocally wrong to say the leering, disgusting things he said to me. (I would physically harm anyone who spoke that way to my daughter today.) But somewhere in the depths of his redneck brain, he believed he was helping me. And in many ways I believe that too.

Joe followed up on that conversation in the weeks and months that followed. We didn't have money for defense-type classes. So Joe taught me a few moves at home, including how to make a man sing soprano with a well-placed knee to the groin.

———

The second big change in my life involved a move I didn't want to make. At the beginning of my sophomore year, Mom bought one of the few houses she could afford in a middle-class area of Huntington Beach. It was near the pet store and the ugliest fixer-upper in the neighborhood, desperately in need of an overhaul. For a while she drove back and forth between it and our rental in South Gate, where I was staying with Grandma, but I knew that wouldn't last. I knew she wanted us all to move into the Huntington Beach house together.

Mom did her best to convince me that starting a new school would be fun, a chance to start over. I wasn't buying it. Why should I have to move away from my friends and into a house with a man I couldn't stand?

I pleaded my case to at least finish out my school years where I was and threw in an extra dose of guilt. I must have been somewhat successful, because she maintained both residences until it became too expensive. But in the end my arguments changed nothing. Toward the end of my sophomore year, Grandma and I moved to Huntington Beach to live full time with Mom and Joe in the fixer-upper, and I lost the support system I'd come to depend on, the cheerleaders who'd been like sisters to me.

Shortly after the move, Grandma became a kleptomaniac, according to Joe. He claimed she was stealing from him. And sure enough, we found random tools, belts, loose change, his partial dentures, and other things—never Mom's or mine—in her room.

Grandma claimed Joe was framing her. I thought Grandma was brilliant and even encouraged her.

Joe's teasing about my appearance went from bad to worse once we were all living together. So did the response from others, especially classmates at my new school. I was bewildered that something as normal as physically growing up could wreak so much havoc in my life, but it did—especially since my "growth" seemed to be concentrated in one particular area. My boobs had gone from big to even bigger, and no one, it seemed, was going to let me forget that fact.

Imagine my surprise at being called a b*tch for daring to talk to one of the cheerleaders my first day at my new school. Someone even spit on the ground in front of me as I walked by! I had been one of them, a cheerleader. Now, suddenly, I was no one. Actually, I was worse than no one. I was the girl everyone liked to make fun of, harass, and call names. Being no one would have been a welcome relief.

I had been an outcast most of my life because I was a skinny nerd. Now I was becoming an outcast for the opposite reason: because I was overdeveloped. I couldn't regain my previous status as a cheerleader, and going unseen didn't seem to be an option either. Instead, I was subjected to the high court of school royalty, who relegated me to the status of Stuck-up School Slut.

That's when I began to hate school again. I'd walk with my books clutched close to my chest and speak to no one. The only times I felt I had a voice at all was if I was venomously lashing out in anger.

I struggled in my studies for the first time since third grade, not because I wasn't smart enough, but because I couldn't focus. When Tommy, a freckle-faced boy who wore glasses, gave me the nickname Jugs at the beginning of the year, it stuck. So Jugs was my nickname in high school, and Sexy B*tch was my nickname at home.

I had the perfect ingredients for a code-red identity crisis. I began accepting the definitions others had for me—at least outwardly. Rather than fight it, I began rolling with the idea that my body was free territory for anyone to gawk at, joke about, comment on. My physical features became my identity. Sexy was what people expected me to be, a standard for me to live by. Sexy B*tch brought it to life.

Living near the beach would have been the one ray of light in my life, had it not been drowned out by the overwhelming drama not only at school but also at home. I despised Joe's crude jokes. I despised their chain-smoking. Even more, I despised all the fighting. It was nonstop—between Mom and Joe, between Joe and me, and between Joe and Grandma. Basically same crap, different day. Our house was not a home, not a place of comfort and safety, not a place I wanted to bring friends to hang out. On top of that, the place was always under construction. Nothing was ever *done*, and boxes full of lord-knows-what cluttered the hallways.

One memorable evening, when I had finally taken a chance on inviting one of my few friends over, Mom and Joe got into a rip-roaring fight over his irrational jealousy. He shoved her and then, as an exclamation point, he threw something at her TV. And that's when the sparks really began to fly. Never mind that he'd been in the Special Forces; my mom was a special force all her own. As muddled as her boundaries were about many things, they were crystal clear about macho, "power over others" BS.

When my friend and I walked down the hallway to check on the commotion, Mom was on Joe's back, and had him in a choke hold. "Pack sand in your a**, you SOB! And don't ever put a hand on me again, or I will pack it for you!"

"Get off of me, you crazy b*tch! You're choking me!" He literally choked the words out, sounding more like Mickey Mouse than a war-toughened vet.

They spun around with Mom on his back, screaming like a banshee. Dizzy, he fell onto the bed, she let go, and they both burst into laughter for a moment before picking up where they'd left off, screaming and threatening.

I was totally embarrassed, but my friend was totally enthralled. Later she laughed so hard that I thought she was going to pee her pants.

"Your mom doesn't take crap from anyone!" she said.

It's true that you did *not* want to cross Mom, but after the incident with Dale, we both were feeling vulnerable. And Mom faced the never-ending responsibilities that came with keeping us afloat financially even while she was trying to parent a precocious, overdeveloped teen. She would later tell me that part of the reason she kept Joe around—even after learning that he'd lied to her about being married—was that she thought he would protect me. In other words, I wasn't the only scared little girl in that household. Mom had been white-knuckling her way through life for twenty years.

Before long, Joe became a partner in Mom's business. The pet store she'd purchased several years earlier had a grooming parlor in the back that became one of the most lucrative in the area as a result of her "never say no" policy. We didn't just groom dogs. We groomed *mean* dogs, cats, bunnies, and any other furry creature someone happened to bring in, including an opossum. And we were open seven days a week, including holidays.

By the time I was eleven, I knew how to sell every product in the store and could upsell most. As a result, Mom started making me work every weekend and anytime I wasn't in school. When I complained about the long hours, she said, "I can teach product knowledge, but I can't teach sales *instinct*. You get that from me, kid. Our sales are almost 30 percent higher when you're here. Besides, you gotta be here so I can be in the grooming parlor."

Our grooming business spawned yet another business opportunity that Mom jumped on with her usual energy. The chemical-laden grooming products available at that time were harsh. Their toxicity wasn't good for the dogs, and it was even worse for my mom and the other groomers who had to use the stuff every day. So Mom asked Joe, who had a degree in chemical engineering, to help her make the products less toxic. He invented a safer formula, and Mom started producing it in our garage, storing it in fifty-gallon drums gathered from an industrial park. They found a partner to help with distribution until they eventually bought him out.

As other stores started buying the solution, we slowly but surely made our way out of poverty on a combination of elbow grease and ingenuity. It was mostly Mom's hard work, but she always credited Joe because he helped her create the formula. Within a few years Mom had bought a small industrial building (which she would later keep as an investment property), leased a large manufacturing plant, and expanded the operation to include international distribution.

That success did not happen overnight, however. As always, it was Mom working long hours in both businesses while Joe sat at the kitchen table in his robe, listening to the news. His caustic teasing of me never stopped, which gave me ample opportunities to practice my caustic responses. But we arrived at an unspoken understanding. He never tried to touch me and continued pushing me to protect myself. And while I still thought he was an inappropriate jerk for making crude comments, I also knew he would protect me if necessary. It was the first time in my life I could say that with certainty about a man.

The point was proven again one summer night when I was outside and one of the skinheads next door leered at me a little too intently. Ignoring them, I went in the house and watched through the open window as Joe lingered in the yard. He always carried a .45-caliber pistol that he wasn't subtle about concealing.

"You better pray that nothing happens to that girl," he said gruffly to the neighbor. "In fact, you should probably *protect* her. Because if something happens, I'm going to assume you're behind it. And I will rip your f***ing head off and sh*t down your neck. Got that?"

———————

A few months later I was walking to school on one of Huntington Beach's main streets at eight thirty on a typical November morning. My oversized hobo purse was stuffed with my Pee-Chee folder and a textbook. The sun was out, and the cool breeze from the ocean swept down the boulevard among the moderate traffic. The two-mile walk past a few houses, a strip mall, and a few apartment buildings was usually uneventful.

As I approached the alley separating twin apartment buildings, a guy swerved a blue Nissan 300ZX to the curb next to where I was walking, parked, and quickly got out. Surprised by the maneuver but assuming he was headed into the apartments, I ignored him and continued walking—until he ran to catch up with me. He was maybe six foot two, early thirties, wearing a business suit. He wouldn't have stood out in an Orange County crowd.

"Hey, beautiful, my name's John," he said, "and I'm a real-estate loan rep heading for an open house. Will you join me?"

As pickup lines go, I'd heard worse. *But why do these idiots think this works?* Like there was any way I'd go anywhere with this dude.

"No," I said and tried to walk past him. But he caught up and fell in step beside me.

"Come on, I really want you to join me."

"I have a boyfriend." *Just blow him off. Walk faster. He will go away.*

"Does your boyfriend control everything you do?"

"No, actually I just don't want to go with you!" I said with a roll of my eyes.

"You're so beautiful. Why won't you come with me?"

"Um, because I'm fifteen and going to *high school*."

"Come with me," he persisted. "It'll be fun."

By this time I had passed the first building in the complex and was standing where the alley met the sidewalk.

Dismissing him, I raised my chin and looked away as I increased my pace, putting him behind me. That was my mistake. Suddenly I felt one hand clamp between my legs from behind, pulling me closer, and the other groping my chest.

What the—

"I love you so much," he said with a Hannibal-Lecter-in-*The-Silence-of-the-Lambs* sort of smile.

Spinning around, I slapped his face hard and viciously screamed several curse words at him.

He laughed an eerie laugh and grabbed my sweater, stretching it, yanking me. A deep rage welled up within my gut. Through a haze of anger, I realized if he got me into the bushes, nothing good was going to happen. But I was oddly devoid of fear, at least consciously.

In a crisis, it's been said, we all have either a fight, flight, or freeze response. In that moment I discovered which defined me: I had a major, go-completely-psycho, I-will-rip-your-face-off *fight* response. I screamed. I shook. I pushed. I scratched. But he only came toward me again, laughing smugly at my lame attempts at self-defense.

"Oh, yes. Like that! I love that. I love you so much."

I was fighting for my life along a main boulevard. Cars were driving past, even stopping at a light just ahead, but no one stopped. I was on my own. I tried kicking him in the groin but missed. I kicked his thigh.

He stopped laughing. His eyes turned to stone, his laughter to rage. He grabbed my shoulders, shaking me like a rag doll, and shoved me toward the bushes. In a flash, I knew with perfect clarity what would happen next.

In a brazen move that was part confidence and part desperation, I grabbed his shirt, pulled him toward me, and brought my knee up into his groin as hard as I could. He stared straight ahead, frozen with pain. Then he released me as he doubled over with his hands over his crotch.

It was the second of freedom I needed. I kicked off my useless high heels and ran—not to school, but to my mom's pet store a couple of blocks away. When I walked through the back door about ten minutes later, I was peculiarly calm.

Mom looked at me, confused and immediately on high alert. I didn't have my shoes on. Her eyes darted from my stretched sweater hanging cockeyed off my shoulder to my broken nails and oddly tousled curls.

"Tana? What happened?"

I had a stupid, empty smile on my face. My expression didn't match my disheveled body. It was like that of a severed doll's head lying bodiless on the floor—violated, broken, but still smiling.

"The weirdest thing, Mom," I said calmly. "Some guy just attacked me on the street."

My mother's scream startled me out of my shock and into the reality of what had happened.

"What the hell?" she screamed. "What the hell?"

Finally, it hit me that I had been assaulted and nearly raped. On a main boulevard. In broad daylight. On my way to school. And no one had paid any attention.

The tears finally came, and they wouldn't stop.

———

When the police arrived to take my statement, the male officer said, "I need to know exactly what happened, as clearly as you can recall the details."

"No, I can't tell you. My mom's here." My face flushed, and I started shaking at the thought of repeating what had happened. I'm not sure why I didn't want to talk about it in front of my mom, whether it was shame, fear, or embarrassment.

"I guarantee your mother is not going to be mad at you for what you say. If anything, she's proud that you fought."

My eyes shifted to my mom's tear-stained face. Almost imperceptibly, she nodded.

The officer said that he'd taken scores of reports from women who'd been raped or attacked. Most had told him, "I thought if I was quiet and coopera-tive, he wouldn't hurt me."

"But we know that's never the answer," he said. "You're just fifteen years old, and somehow you knew that fighting was the right thing. What you did saved your life."

These are words I have never forgotten. The officer validated my fighting for my own protection, as unladylike as it may have been. Whatever shame and embarrassment I felt melted when I heard, "What you did saved your life."

I told him it had seemed like the attack lasted for ten minutes. I could see the man's face clearly, the material of his suit, his disgusting smile. The officer explained that actually it had probably lasted less than ten to fifteen seconds.

"No way! How can that be?" I asked.

"When we are physically attacked and terrified for our lives, our percep-tion of time is distorted."

The police never found the guy who assaulted me. For a few weeks after the attack, Mom and Joe were hypervigilant, not allowing me to walk anywhere. They were scared. I was scared. Meanwhile, Joe conducted his own search, and everyone was a suspect: delivery people, the exterminators, and the construction crew working on the neighbor's house. He questioned everyone he could think of, to no avail.

Who *was* that guy? Had he been watching me? Was it premeditated? Would he come back? Not knowing made it hard for any of us to let it go.

And then one morning my fear suddenly turned to a second wave of rage. I grew furious that someone had claimed the right to take away my innocence, my freedom to walk safely down the street, my sense of security, my dignity. Why, I wondered, was I the one who had to go through life feeling scared? I wasn't the psychopath in a suit. He was. This wasn't my problem. It was his.

Enough! My nickname Sexy B*tch took on a whole new meaning. If I was going to be sexy, it would be on *my* terms. And if anyone ever tried to assault me again, the only b*tch they would encounter would be a scary one.

One night I lay in bed, discombobulated by what had happened and by the general chaos in my life, by the seemingly impossible challenge of being myself without feeling exploited at every turn. I wasn't certain if it was my fault or if I was a victim of circumstance, but I was clear about one thing: *Tana, being nice ain't gonna cut it.*

I might have still been something of a scared little girl, but I had learned to use my voice. Now I vowed to never, ever give it up.

I had also learned that scared little girls don't always need to be nice. Sometimes they need to fight. And if that meant I was a b*tch, I could live with that.

CHAPTER 7

FALLEN STAR

If you never heal from what hurt you, you'll
bleed on people who didn't cut you.

—Unknown

By the time I was sixteen, I had heard almost every boob joke there ever was. Most of them suggested that females were bubble-headed bimbos, but I quickly learned who the real airheads were: the guys making the jokes. I noticed that when a woman with large breasts walked into a room, it was the men who were tripping over their tongues or making incoherent Neanderthal sounds. I witnessed intelligent men suddenly drop twenty IQ points when breasts were involved.

I even had a counselor at our school ask me out right in front of the few friends I'd finally managed to make. Though he'd flirted with me before, I could only hope he wasn't serious. I openly rejected him, but of course the rumor mill didn't spin the story to show that he was a pig. Instead, I was a slut.

Another time, when I tried to buy a bedspread—a special treat that Mom had agreed to charge on her credit card—the man at the counter handed the card back to me.

"I don't want your money," he said. "I just want your phone number."

I wasn't stupid. His intentions were clear. Even then I knew that the most expensive things in life were those advertised as free.

I insisted he take the card. He vehemently refused, harassing me for my number. *Okay, fine, idiot.* I wrote down a fake phone number and walked out of the store with the free bedspread.

Mom's reaction? She was angry with me for not paying, insisting I had stolen the bedspread. Joe, rolling in laughter, suggested the "ethical" reaction would have been to accept the free bedspread and give the guy my actual phone number. I couldn't win.

One day Mom surprised me and told me she was taking a rare day off to hang out with me at the beach. As we walked on the boardwalk, enjoying our mother-daughter bonding moment, a guy shouted at me, "Magic Johnson! Look at those basketballs!"

"Where do you store the ice in that chest?" his friend yelled.

Nearby, a guy on a bicycle rode straight into a wall. I'm not sure if he was distracted by my boobs or by the other two idiots making a scene.

By that point, I was almost numb to this type of adolescent exchange. Almost. But with those assaults coming at me faster than one-two punches, I wanted to disappear. Instead, I was stuck on display in the middle of it all, and my own mother was doubled over with laughter.

I wanted to say: "Mom! Hello! You're supposed to be supporting me, not encouraging them." I felt like I was some circus animal and my mom had joined the crowd outside the cage like a tour guide happy to see the tourists enjoying themselves.

Though I wasn't a goody two-shoes in high school, I didn't sleep around either. I didn't even date much before finding a boyfriend, and he was the only one I had until I graduated. I certainly didn't party all weekend or do drugs like many of the other kids. Yet I was the one who was labeled a slut—because of something about my body I could do nothing about.

Some people remember high school as a wonderful coming-of-age time when they clung to innocence or, if they preferred, leapt to independence. I remember it as four years of hell. I couldn't wait to graduate. At least in the "real world," I thought, I'd have a chance to blend in a bit. At this point I not only looked older than my classmates, I also "thought older." High school felt trivial, classmates immature, and teachers untrustworthy.

Then a modeling opportunity presented itself. Several photographers and managers had told me I had potential, and as far as I was concerned the prospect beat the heck out of cleaning dog kennels at Mom's pet store, now a small but thriving business. I'd been working from the age of eleven, and I'd even spent a summer washing windows to earn enough cash for school clothes when money was particularly tight. (I was my mother's daughter after all.) But the idea of making money by modeling was both surprising and intriguing.

I'd never thought I was particularly pretty and usually thought men were patronizing me when they said I was beautiful. I also knew that having big boobs and having a pretty face weren't the same thing. But if people were seriously willing to pay me to smile pretty, I was game. It sounded easy enough.

As I was modeling a bathing suit on a runway at the Long Beach Convention Center, an average-looking guy who appeared to be in his early forties approached me. I was sixteen years old at the time.

"I'd like to photograph you," he said. "I'll be honest. I'm just getting started in photography after retiring from my career. I need some photos for my portfolio, and I will give you a copy for free. My studio is in Beverly Hills."

It sounded a bit suspicious, but I'd already learned that good photos were expensive—and they were the key to modeling offers. I accepted, and Mom agreed to take the day off work to accompany me to the guy's place of business.

"Jim" had a studio built into his huge Beverly Hills mansion—a fact he'd conveniently forgot to mention. Mom and I were confused as we were called in through the security gate and made our way up the winding driveway into the hills off Benedict Canyon Drive, land of movie stars, former Mexican presidents, and five-million-dollar "fixer-uppers." Nothing about the place said "photography studio." Mom and I exchanged sideways glances, trying to play it cool as we walked through the door of the massive estate.

Jim politely introduced himself, took Mom into the "library"—as though it were normal for everyone to have a library the size of an apartment—and told her to make herself comfortable as he took me to the studio. We walked through a backyard that resembled *Fantasy Island*, complete with palm trees, a waterfall, and tropical flowers surrounding a huge rock formation pool. Jim had converted the pool house into a first-rate photography studio.

For two hours Jim took photos and I smiled. He was a gentleman through the whole session, saying very little. When we concluded the session, he told me to return in a week for the photos, and that was it.

As Mom and I drove down the long driveway, I told her about the shoot.

"Well, it appears to be his house," she said. "And he's a health nut."

"What? How do you know that?"

"Because I went through his mail and his refrigerator," she said matter-of-factly. "You didn't think I was going to let you come back without doing that, did you?"

"What if he has security cameras?" I asked.

"Then he knows I'm watching him," she said, "and he'd better behave."

A week later I returned to Jim's "studio" alone. Mom was confident I'd be safe since she knew where to find him. And her intuition told her he was not a bad person, just lonely.

After giving me the photos, Jim sat down next to me, a little too close. I scooted to the furthest edge of the one bench in the room, uncertain what to do next. He moved closer. *Okay, time to figure out an exit strategy.*

"Tana, I like you," he said. "You seem like a nice girl."

I didn't respond.

"I don't like going out. I don't really like this town. It's hard to meet people. And there are so many germs. So many diseases."

What on earth is this dude talking about?

"I'd like you to date me exclusively. I would make it worth your while."

"Excuse me?" I said, heart racing. "I don't follow."

He made no move toward me. He wasn't threatening. He was just—pathetic.

"Don't worry. I'm not going to hurt you. I want to date someone young who hasn't had a lot of boyfriends and who isn't from this town. I could take care of you."

I felt like Dorothy on the yellow brick road: I definitely wasn't in Kansas anymore. This guy could go to jail or worse—*and* he had met my mom, though he clearly didn't know her.

"Think about it," he said.

I mumbled something about needing to get home before my mom started worrying and left. When I got home and told her, she wasn't surprised. She said she had sensed sadness in him but nothing sinister.

"Just stay away from him," she said.

Joe disagreed. "Having a rich older guy take care of you wouldn't be the worst thing," he said without a hint of a smile.

What happened next, in the form of a new friend named Tiffany, drove me more toward that direction than away from it. Tiffany and I had met through my best friend, Jill, shortly after I started modeling. Jill knew her from the equestrian center where they both boarded their horses. Tiffany, a twenty-four-year-old self-proclaimed star, offered to give me career advice about acting.

When we met at the stables, Tiffany's long platinum hair was teased into a huge mane. She wore a Barbie-sized cropped tank top that stretched over her enormous silicone breasts, accented by Daisy Duke shorts and four-inch heels. Not surprisingly, she was the fastest-talking human alive.

To me, Tiffany looked more like a prostitute than a movie star. But she was holding the reins of the most beautiful Arabian horse I'd ever seen and standing next to a candy-apple-red Ferrari Testarossa, so I assumed she must know something. Turns out Tiffany had—wait for it—married a very wealthy older man who wanted her out of his hair while he worked, so she'd taken up acting as a hobby.

Tiffany said I would need a new wardrobe before we made the rounds in Hollywood. But when she tried to dress me as the junior version of herself, I politely declined, opting for my standard sweater and jeans. I didn't want to look like Tiffany. But she seemed to genuinely like me, and I believed she was only trying to help.

When Tiffany came to pick me up early one Monday morning, Joe and Mom eyed her suspiciously. While she and Mom talked, Joe quietly pulled me aside. "Why is there a hooker here asking for you?"

"She's not a hooker. She's an actress. She's helping me find an agent."

"Or a pimp," he said. "Well, if you get into trouble, call. We'll come get you."

The first agency "connection" Tiffany made for me was with Central Casting Agency, known for casting extras. Being an extra didn't sound all that appealing to me, but Tiffany said it was good pocket change and a great way to hang out with the stars.

"I do it all the time," she said.

"But you're married."

"I didn't say I want to screw them. I just like to party with them." She shrugged. "Look, if you can't handle it, you can go home to Mommy."

"I didn't say that."

"Good. When you fill out the application, you need to say you're eighteen, which isn't much of a lie. You'll be seventeen in a couple of months, and they probably won't check."

A few days later we booked our first job together on the set of a new prime-time cop show. The two lead characters were male detectives.

"Perfect," Tiffany said smugly as we walked from her car to the set. "Just leave this to me."

"What's perfect?" I asked, but she didn't answer.

By lunchtime, Tiffany had worked her magic. The two stars, Harry and Dick (not their real names), still in makeup and sporting fake rubber guns, chatted us up at the craft table during one of their breaks. As the director called them back on set, Dick handed Tiffany a piece of paper with an address and phone number. "You two should join us tonight. We're having a party."

"We'll have you hooked up in no time," Tiffany said. "Then we'll both be driving Ferraris."

"I don't want to date either of those guys! And I definitely don't want to go to their party!"

"We'll just stop by for ten minutes. Just long enough to get invited to another party."

Tiffany turned a deaf ear to my arguments. By the time we left the set and made our way through LA traffic, it was after eight.

The party turned out to be at an old hotel on Sunset Boulevard.

"I'm *really* not comfortable with this," I said as we pulled up in front of it. She ignored me.

As we entered the dark foyer, Harry was coming out of the elevator. "Hello, ladies," he said, opening his arms wide. Tiffany gave him a big hug and planted a bright-red kiss-shaped smudge on his cheek.

"Isn't this place cool?" Harry asked, not really waiting for an answer. "The history here is mind-boggling. Rod Stewart lives here. They turned this historic hotel into concierge apartments."

I assumed he was lying. Not that it mattered.

"Come on up, and we can have a drink. We have a spectacular view."

With his arm around Tiffany, Harry proceeded to the elevator. When the door opened on his floor, Harry walked ahead. Grabbing Tiffany's arm, I whispered, "Please *do not* drink. You don't know these guys, and you're driving."

Yanking her arm away, she hissed, "Knock it off, or I'll never bring you with me again. You're acting like a child."

I glanced around the sparsely decorated bachelor pad, noting that—surprise—we were the only people at the "party." When Dick met us at the door with martinis, Tiffany accepted gleefully. I declined, ignoring the daggers Tiffany shot my direction. While Harry gave Tiffany a "tour" of the three-room suite, Dick moved closer to me, attempting to put his arm around my shoulder. Sidestepping the gesture, I told him I was sixteen.

"I can keep a secret," he replied with a shrug.

When I backed away he didn't pursue, but he didn't retreat either. "You don't look sixteen," was all he said. "And your friend—" he took a swig of his cocktail—"She's definitely been ridden hard and put away wet a few times."

"She's been what?" I asked, confused.

Laughing, he said, "Never mind. You really are a kid." As if on cue, Tiffany's shrill giggle emanated from what I assumed was a bedroom. Dick added, "You might want to keep different company if you don't want trouble."

Tiffany emerged with faint red lipstick stains smeared around her mouth. "We'll be right back, boys," she said flirtatiously and winked. Tiffany toddled to the door unsteadily, motioning for me to follow her. Confused, but not wasting time, I clutched my purse and complied. She giggled loudly all the way to the elevator, stopping only long enough to say, "Go along with it."

"Go along with what?"

Once in the elevator, Tiffany said, "They drugged my drink. I think I'm going to be sick." She grabbed onto me, steadying herself, almost taking us both down. "I told them I had cocaine in the car so they'd let us leave to get it. We need to get out of here."

"Are you out of your mind?" I screeched. "Why would you tell them that?"

Tiffany didn't answer. She just climbed in the passenger seat and tossed me the keys.

"I can't drive a Ferrari," I said.

"You're going to have to. It's like any other stick, only cooler. Ugh! Everything is spinning." She crumpled into the seat.

I jumped in the car and locked the doors while deciding what to do. Tiffany's story about being drugged sounded highly suspicious. I wondered, *Why would they drug only one of us?*

I was beginning to think that Tiffany might be more dangerous than the fake cops. It was obvious Dick and Harry had been planning for us to be the evening entertainment, but if they'd drugged Tiffany, why would they have let us walk out without an argument? And even though Dick had been undeterred by my age, he hadn't pushed himself on me either. My biggest concern now was getting home—and getting as far from Tiffany as possible.

Feeling like a gangster in *Scarface*, I quickly checked the glove box and under the seats, checking for a baggie of white powder or anything I assumed might be a concealed cocaine container. I wasn't sure if Tiffany was serious, and I didn't want to get caught with it in the car. Relieved to find nothing, I decided my best option was to drive the Testarossa.

Tiffany was sound asleep in the passenger seat, snoring softly. Grateful that the car Mom had recently bought me had a stick shift, I pulled onto Sunset grinding the gears, then promptly stalled.

Somehow we survived the fifty-plus-mile drive home. I parked in front of her house and left the keys in the driver's seat and Tiffany in the passenger seat sleeping. When I finally walked through the front door of my darkened house, I was nearly three hours late. Entering as quietly as possible, I made it two steps before our new Doberman, Baron, started his ferocious yapping. The lights clicked on. I cringed—more at the sight of Joe standing in his underwear and open robe than at the .45 he was holding.

"You said you'd be home by nine," Mom said. "Where have you been?"

"It's a long story. Basically, Tiffany is psycho. I won't be hanging out with her anymore."

"Good," Joe said. "I told you she was a bimbo."

Mom kissed me on the cheek. "I'm glad you're home safe. You're smart, and we trust you. But next time try to call if you're going to be late." She grabbed Baron's collar and headed back to bed, followed by Joe.

A few weeks later I auditioned for a part in a movie. Within a week I had met the producer at a callback. Don (again, not his real name) gave me the number of an acting coach and paid for my lessons, saying it was an investment. He seemed legit, but how would I know? Maybe I should have been suspicious when he paraded me around, introducing me to several of the who's-who types in Hollywood. Within a week I had met Aaron Spelling, more producers, and a couple of other "important people" I didn't recognize. Not that they had an inkling—or cared—who I was. They probably assumed the worst, which hadn't happened. But the people Don introduced me to confirmed who he was and said he'd produced many films.

I was excited. I finally had a shot.

Don soon called and said he wanted me to meet an investor at a business dinner. I should wear a dress and meet him at his house so I wouldn't have to drive separately. I foolishly thought I was special because I had talent, but when I arrived at his house, another girl was already there. Red flag. Somehow, she'd become part of this "business dinner." As we drove, I quickly discovered the other girl wasn't the brightest bulb, and I found myself increasingly annoyed by her incessant giggling.

When Don said we needed to make a stop and meet a "friend" before dinner, my heart raced. Worst-case scenarios came to mind, and I started planning exit strategies. But when he drove us to a huge arena called the Forum, previous home to the Lakers and site of a bunch of killer concerts, I relaxed a little. Whoever the friend was couldn't be that bad if we were meeting him at a public venue.

Don then led us to a large room where I expected a meeting or a dinner. Instead I found a group of people mingling at a party.

"Surprise!"

He looked at the other girl, who was clearly excited, then at me, who wasn't at all amused.

"Why are we at the Forum—in a back room?" I asked.

"We've got ringside tickets to the fight tonight."

"What? I'm dressed for dinner, not a boxing match."

"Relax," he said. "Everyone dresses up when they're ringside. That's why I told you to dress for a nice restaurant."

Highly annoyed, but even more hungry, I made my way to a buffet line. That's when I noticed there were two to three girls for every man in the room—the operative word being *girls,* most who looked about my age if not younger. At this point I felt too queasy to eat.

As the evening progressed, Don introduced me to his "friends," a couple of whom I'd seen in recent headlines—not uncommon for some of the playboys that hung out at the Forum in the eighties. Common sense and intuition told me I was in *way* over my head. These guys were powerful and likely not fazed by little things like statutory-rape laws. I felt like a fly headed straight for the spider's web.

Relieved when we made our way to the boxing match, I found my seat—ringside, where I felt the sweat of the boxers sprinkling me and my new dress each time one landed a powerful strike. It was then that I knew any schoolgirl fantasy I might have had about being an actress was over. I don't remember who fought or how many rounds the fight lasted. I was scared and disgusted, so I went to the bathroom and lingered as long as I could. When Don's other date—I realized that's what he considered us, *dates*—came in to check on me, I told her I was feeling sick and had just thrown up.

"I'm not leaving here until it's time to go," I said.

She frowned at my killjoy attitude, but that didn't bother me in the least.

At the end of the evening we drove to Don's house in silence. When we arrived he kissed "giggle girl" on the cheek and sent her on her way. Then, without asking how I was feeling, he turned to me.

"A lot of girls would do a lot of things for an opportunity like this. I've created a lot of stars."

Hindsight has shown me many graceful ways I might have responded, but not one of those came to me in that moment. Instead, channeling my mother, I unleashed my fury on the narcissistic, predatory a**.

"F*** you, motherf*****. How dare you! You and your friends are disgusting pigs and should be arrested."

He put his hand up to stop the litany of foulness directed at him.

"Put your hands over your ears," he instructed.

"What the—"

"Just do it!"

For some unknown reason, I complied. Then he started screaming.

"F*** you, b*tch! You are a pain in the a**!"

Something about the absurdity of the scenario struck me as hilarious. I started laughing, and I couldn't stop. I had been traipsing around LA with a producer, being introduced to the Hollywood elite, who probably thought I was sleeping with the guy. And here I was in the front yard of his Hollywood Hills mansion with my hands over my ears.

Why? So he wouldn't offend my delicate senses with his curse words? It was both hilarious and tragic.

"A**hole," I said as I walked to my car, still laughing.

———

Believe it or not, my interactions with men only got worse after that. Just before Christmas, and just after my seventeenth birthday, I met Dylan. He was twenty-six, six foot two, charming, a body builder, and gorgeous.

We met at the mall when we were both Christmas shopping. I knew I should decline when he asked me out. But I was intrigued, and he didn't seem to care about my age, so neither did I. I knew I should tell Mom about him, but I didn't. And since she trusted me, she rarely asked where I was going or who I was with.

By our second date—technically the third if you counted our impromptu lunch on the day we met—I was smitten. I'd never been out with anyone as attentive and polite as he was—a true gentleman. He was a bit bold with his first goodnight kiss that night, but nothing triggered alarm bells, and he stopped when I pulled back. Not that I actually *wanted* to stop, but I felt it was too soon. I really liked this guy and had a feeling that what we had would eventually develop into a relationship.

For our third date, Dylan planned an early dinner and movie. After dinner he asked if we could stop by his house, saying he needed to give one of his roommates rent money. While we were there he offered a quick tour of the place. And when we were in the doorway of his bedroom, he grabbed me in an aggressive embrace and kissed me hard. With a flip of a switch, the polite, charming guy was replaced by a guy who forced me into the room and onto the bed, covering my mouth with his to drown my screams.

Trapping me under his weight, Dylan seemed unfazed by my attempt to fight. No match for his size and aware that I was losing the struggle, I made a feeble attempt to stop him by telling him I was on my period. It didn't work.

My heart sank as I realized I could do nothing to stop what was about to happen. So I stopped fighting and just lay still.

The ordeal lasted only a few minutes—an eternity, really. He rolled off of me and politely offered, "You're amazing."

I was stunned. I felt broken, betrayed, and confused.

Without a word, I got up and straightened my skirt and sweater, which had never been removed. I left my torn underwear on the floor.

"I'll call you tomorrow," he said sleepily.

He did call the next day and left a message as though nothing had happened. I refused to talk to him or even to leave my room.

I'd heard tragic stories about girls being "date raped" and never understood how they could put themselves in that situation. How they could date a guy without seeing any signs that he was a creep. How they couldn't fight and get away. Now I'd joined the same tragic club. The shame was overwhelming—shame over being violated and used and feeling powerless to stop it. But the shame wasn't nearly as paralyzing as the self-loathing.

I shouldn't have dated him.

I shouldn't have dressed sexy.

I shouldn't have gone to his apartment.

How could I have been so stupid?

Maybe I deserved it.

I even tried convincing myself it wasn't a big deal. After all, I wasn't a virgin. And I'd even imagined having a relationship with him.

Mom interrupted my endlessly looping thoughts. "Sweetheart, do you want to talk about anything?" she asked, sitting next to me on the bed.

"No, Mom. I just want to be alone."

"I'm not sure who he is, but this is obviously about a guy—and, I suspect, a decision you regret."

You have no idea, I thought. But there was no way I could tell her. She would freak out. Joe would kill the guy. And I couldn't help but think I was to blame.

Stroking my hair gently, she said, "I'm here to talk when you're ready. In the meantime, I'm going to give you the best advice I can: don't waste any more time on this guy. Learn from this and move on. Please don't screw up your life for a piece of a**!"

As Mom left my room, I pondered her unorthodox advice. She might not have known the context for her counsel—or maybe she had. Either way, the idea of mentally reducing Dylan to a "piece of a**" felt better than feeling violated and broken.

Just like when I was twelve, when Dale climbed in bed with me, I felt confused and unsure of the truth. Had I been raped? Had I asked for it? Was I a tease? It was easier to convince myself that I'd given in voluntarily—that I'd been the one to use him, even—than to continue the torturous, looping victim dialogue. But deep down I knew that wasn't true. I just couldn't get my head around what had happened.

Over the next few weeks I began to feel more scared and powerless than I had in years. My life felt out of control. Why did I continually find myself in circumstances beyond my ability to manage? Other girls didn't seem to attract the trouble I did, or at least they didn't make the same stupid decisions. A thought I hadn't had since third grade began plaguing me: *Maybe I'm just not very smart.*

Several times after the Dylan "incident"—I was reluctant to label it a rape—I tried to go out with friends but would become overwhelmed with fear. I would wonder if people were staring at me or talking about me. Panic would envelop me, and I'd go back home and hide. Just like when I was a kid, my world basically shrank to the safety of my room.

My timidity from childhood had all but evaporated over the previous five years. But this new bout with anxiety practically paralyzed me. I was miserable at school. I was miserable at home. I was miserable when boys gave me attention and when men gawked at my body. And confusingly, I was even more miserable when they didn't. I'd begun craving the attention I hated.

I felt no outlet for the anxiety, chaos, and rage that swirled within me. Until, that is, the day I found myself over a toilet bowl with my finger down my throat, throwing up a half pint of Haagen-Dazs—and experienced instant relief. It was gross and humiliating, yes, but also strangely comforting.

I wasn't trying to lose weight. My weight had never really been an issue for me. And though my food habits had never been especially healthy, I wasn't driven to binge on junk food. I just felt relief, somehow, in the act of purging. (Looking back now, I know it was about having some kind of control in my life.)

Joe's food didn't help, though. Before he entered our lives, Mom and I had subsisted on a diet of Big Macs, Cap'n Crunch, and frozen pot pies. But Joe liked to cook his hometown favorites: chicken-fried steak, mashed potatoes, gravy, and pie. Everything he made was either fried or filled with sugar and fat—except for the canned food in the pantry, which was downright scary. As a Vietnam vet, Joe had taken a liking to canned snake, eel, snails, Spam, and an array of other wartime delicacies.

To say I wasn't a fan of Joe's weird food would be an understatement. Soon I was back with my old childhood friends—the clown, the tiger, the leprechaun, and the Cap'n. But now, on top of the comfort they gave, I had the intoxicating sense of cleansing and control that purging gave me. Unaware of the dangers, I began to rely on it as my new coping mechanism.

At first no one seemed to notice. A few months later, though, Mom's intuition kicked in. I suppose my timed trips to the bathroom at the end of large meals might have tipped her off. Later she told me that she'd noticed I was getting chipmunk cheeks—a side effect of purging. In any case, one day she followed me to the bathroom of our fixer-upper, which was still under construction. I was mortified when she busted the make-shift lock, burst in, and saw me on my knees, the contents of my breakfast still in the bowl.

True to her nature, she burst into tears. "Why, Tana, why?"

She kept asking that over and over but didn't wait for an answer. Apparently I'd broken the one "good girl" rule Mom had: I'd caused a problem for her. She had to take precious time from work and more precious funds from savings to get me help. And I didn't even think I needed help. Despite shame, guilt, and overwhelming sadness and anxiety, I figured I could handle it the way I'd handled most things in my life—on my own.

———

I actually enjoyed the long drive to UCLA's Resnick Neuropsychiatric Hospital, where I would be assessed for their eating disorders program. I hadn't been alone with Mom for that long in quite a while, and it felt good, despite the humiliating circumstances. We talked about many of the challenges I'd been facing. Mom was actually good at giving advice when she could take time to listen, and when she wasn't freaking out because she was scared. That day on the drive, I felt closer to her than I had in years.

When we arrived at the hospital, I had to remind myself why we were there. Walking inside felt eerie. Everything was so . . . white! And so cold.

We filled out paperwork and waited. Finally we were led to a white room with a table and several chairs. A woman with short hair and a white coat came in and introduced herself. She wasn't particularly kind or inviting as she explained the dangers of bulimia, a word I hardly recognized.

Wait! Back that train up. Do I actually have this disease with the ugly-sounding name? I haven't done it for very long. I can stop. I thought I was coming in to learn how to deal with my anxiety, not to be labeled as sick.

Halfway into her speech about how purging could rot my teeth (I had no idea), cause heart problems (really?), and make my hair fall out (who knew?), a voice crackled over the intercom. "Code Blue! Code Blue!"

I didn't know what it meant, but the lady in the white coat jumped up and ran out of the room. I sat there, wallowing in my humiliation over being at such a place. *Bad girl!*

Sometime later the woman returned, interrupting my self-flagellating thoughts. She looked me in the eye. "We just lost a patient."

"What do you mean you *lost* her?"

"One of our girls went into cardiac arrest. She was seventeen."

"*What?*" I was seventeen.

The woman made a few appointments for me—psych assessment, therapy, blah, blah, blah. I don't remember much beyond the young girl whose heart had gone into arrest. When Mom and I left, which felt like an eternity later, I begged her not to take me back to the hospital. I swore on my life that I would be honest if I couldn't control whatever it was I had. (I refused to use the b-word.) I promised I would do whatever it took to stop making myself vomit, and I would go back to the hospital willingly if I couldn't.

And I did stop throwing up. Unfortunately, I didn't really stop purging. I just switched to a different form.

I didn't know it at the time, but there are many ways to purge, including exercise. I begged Mom to buy me a gym membership, and working out became my drug of choice. Who could be mad at me for doing that?

Exercise fit my goals in many ways. It helped me feel stronger—and to *be stronger,* as I'd pledged to become after being nearly raped at fifteen and then "forced into sex" (or whatever—I still hadn't decided how to define it) at seventeen. It also relieved my sadness and anxiety and eliminated my compulsion to make myself vomit. Plus, it made me look great, something that was becoming increasingly important to me. If I couldn't make peace with my body, I figured, I'd make peace with the attention my body got me.

So, while my friends were striving to look like Victoria's Secret models, I taped a picture of Rachel McLish, the reigning Ms. Olympia, to my mirror and hit the weights for two hours every day. I never did look like Rachel McLish, but I was fit and strong. And I kept my promise to stop making myself vomit—at least for the time being.

―――――――

When graduation time came, I put my high school years in the rearview mirror and looked forward to living on my own. But perhaps it was a premonition of doom when my father showed up, ready to patch up our differences and put on the dad hat again.

Since the summer when I was twelve and fought with him about coming home early, I'd rarely seen him, and eventually our visits had dwindled to occasional phone calls. Now he showed up in a new Cadillac, wearing a silk suit—apparently courtesy of tithe money he'd "borrowed" from his former congregation—and informed me he was leaving the ministry.

Though I'd always found it laughable that he became a pastor in the first place, I'd at least given him credit for effort. And he'd stuck with the ministry for fourteen years, the longest he'd stuck with anything. But this new effort to reinvent himself again just seemed ridiculous—and more than a little worrying.

He asked me to meet him at one of the swankiest restaurants Huntington Beach had to offer. The venue didn't impress me in the least. And as for the "cool dude" persona he'd adopted to match the car and suit—that was just bizarre. What was he up to?

"Let's see," he said to the waitress, "I believe I'll go with the swordfish." I squinted with suspicion. Silk suit, Cadillac, swordfish—something was definitely up. I remembered seeing Jim Bakker in the news for embezzling money from his congregation and had a light-bulb moment. *Maybe Dad's gone off the deep end and become a televangelist.* The idea was preposterous, of course, but so was this dinner.

"And your lovely date?" the waitress asked.

"Isn't she beautiful?" Dad laughed and put his hand over mine.

"I'm not his date," I said, snapping my hand away. "I'm his *daughter*." I glared at him. "And I'm fully capable of ordering on my own."

I'd had years to work out a strategy for dealing with my dad when (or if) he reappeared, but I wasn't prepared for the man in front of me who *wasn't* preaching to me about how my mother had been a bad influence with her worldly ways or how my music was satanic and brainwashing me with subliminal messages.

Instead, I suspected this guy was hiding something behind the permasmile and quick laugh. As he tried to act cool and calm, my wariness increased, and I probed for the truth. I'm sure he felt I was being particularly ornery, but I had no interest in hearing about his "self-improvement" detour from the responsibilities of life. I wanted to know the truth about why he'd shown up.

By this point in my life, I really didn't have much use for my dad. I resented his absences nearly as much as I resented his self-righteous criticism of Mom and me when he wasn't absent. He'd seldom paid child support. He'd overlooked numerous birthdays. And when he did show up it was usually some lame attempt to gloss over the past, as if his negligence were nothing but a bug splat on a windshield that could be wiped clean with a spritz of Windex.

I didn't trust him in the first place. And now, as the night deepened, my mistrust grew. Since I was now eighteen, he didn't owe child support, and it wasn't my birthday, so I suspected he was there with a different agenda.

As we were finishing dinner, he informed me that he and Kathy were getting a divorce. And the reason he was leaving the ministry was to become a motivational speaker.

That made me laugh out loud.

"You're leaving another family? So you can—let me get this straight—motivate others on how to make their lives more successful?"

"Kathy broke up our family. I didn't. She's the reason I was forced to leave the ministry." He seemed defensive and genuinely disappointed that I wasn't happy for him.

I didn't bother listening to all the horrible things he tried to tell me about Kathy after that. His entire life—all the missed and failed opportunities—had always been someone else's fault as far as he was concerned. And the truth was, I liked Kathy. No, she wasn't perfect, but she'd at least spent time with me when I visited. He had not.

I still did not know what this man wanted from me. I only knew I couldn't listen for another minute. I cut the dinner short and walked out.

The next morning I was still seething. So I pulled out pen and paper and wrote him a letter whose theme was simple:

I am done being your daughter. Being a sperm donor doesn't make you my dad. You were a loser when I was growing up, and you're a loser now. Stay out of my life. *Do not* misinterpret this as some desperate cry for help or invitation for communication. And don't ever call me again.

When I told Mom about the letter, her reaction surprised me. She was horrified that I would consider sending my father something so vicious.

"You can't send that," she pleaded when she'd heard it.

"Of course I can."

"No, it's too harsh. You'll regret it. I would die if I ever received a letter like that from you."

"Harsh?" I said. "Harsh is him calling you a whore in front of the neighborhood. Harsh is me showing up for every school event where fathers were invited and being the kid without one. Harsh is his thinking he can come and go like a seasonal flu and then take me to dinner last night like I was an end-of-December tax write-off."

"Tana, you need to face him and tell him how you feel—in person, not in a letter. Scream at him if you must. Just do it. Please, Tana. If you don't, it will haunt you and affect your future relationships with men. You simply can't send that letter."

"Mom, he doesn't deserve my time. And talking to him wouldn't change anything."

Suddenly my anger at Dad was spilling over to her, too, and I couldn't seem to stop. "Why do you always feel the need to collect losers anyway?" I ranted. "I don't share your affliction for fixing people. And I need you to support me, not him. I wasn't the one who neglected my job as a father. He was. And I *endured* that neglect. I know you did your best to protect me, but don't make me feel bad for protecting myself. And please don't try to guilt-trip me for cutting ties with a guy who essentially cut ties with me eighteen years ago. It's done! I'm not you. I don't feel bad for not catering to losers. For all your tough talk, when it comes to men, you keep taking crap."

I knew my words hurt Mom deeply, but I felt I needed to say them. She saw herself as caring, and she was, but I'd come to see her as codependent also. And for now, because of my pain, I could only focus on that, not on her loyalty and love for me. I needed to prove to myself that I was a big girl. That I could take care of myself.

I sent the letter.

A couple of weeks later I discovered Kathy had recently been released from a seventy-two-hour hold at a psychiatric hospital. Dad had filed a report claiming she was suicidal. By the time she was declared mentally stable and released, Dad had kidnapped both girls and taken them to New Mexico, where he had family.

Two weeks after that, Kathy finally got an emergency custody order. Showing up with a police escort at the new school where the kids had been enrolled, she withdrew them from class and left without notifying Dad.

This incident prompted me to start trying to connect with my half sisters more regularly. Kathy seemed more fragile and unhappy. A few years later her weight fell alarmingly low and I suspected drugs, though I never confirmed it. As the girls entered middle school, Kathy would occasionally call asking for my help, claiming she couldn't handle her girls. Not certain what I, a young adult, was supposed to do with a couple of tweens, I'd occasionally drive a couple of hours to their house in Santa Paula where they'd moved in with Grandma Jane, pick them up, and try to entertain them with a trip to the beach or a concert.

A couple of months after that dinner with my father, I met an older—okay, okay, *much* older—man with whom I began jet-setting around the world. He wined me and dined me, and under his influence I became a bit more sophisticated. Deep down I knew the relationship wasn't going anywhere, but mostly it felt safe and structured, and it gave me the false belief that my life was no longer out of control.

It didn't take a shrink to recognize a classic case of "daddy issues." But this relationship was also the least drama-filled of my life so far, which wasn't saying a lot. And I was a little afraid to be on my own for fear that I would somehow regress to the dark years of my childhood, but I also didn't want to live at home with Mom and Joe any longer.

To me any progress was a win. And I didn't believe I deserved better.

At the same time, I was beginning to think about what would come next in my life. I knew I needed to work—I currently had a job as an aesthetician. But what about higher education? Was that even possible for me?

I took a few classes at the local community college and realized three things.

First, I had already wasted a lot of time, although I had to admit I'd had some fun.

Second, I was college smart. I could definitely do the work. In fact, the college-placement counselor suggested I was far brighter than I gave myself credit for and should consider shooting higher than I'd imagined. Buoyed by those words, I even began to dust off an old dream that had seemed so ridiculous I'd never shared it with anyone. Could I possibly go to medical school?

The problem was that, third, I simply couldn't afford to go to school full time. I needed to *work* full time, which would only leave me time to take classes here and there. I didn't think there was any way to do that and have a career in medicine too.

I called the local ROTC office, thinking a stint in the air force might enable me to have the military pick up my college expenses. But when I mentioned my dream of going to medical school to my jet-setting boyfriend, he scoffed.

"Yeah, right," he said. "The only way you're going to get through med school, or any school, is on your back."

Ouch. I would never forget that comment.

Never.

CHAPTER 8

WHAT DO CANCER AND *PLAYBOY* HAVE IN COMMON?

This isn't life in the fast lane, it's life
in the oncoming traffic.

—Terry Pratchett

I was walking on the beach, pondering my miserably uncertain future, when I was approached by a photographer who said he did freelance work for *Playboy* magazine.

"Would you be interested in posing for some test shots to see if you might be picked to be in the magazine?" he asked.

I rolled my eyes. *When will these guys come up with a better line?*

Back in 1992, in the days before the Internet, it was more common for girls to be "discovered" as models and actresses when they were walking around in public, but it was also more common for them to become victims of predators posing as producers, directors, and yes, *Playboy* photographers.

Sensing my skepticism, the guy on the beach gave me several phone numbers to call that would verify his story. I did. He was legit. So I began mulling the possibility of posing.

I had been seriously considering what it would take for me to become a doctor, but I didn't have the kind of money it would take. At twenty-three, I might also be too old to endure the eleven to fourteen years of training—bachelor's degree, med school, and residency.

Joe thought the whole idea was ridiculous. "Why waste all that time and money on an expensive education when you're just gonna have babies and not use it? You're better off snagging a rich husband, which you *could* do. And if you can hold on to the schmuck for at least ten years, it's a long-term marriage, and he'll have to support you forever. If you're smart and take care of him"—he elbowed me in the side—"you have about that long before he starts screwing around."

I turned a deaf ear to Joe's degrading comments. It was a waste of time explaining to him that I didn't even want babies—why put someone else through what I'd been through? But his "advice" inadvertently made my dream of a college degree burn brighter, because it set me thinking of obtaining a bachelor of science degree in nursing. I could become a nurse first, and then, if my circumstances changed for the better, go on to medical school. And if that was not possible, I'd still have the option of becoming a nurse practitioner. I liked having options.

When I discovered that my boyfriend had gone on a "business trip" (a.k.a. a vacation with another woman), I recognized that relationship was DOA. *Maybe Joe's right. All men cheat. It's only a matter of time.* I packed my bags, got my own place, and found a couple of roommates to help pay the rent. That's when the *Playboy* photographer's offer started to appeal to me.

Playboy, I reasoned, could simply be a way to finance college. If I were chosen as a Playmate of the Month, I'd get twenty-five thousand dollars. If I made Playmate of the Year, I'd get a hundred thousand. In the early nineties, that would pay for a lot of school.

I'd finally come to the realization that I had more to offer in life than a pretty face and big boobs. But maybe I could *use* my face and boobs to get me where I wanted to go. Even if *Playboy*'s offer confirmed once again that others assumed that's where my value lay, I could still take the paycheck and invest it in my future.

My mother tried to dissuade me from that plan, but not because she was a prude and thought that baring my all was a bad idea. Instead, she said her "intuition" was telling her that doing so wouldn't be wise.

"I sense that you're going to marry someone extremely important," she said, "and this would not be good for you in that respect. This could interfere."

Seriously? I had no idea what she was talking about, and I wasn't about to pass up a great opportunity based on another of her premonitions.

"Thanks, Mom, but I'm not waiting for a man to take care of me. I've seen how reliable they are. I've got to rely on myself."

I said yes to *Playboy*.

The day of the test shoot was surreal. In the early nineties, the *Playboy* headquarters were in a high-rise building located on Sunset Boulevard. Beautiful women walked around in fluffy robes and slippers so that clothing lines wouldn't crease their bodies. The only men I ever saw were the photographers, and I was never alone with one. The atmosphere was totally professional. I saw no signs of the alcohol and illicit drugs I'd been warned about. It was all business. And I was made to feel like a princess. As a makeup artist applied thick cat-eye liner to my eyes and creamy peach gloss to my lips, one of the assistants popped her head in to take my lunch order. I was told I could order from any restaurant I wanted in the vicinity.

"I can't imagine eating," I said. "I'm so nervous I'm crawling out of my skin. I think I'd throw up if I ate anything." I wrung my hands as the knowledge that I'd soon be disrobing sank in.

"Don't lose the skin," the makeup artist joked. "It's what we're selling. As for throwing up, don't tell anyone." She gave me a playful wink.

All in all, the day with the *Playboy* people turned out to be enjoyable. Everyone was really nice. The men who congregated outside the building, waiting for their opportunity to snag a Playmate, were a different story entirely. But if I'd had doubts about my decision to pose for *Playboy*, they vanished after the test shoot.

I was told it would be several weeks until I heard whether I'd been chosen.

It seemed like forever! And while I waited, I realized that I really, really wanted the job. An implausible idea had taken root and become a coveted dream, a dream on which I'd hung my plans for college.

But during that same time, I also noticed I wasn't feeling right. I was losing weight for seemingly no reason. I had a slight tremor in my hands. Something was *off.*

I went to the doctor without telling Mom because telling her would've meant dealing with questions, possibly even tears. I was already tired without having to console her.

The doctor felt my neck and found a lump. I was quickly referred to a thyroid specialist. Multiple needle-aspiration biopsies were taken, conjectures made. Like the *Playboy* shoot, the experience was surreal, but this time I did not feel like a princess being pampered. I felt like a prisoner being tortured.

Three days later I was holding the phone in my hand, frozen in disbelief.

"I'm sorry," the doctor had said, "but you have thyroid cancer."

I wasn't even sure what my thyroid was supposed to do. The only reason I knew it was in my neck was that they'd stuck the biopsy needles in there.

Just a few days before, I'd had the world by the tail—*Playboy,* school, a future career, who knew what beyond that. Now what did I have? Chemo? Radiation? Surgeries? Death?

My mother walked in as I was standing there. She had no idea who was on the line. As if on cue, though, she began screaming.

"You have cancer, don't you? Oh, my god! You have cancer!"

When I nodded yes, she wailed even louder. It was so typical of my topsy-turvy life. There I was, the person who'd just been informed she had cancer, trying to calm down my out-of-control mother. Tough as she was, she was just not good at handling bad news, especially where I was concerned. So at a time when I desperately needed to process this information, I had to focus on consoling her.

My father heard the news through a well-meaning family member and called me a few days later. It was the first time I'd heard from him since sending the "Dear Dad" letter five years prior. The conversation was awkward and hollow. I struggled to make small talk as he told me he loved me. As much as I wanted to return the sentiment, I just couldn't.

My sister Tamara cried when I called to tell her the news. When I asked to talk to Kathy, Tamara said, "She's not home. She's never here anymore. She's different. Always working or partying."

"Really? That makes me sad," I said.

"Yeah, it is sad. She fights with us constantly. And she hardly sleeps."

"I'm sorry. I'll try to come out and see you in a few months, after this is behind me."

"I'm leaving in a few months. I'm going to live with Dad," she said. "Maybe I can visit you before I move."

That visit didn't work out. And though I was concerned about the situation with Kathy and the girls, I was too busy with what was going on in my own life to dwell on it.

On my next visit, the doctor was quick to assure me that I wasn't going to die. In fact, he told me that thyroid cancer was one of the safest kinds of cancer to have because it was slow growing. One surgery, one treatment, and my life would be back to normal. At least that's what I heard him say.

"Great!" I told him. "That's a relief! I'm going to postpone surgery to do a *Playboy* shoot." With this new diagnosis, I knew I'd need the money even more.

"Not a good idea," he said, "especially since we're not finished with the diagnostic tests. Things could change."

Seven days and a lot more tests later, they had.

"It *can't* wait a couple of months," the doctor said. "Even though a tumor like this is generally slow growing, we found cancer in the lymph nodes of the neck and chest. It's uncommon for thyroid cancer to metastasize in this pattern, but it can happen, and it has. It's probably been there since early adolescence. If it moves into the lungs, it's no longer safe or slow growing. So you need the surgery now. Within six months or maybe a year, I hope to have you back to your normal routine. But for now you should drop your classes and focus on this. It's going to be difficult to keep up for at least that long."

I just stared at him, stunned. The man was insane if he thought I was dropping out of school. I had finally started taking it seriously. The news was difficult to accept, and I was in shock. How could I look healthy enough to pose for *Playboy*, yet be rotting with cancer on the inside? I drifted through life in a haze for the next several weeks, trying to figure out where I would live, how I would pay my bills, how I would stay in school. Basically, how I was going to manage life.

When I awkwardly told the assistant editor at *Playboy* about needing the surgery—there was no script for explaining why I had to put exploiting my body on hold for a quick detour to save my life—she seemed surprisingly understanding. Or maybe she just wanted to end the clumsy conversation as much as I did.

"Call us when you're well again," she said, "and we'll go from there." It was as encouraging a response as I could have hoped for, even if her tone suggested I was just going in for a teeth cleaning.

The treatment for thyroid cancer back then was far more complicated than it is now. I underwent surgery to remove my thyroid, transplant the para-thyroid glands, and remove lymph nodes in my neck and chest. The surgery wasn't as horrible as I expected. The effects of having no thyroid, however, were devastating. As they say, nobody dies without a thyroid; they just *wish* they had. I experienced extreme nausea, fatigue, and muscle weakness for several weeks following the surgery as the doctor tried to regulate my calcium levels.

As soon as I started feeling human again, it was time for the next phase of treatment: killing rogue cancer cells with radioactive iodine. In those days it was considered preferable for patients with this type of cancer to avoid taking thyroid medication for six to eight weeks before receiving the radiation treatment. After that I could start the thyroid medication, but it would take another several weeks to begin to feel human.

The radioactive iodine I-131 pill was touted to me as a magic bullet. I was told it would kill thyroid cells, including thyroid cancer, but not healthy cells. I would feel no pain, but I'd need to remain completely isolated for a week because the radiation would be harmful to anyone near me who had a functioning thyroid.

I drove alone to the doctor's office, where a man in a biohazard suit removed a little pill from a lead tube and handed it to me. I swallowed it and headed out to stay at a friend's beach house for the week. As I drove there my mobile phone rang; Mom wanted me to stop by her house to pick something up. When I arrived she was on the porch crying. Keeping my distance, I asked her what was happening.

"I have to have brain surgery," she said.

"What?" I wailed. *"When?"*

Standing on the front lawn, totally helpless, I broke down, sobbing. Mom had been having headaches, dizzy spells, coughing fits, and loss of feeling in her hands and feet for months, but we'd assumed the problem was a pinched nerve or a hormonal imbalance. When she couldn't ignore the worsening symptoms any longer, she'd finally seen a neurologist and been diagnosed with Chiari malformation, a congenital condition where the tissue of the cerebellum extends into the spinal canal. She'd waited until I swallowed the radiation pill to tell me the diagnosis, fearing I would refuse to follow through with my treatment otherwise.

For nearly an hour the two of us stood there across the yard from each other, crying, feeling helpless, unable to embrace. I was furious about what had happened with my health. But I was *terrified* about something happening to Mom. For years I'd thought I was self-sufficient. Now suddenly I felt like a vulnerable child again.

Being in isolation for a week when Mom needed me made me feel more powerless than I'd felt in years. We spent a lot of time talking on the phone, making plans for her upcoming surgery. I promised I'd do whatever I could to help her and Joe run their pet shampoo manufacturing business while she was recovering.

Mom's surgery left her physically incapacitated for months. Her pain was debilitating. She lay in total darkness and would vomit when we tried to help her to the bathroom or even just turned on the lights. I'd never seen Mom so weak or Joe so helpless. And I was in way over my head trying to help run a business I didn't have much experience with and also struggling to manage my own health.

Four months after her first surgery, Mom was scheduled for a second surgery to place a shunt that would relieve the fluid that was building up and causing pressure in her head. I'd never seen Mom pray aloud, but she started doing so. Fervently. And often.

After months of postsurgical agony and lying in a dark room—and one week before she was scheduled for her second procedure—Mom's pain completely vanished. One morning I stopped by to see her on my way to the office, and Mom was standing at the window with the drapes open and a big smile on her face. From that day on, she quickly regained her strength and resumed control of her business.

The relief I felt at seeing Mom's newfound energy was overwhelming. Once again she had proved that nothing could stop her. And selfishly, I still needed my mom while I faced another treatment with the radioactive iodine.

"We got most of the cancer," my doctor had said, and the second treatment was expected to take care of the rest. But my body was already paying a high price for the treatment.

I'd managed to show up and help Mom, but just barely. And now, as soon as she found her footing again, I lost mine. After the second treatment I went into a deep, dark depression. I couldn't get out of bed during the day. I had no motivation to even get dressed or get out of the house. My muscles ached all the time, and I felt exhausted.

No one in the medical establishment had warned me that one of the ramifications of having my thyroid gland removed was psychological pain. In fact, when my endocrinologist suggested I see a psychiatrist, I interpreted the recommendation to mean it was *my fault* that I wasn't handling the situation better.

To make things worse, I could no longer access my preferred coping strategy—those two-hour-long workouts. The lack of exercise, combined with my lack of a thyroid, caused me to gain nearly ten pounds, which put me on a roller coaster of anxiety and depression, each fighting for first place on some subconscious level.

Hindsight and medical training have shown me that I likely would have processed the entire situation differently if I'd had more financial support, emotional support, and coping skills—or if my entire identity hadn't come to be based on my appearance. As it was, cancer turned out to be the perfect storm to destroy my world, which I'd built like a house of cards on a windy shoreline.

Then one dark, rainy day I found myself hunched over a toilet bowl again.

I'd sworn those days of adolescent behavior were behind me forever. It had been more than eight years since I'd even thought about purging. Now I was not only thinking about it but doing it. And this time the problem was far worse, the depression magnified by the hormonal imbalance and the knowledge that I had broken my promise to Mom. I'd told her if I ever found myself purging again, I would tell her. But I couldn't. And I couldn't stop.

You stupid, weak, fat pig! When I wasn't in bed or over a toilet barfing up Cheerios, I would stand in front of the mirror yelling at myself, trying to will myself to stop. Instead, the emotional pain grew so severe that I wanted to squeeze out of my body, rip my skin off—anything to make it stop. But it wouldn't.

Depression was unlike any other pain I'd ever felt. It gripped my soul. I was living in a dark hole and felt paralyzed, like I was stuck in one of those dreams where you know you need to run but you're helpless to move.

The doctor had been right about school. I had to drop my classes because I couldn't think straight for ten minutes, much less sit through lectures and tests five days a week.

Mom, seeing my inability to bounce back after my cancer treatment, told me I needed to snap out of it, to push through. She was relieved and grateful that we'd both been given a second chance, that I wasn't going to die of cancer. After all we'd both overcome, she couldn't understand why I didn't feel or act the same way she did. She thought I was either lazy or feeling sorry for myself.

Maybe Mom is right. The thought only caused me to sink deeper into despair. The hurricane of thoughts spun in my head, threatening to fling me into some black abyss of no return as I rehearsed all the reasons why I *should* feel lucky (but didn't).

You're so lucky your stepdad didn't actually rape you; it was only a "close call."
You're so lucky you fought that predator! He could have killed you.

It sucks not to have your dad, but you're so lucky to have your mom.

I know you had to give up Playboy, *but maybe that was a blessing in disguise.*

You're so lucky that the cancer you have is easier to treat than most cancers.

I couldn't even get fricking cancer in a way that made sense. Everything in my life seemed to fall into some gray, murky swampland. I couldn't see the monsters, but I knew they were just under the surface. And yet I felt compelled to be grateful because at least my raft was prettier, bigger, sturdier than the ones others had.

The truth was, I did not feel grateful. I felt hateful, mostly toward myself. And unlike my mom, I couldn't even bring myself to cry out to God. If there even was a God, I decided, He had forsaken me. If there was a God, He was either punishing me or had abandoned me. I hadn't been particularly good, but then I hadn't been an awful person either. *If* there was a God, why would He let all of those things happen in my life?

Maybe He was punishing me for posing nude, even though the photos had never been published. But if that was the way He worked, then why hadn't He punished the people who had hurt *me*? Maybe God was just like all the other men in my life—present when things were good and absent when things were not. Either way, I decided, He didn't love me, so why should I love Him? How *could* I love Him?

Even as I sank deeper into despair, I knew I couldn't kill myself—my mother had made it clear that she would die if I did that. But I did pray that someone else would kill me. When I saw an eighteen-wheeler next to me on the road, for example, I found myself fantasizing about an accident. *Just a slight turn the wrong way, and it would all be over. And it wouldn't be my fault.*

As it was, I saw myself as wasting the planet's oxygen. I had no purpose, no sense of worth, no expectation for what was to come in my life. Nothing but perpetual fog and darkness.

Then came a bizarre, momentary parting of the storm clouds. *Playboy* called, asking me to do another test shoot. Initially I resisted. I hadn't lost the ten pounds I'd gained after my last treatment, but I knew I wouldn't get another chance if I turned down the shoot. So I accepted and returned to the *Playboy* headquarters, which had recently moved from Sunset Boulevard to a less glamorous location in Santa Monica. After another stunning transformation, the makeup magician—that's what I called her—escorted me to "wardrobe," where a pair of high heels and some accessories awaited me. As the magician added some final touches, the editor walked in and applauded me for the weight gain.

"You were a little too skinny last time we saw you. You look healthier now." Turning to the makeup artist, she said, "She has an *amazing* body. Her face is all right"—she made a waffling sign with her hand—"But we can work with it."

The only thing I took away from that conversation at the time was "her face is all right." It was another blow to my fragile and battered ego. I'd been reduced to average, and barely that. Those words confirmed my worst fear: *Tana, you're not good enough—almost, but not quite.*

I could see it when I looked around the *Playboy* studio at all those robe-clad girls. I was average at best. In my little world people may have thought of me as beautiful, but in the international world of *Playboy* beauties, I was barely passable.

In some ways, a decade of being valued mostly for my looks had culminated in my coming to believe, on some level, that my appearance was the only standard by which I could be measured. Deep down I knew I was smart, resourceful, and resilient—or at least I had been. And I couldn't help but dream that somewhere out there was a man who would see beyond my book's cover and read my heart and my soul. But the world didn't seem bent on rewarding women like me for who they were inside. So I blindly kept playing the game, a game that at the time I didn't realize could never be won. My "assets" were as fleeting and unreliable as my health had been.

When I looked in the mirror after months of cancer treatment, purging, and not working out, I saw an "all right," fat-faced, not-quite-good-enough chipmunk of a girl staring back at me. I left the studio, bought a couple of doughnuts—which I promptly threw up—and went back to bed for three days.

CHAPTER 9

TRAIN WRECK

My brain is experiencing technical
difficulties. Please stand by.

—UNKNOWN

Mom had had enough of my aimless moping. She was tired of my listlessness, my sleeping in a dark room all day, my absolute lack of forward motion. She wanted me to push through my gloom, to shake it off.

One afternoon she all but forced me out of bed to do some shopping. In a haze of hopelessness, I shuffled past a sidewalk sale at a secondhand bookstore, praying for the day to end so I could retreat from the assault of smiles and sunshine back to the obscurity of my room. But a book on clearance suddenly caught my eye: *Listening to Prozac.*

I never read beyond the first few pages. That's all it took for me to come up with a solid self-diagnosis: *I have a Prozac deficiency!* Inspired for the first time in months, I went home, pulled out the yellow pages, and made an appointment with the first psychiatrist who offered a cash discount and could see me that week.

In hindsight, the fact that this doctor was cheap and readily available should have been a red flag, but that never crossed my mind. Besides, I already *knew* what I needed. I just needed the doctor to write the prescription for me.

Five days later I was sitting in front of a Doogie Howser lookalike, impatiently trying to convince him of my diagnosis.

"I'm so depressed I want to die," I said. "I have no purpose for living. But I'm not *actually* suicidal. Killing myself would kill my mother. If you can feel guilt in the afterlife, she'd make sure I spend eternity in a guilt-ridden hell."

An awkward pause ensued, suggesting I fill the void.

"I read about Prozac, and I think it would help me. I'm pretty sure that's what I need. I need something to snap me out of this fast. I have no intention of sitting on a couch, banging my head against a wall for the next three years, telling you how f***ed-up my mother is. I just want to feel better *now*. I want Prozac."

The young psychiatrist said nothing. Certain that my enthusiastic speech warranted some kind of response, I refused to blink first. He wasn't disagreeing with me. That was something.

"How long have you felt this way?"

He speaks!

"Tell me what precipitated the depression. Did you have some kind of breakup? A major life change? Do you live alone?"

Oh, here we go! Reading the situation, I quickly realized I'd have to trade information for my prescription. If he needed me to be screwed up enough to get Prozac, I would accommodate. For the next twenty minutes I word-vomited all the crap that had gone on in my life for the past year and a half, starting with cancer treatment and a wicked breakup with a jet-setting boyfriend, continuing on to my obsession with hugging the toilet bowl, and concluding with a *Playboy* deal that was still in limbo.

Surprise! I was screwed up enough for Prozac. I left with a prescription in my hand.

Within three days of taking the meds, I had more energy. Within a couple of weeks the world no longer looked dark and hazy; in fact, I had a slightly euphoric feeling. A feeling of hope. Colors were a little brighter. The breeze on my skin felt different. I laughed for the first time in months. The relief of not feeling swallowed by darkness was so overwhelming that it was worth the slightly restless feeling that had taken its place. I felt sexier, yet I had little interest in sex—a bonus since I was swearing off men. Again.

These were side effects I could live with, considering that now I actually wanted to live. For the first time in months I went to bed excited about getting up the next morning. Staring at the ceiling, I remembered being attacked on the street when I was fifteen. The past year had felt similar, but so much worse. Being physically assaulted had been terrifying, but I'd also been mobilized; I had fought for my life. There'd been an enemy to attack, a perpetrator on whom to unleash my anger.

By contrast, being sick and depressed felt like a lonely walk down a dark alley with gangbangers ready to strike. Sucker punches coming out of the shadows, knocking me senseless over and over. Cancer to the right of me, depression to the left. And yet there I was, unable to land a punch on the stealthy predators. I kept taking the blows; they kept trying to kill me.

Now, however, thanks to the energy provided by a little green and yellow capsule, I felt mobilized once again. In my mind I heard the police officer saying, "You fought. That's why you survived." Summoning the fighter in me once again, I began the arduous task of rebuilding my life—all under the influence of my newfound pharmaceutical friend.

Despite my improved mood, other parts of my life changed into something between 9½ Weeks and Carrie. One of my roommates went from being a sweet, wholesome girl to funding her nursing education by becoming a stripper. And I met another roommate, Jackie, after realizing that she and I had—unbeknownst to each other—been dating the same doctor. We ditched the doctor and became fast friends before she moved in. I'm not sure if I attracted the drama or if it attracted me. But it followed me like a faithful hound.

Jackie and I christened our fledgling friendship with a trip to Las Vegas. We figured it would be a good place for us to lick our wounds and have some laughs. On the drive we had a conversation that had a profound effect on my behavior for months to come.

"I hate men," Jackie said, clenching the steering wheel.

"I agree. They can't be trusted," I said. "I think I've been asked out by more married men than single men. Dating requires excellent interrogation techniques."

She nodded her head. "Screw them. We have to be better at their games than they are."

"Sounds like a plan," I said. "Absolutely. Offense sounds like a whole lot more fun than defense. But how?"

Jackie and I spent that weekend in Vegas plotting our new plan to take control of our lives while simultaneously honing the skills our plan would require. Being a "man-eater" turned out to be far easier than either of us anticipated, especially without guilt or remorse. I knew something was changing, but I couldn't identify the change. I wasn't sure if it was emotional or mental, but I wasn't feeling pain. That was something. Considering I didn't want to die, *it was everything*. Feeling numb was better than feeling like my mind was chronically under siege, which was how it felt to be depressed.

By the time we returned from Vegas, I was firing on all pistons, with Prozac fueling the ride. Excited just to *be excited* about going out with friends for the first time in months, I dressed to the nines and hit the town. I was the life of the party—and I had never been the life of the party. I'd frequently been the center of attention, but that's hardly the same thing. I was used to being noticed for my appearance—more specifically, my cleavage—not my sparkling personality.

But now, as the Prozac Princess, my usual shy and reserved demeanor was nowhere to be found. Handling the attention I attracted from the opposite sex was like trying to drink water from a firehose. But instead of being overwhelmed, I felt invigorated. *This is going to be fun! Tana, new and improved.* Flirting with the waiter, I ordered a margarita and convinced the guy next to me to pay for it.

The next day I woke up feeling oddly disconnected. I couldn't remember anything after the margarita. Did that guy drug my drink? An uneasy feeling set in. I woke up Jackie.

"I think I was drugged last night," I said.

She scowled. "You only had one drink."

"Really?"

"Yeah. You were more chatty and flirtatious than usual, but I didn't see anything to suggest you were drugged."

Relieved, I wrote the experience off as an inexplicable incident. Then it happened again a few weeks later. One drink, and the next day I had a hard time piecing together events from the night before.

I should have been terrified. Instead, I was only mildly concerned. Finally I called the psychiatrist, thinking maybe it was a reaction to the Prozac. *He didn't tell me not to drink alcohol, did he?*

Nope. He said drinking *a lot* was not recommended, but it was highly unlikely that this kind of reaction would happen with one or two drinks. I'd never been a heavy drinker, so I figured I had nothing to worry about. *Probably a fluke.* This reaction happened several more times, but I ignored it and continued filling up with premium at the Prozac station.

It did sometimes occur to me that I was becoming the very thing I had hated about men. Uncaring and unfeeling. Manipulative. But it's hard to register remorse when your emotions are on a pharmaceutically induced vacation. Somewhere deep down I sensed my life was becoming a runaway train, ready to jump the track. Yet I was too scared to toss the Prozac—to return to the darkness that made me wish for death.

So I rationalized. Sure, there were drawbacks to the medicine. But there were also major payoffs in addition to the obvious—not being depressed. My friends were enthralled, if not a bit bewildered, with my new personality. Many of them benefitted from the new me. I wasn't afraid to push the boundaries, ask for favors, and flirt my way into free admission, free drinks, even backstage passes. Life was good—wasn't it?

To make matters crazier, Jackie decided to make an appointment with the same psychiatrist I was seeing. She'd been depressed after her breakup with the two-timing doctor and hadn't snapped out of it.

Surprise! The psychiatrist gave her Prozac too.

Do I need to paint the picture? Two attractive, busty young girls on a thrilling roller-coaster ride—with no brakes. The coaster was starting to shake as it reached record-breaking speeds. Numbness and a lack of rational fear were the side dishes that came with the main course. I adopted the mantra "Live fast. Die young. Leave a good-looking corpse." What difference did it make? Long a great respecter of rules and regulations, a person who was anxious about every decision, I was now throwing caution to the wind and following my every impulse.

I spontaneously had my long hair cut short, traded my soft angora sweaters for a leather jacket and spiked heels, and embraced my new social life with a vengeance. When three guys at a country-western bar challenged me and Jackie to a drinking contest, we discreetly arranged for the bartender to serve us apple juice to look like tequila shots. We bet the guys a hundred dollars that they couldn't outdrink us and told the bartender we'd buy him a drink for helping out. The cowboys made total fools of themselves trying to two-step after six shots of tequila each. Jackie and I sneaked out with our hundred bucks while the boys were kicking up their heels on the dance floor.

On Halloween Jackie and I went out on the town dressed as dominatrix twins. Our matching costumes—short leather dresses, a spiked collar and dog chain around my neck, the leash in her hand—were a hit at the Halloween contest held by a local sports bar. When one of the judges asked for our entry number, I told him we weren't competing.

"But we've already voted," he said. "And you won." We left with five hundred dollars and a few phone numbers.

Over the next couple of months such episodes continued. And I just didn't care—or maybe I didn't feel enough to care. Pocket change and crazy stories were about the only good things to come from that eight-month stretch. Jackie and I were too numb to notice the Prozac-sized Band-Aid we'd put over our broken souls. And I was ignoring the root issues behind my prescription-driven behavior.

As the emotional bills started piling up, a warning sign flashed in my account: "insufficient funds." I began wondering if Prozac had been a bad idea. I returned to the psychiatrist and talked about how it was making me feel—or *not* feel—and how I was behaving.

He asked, "Are you still having thoughts of wanting to die?"

"No."

"That's encouraging," he said. "I'd like to increase the dose."

Increase? Yep, he doubled my dosage. Six weeks later he doubled it again. *Maybe he's right,* I thought. So I took the new amount of Prozac, which turned up the dial on my impulsive behavior. And the stories piled up.

———————

I started dating John, a slick playboy from the gym. He had been asking me out for more than a year, but I had always been too intimidated by his predatory vibe to say yes. I sensed he was trouble. On my increased dosage of Prozac, though, John didn't seem so scary. Nothing did.

One afternoon he asked if I could take him to the airport for a quick business trip he needed to make to Costa Rica. I obliged. We left early to have dinner at the Peninsula Hotel. We sipped Cristal champagne with appetizers, and he ordered a bottle of wine to be served with dinner—the cost of which would pay my rent for two months. By the second glass of champagne, I was feeling no pain—or anything else, for that matter.

"Come with me," he said.

"Where?"

"To Costa Rica."

"What?" All I knew about this guy was that he was eccentric, something of a jet-setter, and had great abs.

"Come to Costa Rica with me," he said. "We leave in three hours."

"Right!" I laughed and shook my head no.

"Come on. Be spontaneous."

"Not possible. I don't have my passport or any clothes, and there's no time to go get them."

"You're such a goody two-shoes."

I bristled, but he just laughed. He called the only sane roommate I had at the time and offered him a handsome tip if he could get my passport to the Peninsula in time. Then he laid a wad of cash on the table.

"Here's money for incidentals and clothes, and I'll get you a first-class ticket if you get on the plane with me without packing a thing."

Before I knew it, I was sitting in first class, sipping more champagne.

The next morning I called my mother before she could have an all-points bulletin issued.

"Mom, I'm fine, but—" I paused awkwardly as I tried to offer an explanation that would make sense.

"What do mean you're *fine?*" she asked suspiciously.

"Well, I'm in Costa Rica."

Having just seen me the day before at the office, she was confused.

"You mean Costa *Mesa?*" she said, referring to a city near where I lived.

"No, R-r-r-rica," I rolled my *r*'s playfully. "Costa Rica."

"The *country?* What the hell are you doing in Costa Rica? Have you been kidnapped?"

"No, Mom. I'm safe. I was sort of dared to go."

No point explaining something I had no clue about.

"Are you out of your mind?" she asked, then answered her own question. "Of course you are out of your mind! You've been out of your mind for months."

She'd only just begun. "Tana, you were such an easy teenager. I thought I was out of the woods. But now? *Now* you start acting adolescent? You're nearly twenty-five! You were already a toddler when I was twenty-five. I wasn't running off to foreign countries!"

Precisely why I do not plan to have children. I did my best to reassure Mom that I hadn't married some cartel drug lord or been sex trafficked. Then I went shopping for clean underwear and a toothbrush.

That night John and I had a few laughs and a wild night on the town, during which I lost my passport. And the next day, instead of trying to help me find it, he was indifferent; his priority was his getting back to Los Angeles. He left a wad of cash with me and a credit card with the hotel manager, telling him to let me stay there until I figured out what to do about my passport. Then, poof, he left me alone in Costa Rica.

Fortunately someone found my passport and turned it in to the American Embassy. I could get home, but I was monumentally pissed off at John for leaving me. Figuring he'd eventually check in, I wanted to make him sweat. So rather than taking the flight I was booked on, I took another flight with a layover in Miami, where I decided to stay for the weekend with the extra cash John had given me. Needless to say, the whirlwind romance with Costa Rica Man was DOA—not that I lost a second of sleep over him.

––––––––––

One afternoon a man stopped me as I was coming out of the grocery store. I found his slicked-back hair, sexy Italian accent, and new Jag alluring, so when he asked for my number, I gladly obliged. Soon after I heard "Ciao, Bella" on my answering machine, and I was fascinated. For the life of me, when Damiano came to pick me up, I couldn't figure out why my friends thought he was scary. I'd never been drawn to bad boys. In fact, I'd played it surprisingly safe with men in the past. Not necessarily smart. But safe.

Though the Prozac argued to waive my concerns about Damiano, I gave in to them a few weeks later, when I suspected he'd stolen my passport. This happened just after I'd found a duffel bag full of cash in his car and he'd shown up with his face beaten pretty badly. I searched his apartment and car for my missing passport but didn't find it. However, I *did* discover that Damiano's driver's license, passport, and car registration had different last names.

Using fictitious jealousy as an excuse for my snooping, I confronted him with defensive outrage and demanded an explanation. Damiano told me a convoluted story about a bungled business venture, a burglary, and an unfortunate slip in the shower, which did little to allay my growing apprehension or explain what I had found.

With an icy grin and no explanation, Damiano finally admitted to taking my passport. The once sexy accent suddenly sent a chill down my spine. "You pass-a-port ees at my home. You need to come weeth me if-a you want eet."

"I'm late for a doctor's appointment," I responded nervously. "I'll have to come back tomorrow." Then I hightailed it home. For a girl who felt very little, my survival instinct was on overdrive. So I called the one person I'd always been able to count on in a crisis.

Mom.

She made the two-hour drive with me in stop-and-go traffic to Calabasas. We met Damiano at the restaurant he owned. And when Damiano approached her to introduce himself she choked—literally. She started coughing and seemingly couldn't stop.

Putting a hand over her mouth and waving the other, she excused herself to go to the restroom. Concerned, I followed to check on her. When she finally stopped coughing, she said, "I was looking into the eyes of Satan."

"Excuse me?" If Mom hadn't been so upset, I would have laughed.

"Tana, that man is pure evil," she sputtered, "and he knows I see him. We need to get out of here. Just tell him I'm really sick. Let's go." She walked out, resuming her coughing fit. I followed.

Then Mom realized we had driven several hours and not retrieved the passport. She was livid—and panicked. "Tana, when you told me about all the weird stuff going on with Damiano, I thought maybe it was drugs. After seeing him, I know it's girls. He runs girls!"

"Mom, calm down. Seriously. You sound crazy. I think I'd know if he was a pimp."

"I'm right, and he knows I know. He's not going to let this go."

"What is this, some kind of psychic party game? Are you reading each other's minds?"

"You know I'm not psychic, but I do have a gift. So does he. But he is *evil*, I'm telling you. You can't go back there for any reason."

It's not that I necessarily believed her, but under the circumstances I also couldn't *ignore* her. And I still needed my passport. So we decided to involve someone who could be pretty terrifying himself—Joe. Though he often overplayed his hand and could create embarrassing scenes, I knew that if I really was swimming in the deep end with a shark, I needed a killer whale on my side.

Less than twenty-four hours after we told Joe about my predicament with the missing passport, I stopped by Joe's office to find two of Joe's "friends" there. Usually I was put off by his ragtag group of buddies, which included a couple of retired cops and a few ex-cons. (Sometimes it was hard to tell the difference.) But not that day. That day I was relieved. Comforted.

"Tana, give me the a**hole's phone number and address, then leave." That's all he said. And I complied. No snarky comments. No arguments.

The next day Damiano called. "I put your passport in the mail today." There was an awkward pause. Just as I was about to hang up, he said coolly, "Your papa . . . ees not a nice man!" He hung up, and I never heard from him again.

Days later I asked Joe, "What happened with you and Damiano?"

He looked at me, stone-faced. "No idea what you're talking about." And I knew that conversation was over.

A couple of weeks later I was with several friends at an exclusive nightclub in Los Angeles—my name on the coveted guest list a remnant of the *Playboy* saga. When I arrived, Johnny, the club promoter who had added me to the list, made his way over and gave me a kiss on the cheek.

"I didn't think we'd be seeing much of you any longer," he said.

"Why is that?"

"Because I heard you were one of Damiano's girls."

What? "Does that mean what I think it does?"

"I guess that depends on what you think it means. To most people it means you're off limits."

Wow! Could Mom have been right? Again?

I never discovered the full truth about Damiano, but I took that conversation as the final warning I needed to stay clear of any place I thought he might be connected with.

I also took it as a sign that it was time to cool my jets—if only I knew how. At this point, I wanted to be free of Prozac, but I was still terrified of being swallowed by depression again.

Hindsight, of course, would suggest that pharmaceuticals weren't my only problem—or my solution. The Prozac was just masking my spiritual emptiness with a hollow laugh track of my own making. By "toying with boys" while hitting the Prozac pause button on my conscience, I had almost convinced myself that I was right where I wanted to be: a party girl with no inhibitions and a thirst for adventure.

The reality? Sometimes the life of the party is the loneliest one there.

CHAPTER 10

OUT OF THE DARKNESS

Nothing happens until the pain of remaining
the same outweighs the pain of change.

—Arthur Burt

As I was trying to figure out how, exactly, I needed to change, a visit from my sister interrupted my big-life musings. Tamara had moved back and forth between her mom and our dad since the divorce, but she had recently landed once again in California after Dad remarried and moved to Texas. At the time she was sixteen and I was twenty-five.

"Tana," she said, "let's go see Dad. I need to get out of here."

"Tell me what's going on with Kathy?"

"The stories you tell about her when you were a kid don't sound like my mother. I think you got the best of her," Tamara said. "It pisses me off that I don't get that."

Kathy's struggles, it would turn out, had started long before the partying or even the divorce. Soon after her sister committed suicide, her brother had died from a cocaine overdose that was suspected—but not proven—to be intentional. Grandma Jane, having lost her husband and two children, had then sunk deeper into alcoholism. Then the divorce and becoming a single mother had finally pushed Kathy over the edge. She'd fallen into a vicious cycle of self-medicating, according to Dad and Tamara, though she never admitted to more than weed and alcohol.

I hadn't seen my father since that awful night he took me out to dinner in his silk suit. The most interaction we'd had in seven years was the two-minute phone call prompted by the big-C diagnosis. But now my sister was suggesting a sort of reconciliation road trip. What could I possibly gain by allowing my father back into my life at this point?

I also felt too exhausted for drama. Since I'd last said sayonara to Dad, I'd ended my six-year roller-coaster relationship, battled metastatic thyroid cancer, and lost a deal with *Playboy*. I'd gone numb on Prozac, filed for bankruptcy because I couldn't pay the mountain of medical bills, and continued to struggle with an eating disorder. I didn't have enough energy to be angry with him. But that didn't mean I was convinced it was a good idea to pick up where we'd left off—which was precisely nowhere.

"He's changed," Tamara said.

"Really? Pray tell."

"He's not the self-righteous jerk he used to be. He even parties with me. He drinks beer, smokes weed, and loves Def Leppard."

"Oh, great. So Dad smokes weed with his daughters and rocks out—and that suddenly makes him a great dad? How is this different from your mom?" I asked.

"Mom is disconnected. Dad is more fun," she said.

"And you said he's remarried? That's number three, I believe. Or is it four?" I thought a minute. "Yeah, four. But then, who's counting?"

Tamara said he had married one of his former "patients," having made the transition from (failed) pastor to (questionably qualified) therapist without ever becoming the successful motivational speaker he'd aspired to be. I couldn't get my head around that. My father advising people about getting their lives together seemed like North Korea's Kim Jong-un leading peace-through-meditation retreats.

But Dad had a new PhD from Emmanuel Baptist University, even though he'd never lived in North Carolina, where the university is located. Dad claimed he'd completed a correspondence program (which no one could confirm) that offered "retroactive credits" for the time he'd served as a pastor. In other words, he got credit for life experience. So in almost a snap of the fingers, my absentee, thrice-divorced dad had obtained a mail-order doctorate and was working as a marriage and family therapist. *Rich.*

Yet, I said yes to the trip with Tamara.

Sometime during that visit, Dad lit up a joint and passed it to my sixteen-year-old sister, who then passed it to me. I found myself awkwardly accepting and taking a small hit, then regretting it. I'd never been one to give in to peer pressure, so why had I felt obligated to give in to it with my *father,* whom I hadn't spoken to for years? I told myself it was my way of showing Dad I had put the past behind me. I *was* ready to put the past behind me—wasn't *I?*

For some reason—maybe I was still too numb from Prozac at the time—I didn't recognize the gravity of the situation, which was that he had been getting high with my sixteen-year-old sister for the past two years. And that I'd just been complicit in the same idiotic act.

When the brief visit ended, I realized I had not found a changed man in the slick-talking, pot-smoking Dad 3.0. Instead I'd found a worn-out man. A despondent man. A tired man. More important, I realized I was done being angry with him. This was no fairy-tale-ending road trip, punctuated with a big group hug at the end. But it did show me that I had let go of expecting him to be the perfect dad, which he never would be. It was simply too tiring to hold on to a grudge.

––––––––––

When the three-day visit ended, my sister and I began our drive back to LA. I drove first, and somewhere on a desolate stretch of I-40 in New Mexico, about an hour after my sister had taken over at the wheel, I was wakened by a nightmare—a living nightmare. I was being shaken like a rag doll in a rolling-over car. Driving seventy-five miles per hour, my sister had fallen asleep.

The world spun and spun and spun to the pounding percussion of crumpling metal and broken glass, while Tamara and I banged around like rocks in a tumbler. We barely missed being T-boned by a forty-foot motorhome as our vehicle flipped upside down and came to a halt.

When the car fully stilled and the dust settled, the two of us were still alive. Bruised. Scratched. Scared beyond words. But alive.

That was my life in a nutshell. At that point I should have been dead for all sorts of reasons, ranging from my drug-dealing uncle's customers to rape attempts to metastatic cancer to wanting to get hit by a truck . . . wait—could this be God's much-delayed answer to my long-ago prayer to die? If so, He'd come close to fulfilling my wish.

But, no, Tamara and I both came out of the accident without the kind of fatal or near-fatal injuries a crash like that might normally cause. In fact, we were able to walk away without any visible injuries. It was as if someone still had work for me to do.

Eventually an ambulance arrived and took Tamara and me to a tiny "hospital"—a converted two-bedroom house in what seemed to be no-man's-land. It had two examining rooms, concrete floors, and cracked fiberglass showers. We were briefly seen by a cowboy/doctor wearing boots and jeans. Then Dad showed up and drove me to the nearest airport. During the five-hour drive he pressured me—to protect Tamara from losing her license and avoid problems with insurance coverage—to say I had been driving.

Rolling my eyes, I realized my dad hadn't changed at all. But I took the blame anyhow—and assumed the financial obligation of the deductible and increased insurance premiums.

The death sentence I'd staved off became my wake-up call to get my act together. The past few years had been the hardest of my life, but I'd already proven to myself I was a fighter. It was time to stand up, brush off the dust, and create some kind of life I could be proud of.

Not that I had much of a clue *how*.

———

Back home, Uncle Bob noticed my new surge of energy and asked me to join him for a retreat he was leading in Hawaii. Yes, Bob, the navy-vet-heroin-addict zombie who had lived with us, had gotten his act together in the last twelve years, and now wanted to help me do the same. After finally kicking his drug habit for good, he'd become a counselor at juvenile hall, then moved to Hawaii and started teaching intensive self-help seminars.

I wasn't sure how much good a seminar would do me, but I figured a trip to Hawaii would be just what the doctor ordered. So I took him up on the invitation and flew to Hawaii.

I learned as much from Bob as I did from that seminar—maybe more. I told him how down I'd been after going through the battle with cancer and that the Prozac I was taking just made things worse. I still had no drive. No vision. No real excitement about life.

Uncle Bob didn't coddle me. Instead he challenged me. "How much responsibility are you willing to take for where your life is at?" he asked.

"Well, it's not like I can take responsibility for getting *cancer*. That wasn't my idea of a good time."

"Got it. But I didn't ask you to take the *blame*. However, what will you take responsibility for?"

Drawing a circle on a piece of paper, he put a line through the middle.

"Responsibility is the ability to respond," he said. "Let's say you take 50 percent of the responsibility for where your life is now." He pointed to one half of the circle. "You still have no control over—no ability to respond to—the other 50 percent, right? Like someone could slap you in the face, and you're not to blame for being slapped. That just happened to you. But . . . if you block the next slap, then you're taking responsibility. You're using your ability to respond—which would change the outcome."

At those words I experienced a light-switch moment that would literally change the trajectory of my life. I realized how much control of my life I'd given up. How sorry I was feeling for myself. How I'd come to see myself as a victim—and victims are never winners; they are *always* victims. Even when I wasn't being a victim, I was still flitting aimlessly through life, *letting* it happen to me instead of *making* it happen.

I didn't want to be a victim, nor did I want to be aimless. I wanted to be a winner. More than that, I wanted to be a *warrior*. That became my metaphor.

So I came home and started kicking butt. For starters, it was time to get off Prozac, the drug I was now sure was responsible for the change in my personality, not to mention my risky behavior. I was still afraid that my depression might return, but not nearly as afraid as I was of where my life would end up in ten years if I stayed on Prozac.

Which is what I told the psychiatrist who had prescribed it for me.

"My behavior is erratic," I said.

"Are you still depressed?"

"No, I'm not depressed. But I'm not happy either. I'm not *anything*. I just don't give a crap. I have no regard for consequences, and my judgment sucks. I'm spontaneous to the point of being reckless. And nothing matters."

"Give it some more time," he said.

BS, I thought. I realized Doogie had some maturing to do, but it wouldn't be at my expense. It was time to recover from the Prozac walk of shame—on my own. I left his office and trashed the Prozac.

(Note: As a nurse, I am now aware that no one should try this at home. Quitting an antidepressant cold turkey, without the help of a trained professional, is a bad idea—really bad. I'm very, very lucky that I got through that sudden withdrawal without major problems. But as a personal choice I'm still really glad I went off the Prozac, which was the wrong medication for me.)

For the first time in two years, the only things I had going for me were a renewed sense of responsibility—and hope. And that was a lot. It had taken months of bad decisions, months of wandering through the fog, but I'd somehow seen that Prozac wasn't improving my life; it was simply obscuring the anguish in a veneer of to-hell-with-everything.

I had always been an anxious person; Prozac had made me a dangerously impulsive person. And now I was another year behind in school. Health problems—both mine and Mom's—and the Prozac haze had derailed my academic progress.

But now that I had my thyroid medication regulated and was free of Prozac, I knew I could focus again. I knew I could get into, and through, nursing school. And now, finally, I knew I was so much more than what men had defined me as being—more than I had *allowed* them to reduce me to.

So once again I swore off men.

"That's nonsense," said Krissy, a friend of mine who was closer to my mom in age.

"Seriously, I'm not dating anymore. Men are jerks. I'm a jerk magnet."

"Your problem isn't the men you meet. It's the ones you give your phone number to."

"What?"

"There are a lot of great men in the world. Your filter is not set to notice them. You *choose* men who are jerks."

Ouch! There it was again—responsibility in a nutshell.

I've often wondered if Krissy entering my life was coincidence or God's doing. I'd first met her when I was nineteen, working as an aesthetician, and I had started a skin-care business using money gifted to me by Mom. Though the business wasn't very successful, Krissy had been one of my regular customers. I'd always looked forward to seeing her, not because of her handsome tips, but because she had an energy that always left me feeling good. I couldn't figure out what or why, but I was drawn to it.

Krissy was joyful despite having gone through significant challenges. She had been through an ugly divorce but harbored no anger or bitterness about it. And it didn't bother me when she talked about God, because I never felt like she was judging me or trying to make me change. She just genuinely liked me.

I reconnected with Krissy soon after I returned from the Hawaiian retreat. She had two daughters around my age who had left for college several years before, and because she and her husband traveled the world extensively, she was looking for a live-in house and dog sitter. The timing couldn't have been better when she offered me the job. I needed to save money while going back to school, and if I was going to get my life together, I needed a break from my two current wild roommates. Moving in with Krissy would give me both.

After I moved in, Krissy invited me to go to church with her. "Sure," I said, not wanting to be rude, though I had no real intention of going. I was happy that church worked for her, but I was pretty sure I was beyond the help of Sunday morning hymns and people yelling, "Amen." No one was going to pull me out of this hole I'd dug for myself except me, and it was going to take a massive one-woman effort.

Besides, just thinking about church triggered thoughts of my hypocritical minister father. I thought of the few times he'd forced me to go to church when I was young, how he'd put on a mask the moment he walked in the door to greet people. *No thanks.* I might be a wreck, but at least I was an authentic wreck.

One rainy Sunday morning when Krissy happened to be home, I was sleeping off a pretty good night on the town when she suddenly poked her head into the bedroom I was occupying. It was seven in the morning.

"Up and at 'em, kiddo," she said.

With great effort I raised a single eyelid.

"Say *what?*"

"Today's the day."

"The day for what?"

"The day you're going to church with me."

"I just got home a few hours ago."

"You promised. I'm in town. So you're going. I don't ask for much."

I wanted to bury my head in the pillow. Why would she choose this morning to coerce me into going to church with her?

Mumbling, I dragged my body out of bed and got ready. Krissy was right; she didn't ask me for much. She had always been a good friend to me, better than I was to her. She gave more than she got. So I figured I owed her. Besides, other than sleep, I didn't have a hell of a lot to lose. It wasn't as if my hedonistic existence had done a lot to improve my life.

I was expecting the usual steeple-and-stained-glass setup, with a choir singing "How Great Thou Art." Instead, Saddleback Church met in a giant tent, and everyone was rocking out. What kind of church was this? I was pretty sure they were going to hell, at least based on my dad's perspective. I'd grown up believing that Baptists frowned on sex because it might lead to dancing and that dancing, of course, leads to hell. Apparently someone had forgotten to send these people the memo that rock music—even Christian rock—would hijack their souls.

On this rare rainy Southern California day, the tent was leaking mightily, and yet the people were partying like I'd never seen at church. *What am I doing here?* I kept asking myself. But then again, what had I been doing in Costa Rica or posing for *Playboy* magazine or dressed up in dominatrix attire at a sports bar or dating a possible gangster?

Eyeing the people around me warily, I walked in and braced myself to be slammed by guilt from some preacher whose life, unlike mine, had been a bed of roses. Or worse, from some preacher like my dad—all talk, no walk. Instead the guy up front spoke of something I'd never heard about: grace and forgiveness. How God forgave us and desired for us to forgive others.

The guy also spoke about brokenness. That definitely hit home. After all, a year earlier I'd been waiting for—hoping for—a Mack truck to end my life. Now I was hearing about a God who offered the hope of new life through Christ. He spoke about taking responsibility for our lives—not by ourselves, but with the help of God.

I was suspicious but intrigued. I listened.

This was the strangest church I'd ever seen, but it felt good—like a warm shower after a long, cold day. And yet I didn't seem deserving of whoever this God was that Krissy worshipped.

"I need to get my life cleaned up," I told her when we talked about it afterward. "Then I'll come back."

"Sweetheart," she said, "you don't get cleaned up so you can take a shower. That's nonsense. You get in the shower to get clean."

"But you don't know what I've seen and done."

"I know that God's less concerned about where you've been and what you've done than about where you're going and what you might do. I know He's in the business of helping us overcome our pasts. Look at King David. He made plenty of rotten choices, including having an affair with a married woman and then having her husband murdered, but God saw him as reconciled and righteous. God is all about second chances."

Well, I definitely haven't been as bad as King David. Maybe there's hope for me.

All this still felt like a little too much God talk for me to feel comfortable, but I was curious. The next week Krissy didn't ask me about going to church; instead, I asked her. I still didn't know how I felt about the whole church business, and I had a lot to learn, but I was open to listening and discovering the truth for myself.

I was starting to realize that there was nothing healing about church per se. A church was simply a group of people who met in a building or, in our case, a tent to worship God and to hang out with one another. Church was a means to a greater end. What it was, I didn't know. But the one thing that seemed clear was that I always left that tent feeling good. I couldn't figure it out, but I wanted to feel good, so I kept going.

Over time I also came to see that I had allowed my experience of my father to cloud my perception of God, my heavenly Father. Why, I asked myself, was I blaming God for my father's imperfections, for his broken humanity? Why was I allowing a single man to define who God was or what my spiritual walk should be? I wasn't sure what a relationship with God would look like, but I wasn't going to sacrifice that relationship—and ultimately my own life—just because I had so little respect for a man who'd purported to be "of God."

My dad is not God! That revelation, weird as it might sound, was tremendously freeing.

———

When some of my friends learned I was going to church, they cringed and then made fun of my new "hobby."

"Church," said one, "is just a crutch."

"No," I said. "It's so much more. It's more like a hospital, a place for healing. And I am clearly a broken mess. I know I'm the last person who should talk about God. But there's something to this."

"Yep," scoffed another. "Opiate of the masses—or the asses."

"Let me get this straight," I fired back. "You're criticizing people for treating church, or God, like a drug? You? The girl who's out drinking and toying with men every night, to avoid feeling *anything*? If it's a drug, at least it has positive side effects."

Even though I wasn't certain how I felt about my fledgling faith, I was irritated that she had disrespected me like that—especially since she was still burying her pain with alcohol and men and clearly not living a life of purpose. Her comment helped crystallize my commitment to explore what my still-shaky faith meant to me.

———

I continued attending Saddleback Church until I moved to Riverside to be closer to the junior college where I would finish taking my prerequisite nursing courses. In Riverside I found a new church—Harvest Christian Fellowship. Harvest drew a bit more of an eclectic crowd—tattoos, long hair, and bikers were not uncommon—and was led by Greg Laurie, whose early life somewhat mirrored my own. He'd been raised by a single mother who had a handful of marriages. And he hadn't grown up in the church but had come to his faith later, on his own. I sensed that many of the stories in the room where we met would make mine seem like an after-school special. And somehow I found that comforting.

The more I hung out with the believers at Harvest, the more I could feel myself changing. For the first time in my life I sensed something I'd never had: personal peace. And when, after three decades of struggle, I finally surrendered my life to Christ, I gained not only a sense of calmness but a sense of purpose and structure. Discipline. A whole new way of thinking. I recalled saying a prayer with my dad, and accepting Jesus into my heart, when I was six years old. It's not that I forgot it or didn't think it was real. But I had been a child without life experience. So many things had happened since then that had me question the reality of a loving God. In a quiet prayer, God became very real and very personal for me.

The Bible, for instance, which I had once seen as the ultimate buzzkill, suddenly started to make sense. God was the ultimate loving Parent. I was like a two-year-old. And the Bible represented the house rules designed to keep me safe. I imagined a toddler who thinks her parents' rules are designed to ruin her fun and who chases a ball into the street—not seeing the semi barreling toward her. When the toddler gets a spanking, clueless about the disaster she was saved from, she thinks her parents are mean.

I realized I was like that two-year-old, habitually running out into the street, oblivious to the danger and the fact that I'd been spared *repeatedly*!

Was it possible that God wasn't the angry, vengeful God my father spoke of? That He was loving? Was it possible that my perceived "punishments" were God saving me from myself?

It was a lot to take in. But it also felt like balm on an open wound.

Along with this new way of thinking and this sense of newfound peace, something even more incredible happened: I lost my urge for revenge. I didn't need to teach men a lesson. I didn't need to teach anyone a lesson. I didn't need to prove I was better than anyone. And I wasn't always waiting and watching for someone to hurt me. I could relax and just be who God had created me to be.

For the first time in a long time the future looked bright.

I was excited about the unknown ahead.

————

I enrolled at Riverside Community College northeast of LA, which was also near where my mother and Joe had moved the now-flourishing dog-grooming-supply manufacturing business. They had bought a beautiful, sprawling horse ranch, so we lived near enough to each other for visits.

I looked forward to my prerequisite courses, but when one I needed was already full, I decided to talk with the teacher, Professor Rivera, who was considered by many to be the toughest at RCC. His class was far cheaper at RCC than at Loma Linda University, where I planned to transfer, so I asked if I could at least audit it. He agreed. He even said I could take the opening quiz, though he doubted enough people would drop to make it feasible for me to fully enroll.

Refusing to be deterred, I came to every class for nearly two weeks, furiously scrawled notes, and went into the quiz with high expectations. I aced it, while other students were dropping like flies. With a skeptical scowl Professor Rivera signed my petition and allowed me in the class—though he might have had some misgivings when, after that first-unit test, I engaged him in a heated discussion in front of the class.

"One of your test questions," I said, "was misleading."

"Is that right?" His eyes locked on mine, challenging me.

I took up the challenge: "Absolutely."

We verbally sparred for a few minutes in front of the class. Then I showed him my copious notes, copied nearly verbatim from his lecture.

In that moment it occurred to me how much I loved college—not just as a means to an end, but as a means of learning. Why hadn't I found a way to be more serious about it sooner?

"Well, okay, *Absolutely*," the professor said. "Since you have the notes to back up what you're saying, I will drop the question."

A smile threatened to emerge on my face, but I held it in for fear of appearing cocky—which, of course, I was. For the remainder of the semester Mr. Rivera referred to me as Absolutely. He was tough and gruff, my favorite professor ever.

One day at the end of the semester, he asked me to stay after class. "Absolutely," he said, "I don't want to be presumptive, but if you'd like a letter of recommendation for Loma Linda, I'd be happy to write one. Honestly, I think you have what it takes to go to medical school."

I beamed—and took him up on the offer.

In 1997, after nearly two years of keeping my head down and working hard at RCC, I was accepted into Loma Linda's School of Nursing—mainly because of my grades but also partly because of the letters of recommendation from professors. I started school at Loma Linda with high hopes, feeling well prepared, confident, and at peace. And all went well—until just before the end of my first year.

At my annual checkup with the endocrinologist, a diagnostic scan revealed "suspicious" lymph nodes in my neck. Based on my history, it was strongly suggested that I undergo surgery to remove the nodes and any other suspicious growths.

Disappointed, but still at peace, I dropped two summer classes and embraced the diagnosis. Fortunately, I didn't need radiation, and the recovery was relatively quick. By fall I was ready to go back to school. I added extra classes to my already demanding load for the remainder of the year—and excelled.

Despite financial challenges, health problems, and a grueling schedule, I had done it. It was a defining moment for me when I graduated with the class ahead of mine—magna cum laude.

I'd learned much in this chapter of my life. Although we hadn't suddenly become Pa and little Laura, I'd forged a peaceful relationship with my father after realizing that bitterness may be harder on the person who harbors it than on the one at whom it's aimed. I'd learned from my uncle about putting on your big-girl panties and taking responsibility for your life. I'd set aside my religious stereotypes long enough to discover that God wasn't some vengeful cop riding the celestial highway looking for lawbreakers but actually concerned about me on a personal level. And thinking back to the former boyfriend who told me I'd never get through nursing school except on my back, I'd learned that success is the best revenge. In fact, I had taped that mantra to my mirror and read it each morning.

CHAPTER 11

VIEW FROM THE TOP

Pride is the mask of one's own faults.

—Unknown

I grew up hating fairy tales. Prince Charming? Oh, I'd met a few of the self-proclaimed variety. But they weren't concerned with rescuing the damsel in distress. Instead, they tried to impress the girl with a slick horse—or, more often, the one prancing on the front of a Ferrari—and an expensive dinner, and they felt entitled to the crown jewels in return. Which is why I was never the little girl who dreamed of castles in the sky or the young woman who imagined some guy would magically pull up in a Bentley to whisk her off to a life of Beverly Hills bliss. I believed what Mom taught me and showed me: *the only path to success is the one you clear for yourself.*

I was fully into path-clearing mode now. I was more stable than, well, *ever,* and life was unfolding with increasing promise. I'd recently moved home with Mom and Joe to be closer to school. I was attending college as a full-time student while working part-time in the family business, part-time as an aesthetician, and attending church regularly.

I'd only been home a few days, but it was long enough to realize that Mom and Joe weren't fighting the way they had in the past. Something had changed between them, but I couldn't put my finger on it. Still, their horse ranch in the country, away from the hustle and bustle, was the perfect place for me to regroup. It was actually peaceful. No half-finished construction, no boxes scattered about like at the house in Huntington Beach. And it was a smoke-free zone, since both Mom and Joe had given up cigarettes.

Grandma still lived with Mom. At eighty-four her health was failing from the effects of diabetes. She needed help walking and showering and rarely left her room. Even with four of us living there, the large house allowed for privacy. I essentially had a wing to myself, except when we came together in the kitchen. With the exception of the political commentary, it was peaceful.

My favorite pastime at the ranch was shooting skeet from the back patio, which was perched above a vast riverbed. Mom had worked hard all her life, and it had paid off. She had gone from being a hard-edged, street-smart scrapper to a humbler, gentler version of herself. She wasn't working ungodly hours. She was enjoying life more. She was still strong, but there was a new light in her eye. She started going to Bible study with me, which created a new bond in our relationship. She'd even scold me if I cursed.

Since I was finally happy being single, I shouldn't have been surprised that a new man caught my attention. He seemed different. No slicked-back hair. No designer clothes. No fast cars. No fast pickup lines. He was a regular guy. I met him at the gym, and he offered to take me to *church* on a date. He drove a pickup and liked country music—very different from the "Guidos in Ferraris" (as Joe called them) I'd become used to. I wanted to get to know him, though I was in no rush to get serious.

For the sake of this story, I'll call him Jeremy.

I was excited to tell Mom—and even Joe—that I thought I'd finally met a down-to-earth man totally unfamiliar with the fast lane in which I'd been driving. As I pulled up the long driveway to the back of the ranch, however, my senses were assaulted by the familiar and obnoxious blaring of Rush Limbaugh through the kitchen screen door. This wasn't uncommon, but it annoyed me nonetheless. I wasn't so much offended by Rush as I was by the volume of Rush competing with Joe's blustering commentary in the background.

Upon seeing me, Joe started ranting about how the country was going to hell in a handbasket because of the "flaming liberals." *Oh boy. Here we go.* Joe and I had called a truce in our tumultuous bickering, but that didn't make his political tirades any more palatable to me. I was opening my mouth to reply when Mom walked into the room, probably wanting to save me from the familiar roar.

"I met someone I want you guys to meet," I said over Rush's report. "I think he's a nice guy."

"Yeah. Like the previous ones?" Joe said. "He'd better not be a d*mn Democrat. You better *never* bring a Democrat home. The Guidos you date are bad enough."

"Even if they're right-wing radical Guidos?" I said sarcastically. "How'd you become such a racist, anyway? Were you dropped on your head as a child?"

"I'm not racist," he said. "I hate everyone: n*ggers, Polacks, Jews, and wetbacks alike. And trust me—you'd be better off bringing home a n*gger than a Democrat! I'll make any Democrat's life hell!"

I flinched at the noxious words, taken back to a time I'd tried so hard to forget. Joe's toxic rants had been one of the reasons I left home as soon as I turned eighteen. I thought I was better equipped to handle him as an adult. I was wrong. Though we'd stopped fighting for the most part, his small-minded discrimination was still a constant point of contention.

As a kid I hadn't *truly* understood how malignant his views were; I'd been too busy hating him for the way he talked to *me*. Joe wore his tough-guy, war-hardened, vulgar bigotry like a badge of honor, and for the most part we ignored it. Not because his racist words had ever been welcomed. I'd always sensed it was wrong, but I hadn't had enough life experience to challenge it—or to understand the damage his words were doing not only to others but to me. Now, as an adult with a lot more life experience, I felt his "jokes" as a caustic assault. And as a new Christian, I cherished God's Word, which taught me that all people are created equally in God's image. So Joe's words struck me as an affront not only to me but to God.

"I feel sorry for you. It must suck to be so ignorant," I said. I turned to my mother, who simply rolled her eyes. This wasn't like Mom at all. I paused, waiting for her comeback, which never came.

Once Joe was out of the room, I asked her, "How do you stay married to that jerk?"

"Being a redneck or even a racist isn't grounds for divorce," she said calmly—too calmly to my mind—and walked out of the room. No screaming. No throwing things.

Confused, I followed her. "Wait. What does that mean, Mom?"

"It means a lot has happened in our marriage. We sleep in separate rooms. We are married in name only. We still work together, but that's all." There was a sad resignation in her voice. I had the sense she was implying infidelity on Joe's part, which didn't surprise me at all. And maybe that explained why he was ornerier than usual.

"Then why stay married to him? Sounds like he's more than a bigot. For me that would be enough. And he obviously doesn't elevate you in any way, like you deserve."

"Because I feel that God wants me to stay. It's the only hope for Joe. Everyone else has turned their backs on him. Besides, his health is poor, and I'm the only person he has. So we don't sleep together as man and wife. And I pray for him—a lot."

Mom had changed in many ways, but one thing hadn't changed: she still felt a need to rescue the broken people of the world, no matter how much those people wronged her. The main difference, as far as I could tell, was that now she was turning to God for the strength to do it.

Maybe I wasn't the only one who was finding a new sense of peace.

———

I did tell Mom about Jeremy that night, and she was supportive. The fact that she didn't have a "vision of doom" about him was a big relief. It felt like permission to forge ahead. So I did.

As Jeremy and I continued to date, our relationship blossomed. He was so different from the other men I'd dated. I desperately wanted a normal life, away from the fast lane of Los Angeles I was rebounding from. Maybe I wanted it too desperately, because I managed to ignore a lot of issues that I should have paid attention to.

I ignored them so well that fourteen months later we were married.

It was a new chapter in my life, a serious chapter. I was now a married, responsible adult, going to school and working hard to get ahead. Money was tight. My new husband made only a modest income from working in his family's business, and I'd cut my work hours dramatically after getting into nursing school.

We worked incredibly hard, but we were sinking financially. Things we needed were sacrificed. Sometimes things we wanted were purchased anyway—with credit cards whose "available cash" needles hovered dangerously on *E* for empty. The hole got deeper. And suddenly our financial instability had become a threat not only to our marriage but to something that I had worked impossibly hard to achieve: becoming a nurse.

I wasn't going to let that happen. My husband and I scraped and scrimped. I took out student loans. And by some miracle I made it through school before we financially imploded. Now I could actually start working as a nurse.

With my exceptional grades and letters of recommendation, I had a job in the toughest unit in the hospital the week after I graduated.

I was hired straight out of school into the Level A Trauma/Neurosurgical ICU unit at Loma Linda University Medical Center. We cared for the most serious neurosurgical patients and the most serious trauma patients, some of whom arrived by helicopter.

Normally working on the unit required at least two years of nursing experience. But I was part of a pilot program to determine if the hospital would be better off hiring and training nurses for that unit straight out of school. The theory was that students who had done well in school would adapt quickly.

The problem was that the patients hadn't read our textbooks, and their conditions didn't follow the rules.

The classroom and books had been nice, neat, predictable. But nothing was nice, neat, and predictable when the doors to unit 8100 swung open. For a girl who had finally learned to create some semblance of order, control, and structure in her world—and loved it—this was overwhelmingly not any of the above. Patients often arrived with their guts ripped open, limbs missing, brain tissue oozing—and worse.

More than half the newbies like me washed out within the first few months, in spite of the one-year commitment made as part of the hiring process. If the blood and guts alone weren't enough, the emotional stress pushed them over the edge. The stories were intense.

One night a man and a woman wound up in our unit after being severely injured in a car accident. This got tricky when the man's wife arrived and realized, as did we, that the injured woman was her husband's mistress.

Another night we treated a cop and a gangbanger who had shot each other. Ever seen a room with cops on one side and a gangbanger's family on the other?

And, of course, there was the day I was assigned to leech therapy.

"Ha, ha," I said when I got the assignment, sure they were messing with the new girl.

"I'm serious," said the straight-faced charge nurse. "Plastic surgeons sometimes use them after reconstructive surgery for tissue transplants. The little suckers are great at improving circulation." She almost cracked a smile as she looked down at her clipboard. "And make sure you watch them. They like to migrate to moist, dark crevices like nostrils, ears, the anus and vagina. If you want to see a pissed-off plastic surgeon, lose one of his leeches so he has to waste his day fishing for them."

I shook my head, speechless.

"Wait up, Ginger," someone yelled as I headed down the hall to serve my time on leech-babysitting duty. Feeling a hand on my shoulder, I turned. It was one of the nurses who had been hired with my group.

"You talking to me?"

"Yes, Ginger—that's who you remind me of. The movie star from *Gilligan's Island*."

I rolled my eyes. I didn't take this as a compliment. I didn't want to be seen as a prima donna.

"Are you kidding?" she said. "If I looked like you, I wouldn't be cleaning crap and blood all day. I'd *use* those looks, honey!"

Oh great. Here we go again. I'm going to have to fight to be taken seriously.

When I got to room 6, the nurse on duty was holding a fat, slimy, gray blob, putting it into a jar of liquid.

"Monica's done. Once they're full you have to put them in this solution to dispose of them and use a new one."

I stared incredulously. *Did she really call the gray blob Monica?*

"And why exactly do they have names?" I asked.

"So we can keep track of them. Monica did a great job. This one is Bill." She pointed to a leech migrating out of his designated work area. "He's pretty sneaky, so you have to watch him. And Hillary, well, she's not sucking very well today. Oh—and sometimes they won't suck if you hold them wearing gloves, so you have to warm them up with bare hands."

You have to be kidding! I did not sign up to cuddle bloodsucking leeches. Didn't I do enough of that when I was single?

Leech therapy actually turned out to be fairly easy, even a source of laughs. But for every "lighthearted" challenge like that, there were ten that ripped your heart out.

One of the saddest cases involved a young pregnant woman who was scheduled to give birth at the hospital where I worked. But when she was nine months pregnant, she was involved in a severe head-on collision and brought to our unit.

Her husband spoke limited English, and when he was notified, all he understood was "your wife is at the hospital." He arrived on the labor and delivery unit smiling broadly, balloons in one hand and a teddy in the other, anticipating the sight of their new baby. Instead he was escorted to the trauma unit, where he found a nightmare. Three nurses were trying desperately to attach lines and drains, transfuse blood and fluids, take labs, apply dressings, and more. Blood covered the floor.

Ultimately, the baby died, and the mother went into a coma. The young father gripped the teddy bear as tears streamed down his face. Afterward, all of us on the medical staff were in tears. I'd never seen or even imagined anything like it.

I wish I could say that I held up pretty well in situations like this. After all, I'd grown up with my fair share of trauma and chaos. But the truth is, I really struggled. I started having nightmares about rooms filling with urine and blood and me not being able to move—or patients dying and me being helpless to do anything. I developed GI issues again—in other words, I started having stomach cramps and rumbles of diarrhea when I'd walk into the unit. Occasionally I'd even throw up—not from an eating disorder but from stress and nerves.

Unfortunately, there was no way to hide my growing anxiety. The more experienced nurses sniffed it out like vultures. And one in particular seemed to relish my pain.

One afternoon I was teary-eyed at seeing a mother on the ground sobbing as a medical team tried to perform life-saving measures on her nineteen-year-old son. He'd been shot twice in the chest because he was in the wrong place at the wrong time.

"You know," the veteran nurse said to me, "you are too soft. Nurses eat their young, and you're going to be the first to go."

I couldn't think of anything to say to her. I hated feeling weak, but how was I supposed to stop feeling for these people?

"You think crying makes you more empathetic," she went on. "It doesn't. It makes you less effective. It makes them unable to trust you. They don't need your tears. They need you to be competent. They need to know you can handle this sh*t."

Ouch!

The truth was, being a good student simply hadn't prepared me for working in a trauma unit. In fact, it seemed to do me a disservice. I had come out of school thinking I was smart and could handle anything. What a joke! Some of my classmates who had struggled in school actually seemed to do better at their nursing jobs than I. Maybe they didn't expect it to be easy, so they were able to roll with the punches.

I was well aware of all my shortcomings and failures. And now this experienced nurse had pointed out another flaw: I was "soft." Maybe I just didn't have what it took.

After four months I'd had enough. I went to my manager to resign.

"I hate admitting this," I told her, "but you picked the wrong person."

"You can't quit," she said. "You signed a contract when we hired you. You owe us a year. You won't get a good recommendation if you quit. Aren't you applying for the nurse-anesthetist program?"

"Yes, but I'm having second thoughts. I'm afraid I'm going to kill someone. This place is a war zone every day."

That was my biggest fear. It wasn't the blood and gore and emotion of the place, though that was bad enough. I just felt incompetent to save lives the way I'd been taught to.

"You're way too scared to kill anyone," the manager told me. "That's why I hired you. You're going to feel totally incompetent for a year, then you're going to be fine. Studies show that the evolution from a novice to a competent ICU nurse in a unit like this requires about a year."

Reluctantly, I stuck it out. And it actually took only nine months for me to feel like I knew what I was doing. I was getting off the elevator one day—the elevator that usually caused my heart to race—when I realized I wasn't filled with dread. In fact, I had a sense of confidence. *I've got this.* Maybe I wasn't the best nurse, but I didn't feel like the worst any longer. And with my competitive spirit, I was determined eventually to be the best.

With this new sense of confidence, I was able to focus on what was really important—the ABCs.

In the past, when the sh*t hit the fan both literally and figuratively, I'd tended to get distracted by menial tasks like cleaning and picking up the bloody rags on the floor. What I needed to be doing instead, I realized, was to concentrate on my ABCs—airway, breathing, circulation. Those were the most important elements in life support, because a patient was way more important than bloody rags.

That was true of life as well. For years I had focused on trivial, unimportant things instead of the things that really mattered. And now my life seemed parallel to my career. Nursing was changing me, toughening me, enlightening me. I was learning, understanding, growing, changing. And just as I grew in skill and competence as a nurse, I was also becoming focused, resourceful, and responsible in other areas of my life.

Dealing with life and death on a daily basis made me see life differently. It gave me dimension and depth and helped me see beyond my own view of the world—my own pain.

———————

There was one person who did not think this new change in my personality was for the best: my husband. As I became a more competent nurse, it became increasingly more difficult for me to come home and flip the switch to "warm and fuzzy." I needed time to debrief from being the hard-charging trauma nurse, to let go of the gore, the violent stories, and the death.

Jeremy wanted nothing to do with that world. He shut me out if I talked about it. So we started communicating less and less, and both of us started working more and more. Soon we were living separate lives, even as we lamented our inability to have a baby together.

After a couple of years trying, I'd gotten pregnant, only to discover at eight weeks that it was an ectopic pregnancy. After an emergency surgery to save my life and to remove both the tube and the unviable embryo that would never become a baby, I realized my chances of having a normal pregnancy—which already seemed challenging—had just been cut in half.

Following a tearful recovery, I resolved that I was fine being childless. I had never wanted kids anyway. Even when I discovered I was pregnant, I'd been ambivalent at best. Mostly I had been trying to conceive as a way to please my husband. And I had no interest in repeating the disappointment of another failed pregnancy. *Why am I so sad over something I never wanted?*

My husband and I had launched a new construction business that, if successful, could help rescue us from the financial burdens of the past several years. Initially we couldn't afford to hire an administrator. So I worked as a nurse several days each week and in our business the remainder.

Eventually, I completed the prerequisites to get into the nurse-anesthetist program, but I decided to postpone applying. This time it wasn't because I was sick or because I didn't have the money. It was because our new business was thriving beyond what we'd dreamed. Our first year in business, we made more money than our combined income for more than the previous *ten* years. And the next year we doubled that. It didn't make sense to go to school for two more years when our fledgling business needed me. Besides, I'd earn peanuts as a nurse anesthetist compared to what our thriving new business was bringing in.

We began making money hand over fist. Our small business was grossing millions—the kind of money that allowed us to essentially airbrush away our problems. We bought nice things that, even if we didn't see it at the time, became inadequate substitutes for what really fuels a marriage: Love. Trust. Communication. Forgiveness. Grace.

Naively, I had believed that regardless of the challenges, we were strong enough—I was strong enough—to fix them. I could *make* it work. Or God could. Because now that I was a Christian, surely God would fix my problems or at least help me do it.

As Jeremy and I drifted further apart and argued more, however, God had gone quiet in my prayers. The sermons at church that I'd once thirsted for began to sound monotonous and hollow.

Understanding that there are three sides to every failed marital story—his side, her side, and the truth—doesn't make it easier to comprehend a truth that isn't yours. The expression "irreconcilable differences" became more personal as the situation grew uglier.

It didn't take long for me to realize we couldn't go on the way things were. I didn't want to be the person I was becoming. The marriage was over, and all I could do was take responsibility for the role I'd played in killing it. I was wise enough by then to know that not doing so would be the equivalent of condemning myself to a self-created hell as a perpetual victim.

Then, just when I had accepted that the marriage was over, I discovered the unimaginable: I was pregnant. It happened shortly after a meeting with a church counselor that had me reconsidering the gravity of divorce, and I had made a last-ditch effort to make things work. After four years of trying, one failed pregnancy, and assuming I would spend a life being childless, I had conceived.

There are many things I'm not proud of doing and ways I'm not proud of responding in my marriage to Jeremy. But I have made peace with my contribution to its demise. And regardless of who did what, I know I did the right thing in leaving. I didn't want to raise a baby in the environment we'd created.

When little Chloe was two weeks old, and I was still physically debilitated from complications following a C-section, I moved out of our house with the help of my mother.

The irony was that even in that short time, Chloe had become the one bright spot in my life. The woman who never wanted kids now found unspeakable joy in motherhood. The moment I laid eyes on her, it was love at first sight—love beyond anything I'd known. In the instant it took for her to take her first breath, she took my breath away, and I knew that I would kill or die to protect the precious miracle I'd undeservedly been given.

But I was also worried. I wanted to be a *good* mother. And though I was convinced I'd made the right decision, I felt tremendous guilt over depriving Chloe of a "normal" two-parent family—as I had been deprived. I dreaded raising my daughter in a "broken home" as I had been raised, facing all the challenges that came with being a single parent. And that's exactly what I was—a single mom working nights to support an infant, fighting an ugly custody battle, and trying to figure out how, at age thirty-five, I had screwed my life up once again.

While I didn't wake up one day with the plan of obliterating my marriage—the disaster had been building for years—the result was total annihilation. I found myself at ground zero, crawling through the rubble while holding a newborn.

Although I wanted to be mad at God for not intervening, deep down I knew God wasn't to blame. I'd felt close to Him at times in my past, but I didn't now. I begged for Him to let me feel His presence, but I felt only a cold spiritual void.

The triggers were just right for my eating disorder to emerge for the third time.

It had been twelve years since I had wrestled with the demon disguised as food. The reemergence of what I'd thought of as an adolescent issue only served to increase the guilt and shame I felt and to add to my ever-growing fix-it list. But now at least I had a new purpose for overcoming—one beautiful child named Chloe. There was no way I was going to let the problems with my ex, an eating disorder, or any other personal issue be the cause of my failure.

Using my "best friend" exercise, I'd managed to keep the symptoms of bulimia mostly at bay—until I couldn't. Like a pressure cooker, the anxiety continued to build until I felt like I would explode. Every couple of weeks or so, I'd give in and purge, temporarily releasing enough pressure to get out of the red zone.

For months I white-knuckled it. As a new mother I no longer had the luxury of going to bed and hiding—or hugging a toilet bowl all day. But I also couldn't let anyone know what was going on. I was in the middle of a custody battle and was terrified of losing my baby for being an unfit mother.

I'd been a master at camouflaging my pain behind a well-structured facade, and I could do it again. I had a job that required intense focus and a baby who needed a mommy with a smile. So that's what I'd do: focus and smile. And it worked: no one noticed I was a broken mess masquerading as a loving mother and trauma nurse. In fact, people frequently commented about how "together" I seemed to be as a single mom. *If they only knew.*

The wound to my soul was festering, and I began to realize that if I didn't get help, my disorder would begin to affect my daughter, something I couldn't allow. I had no idea where to turn. Eating disorders were for teenage girls, weren't they?

I had little respect for psychobabble, regardless of who was offering it, what was being said, and whether it could actually help. It hadn't helped me when I had hit rock bottom. It hadn't saved my marriage. And I didn't believe it could save *me* now.

I needed a quick fix. A miracle cure.

It was then that the custody battle that had raged on for an agonizing two years, starting with our legal separation when Chloe was two weeks old, finally came to an end. My divorce was final, and it was then that I looked back at the devastation of a decade that had shaken my life to its core. I had bent to the point of snapping, but I'd learned lessons that had kept me from breaking completely. My uncle's counsel from more than a decade earlier came to mind: *The more responsibility you take, the more ability you have to respond. How much responsibility do you want?*

I was wise enough to know I needed to take full responsibility for my life. And Lord knows I tried. It seemed impossible not to suffocate under the burden of pretending to be Supermom, but my mask was brilliant. It had to be. My desperation to make sure Chloe had a different childhood experience than I'd had was my motivation to get up each morning, paint my face, and pretend to be strong.

Maybe if I could fake it long enough, it would become reality.

CHAPTER 12

"CAN I SEE YOUR BRAIN?"

You don't know this new me. I've put
back my pieces differently.

—Unknown

Chloe was the one bright spot in what had been a dark period of despair. And the fact that our business had been so successful meant that I wouldn't have to work the way my mother had. I wouldn't be wealthy, and I'd still need to work—I *wanted* to work—but I'd be able to raise my daughter without the help of babysitters. And to this day, I am happy to say I never left her with any hired babysitter or alone with a male other than her father.

In the midst of the chaos, I began grasping for control in the way I knew best: striving for perfection. I believed it would protect me from feeling out of control—and if I couldn't *be* perfect, then I would *look* perfect. I resumed my daily two-hour workouts and primped for about the same. But at the end of the day the nagging thought played in my head like a broken record: *You're still not good enough. You aren't worthy of being loved.*

The glaring truth that gnawed at me was that I wasn't perfect, that having a divorce and an eating disorder made me defective, made me feel like damaged goods with a dirty secret. There was no one to tell and no one to blame, so I stuffed it all deep inside.

Don't talk about your past. Keep everyone at a distance. Don't make commitments. My marriage-gone-bad underscored why the latter was so important; I'd finally made a decision to commit to a man, and it had backfired monstrously.

Despite the pitiful marriage modeling I'd received, I'd thought I could do better. And I hadn't. *Lesson learned.*

The decade of pain I had just endured deterred me from any desire for a new relationship. Not that anyone would want a thirty-six-year-old woman with a baby. A cancer survivor with more issues than there are stars on the Hollywood Walk of Fame who was still entangled with court proceedings involving her ex. I'd gone from *Playboy*'s idea of a dream girl (almost) to the average guy's nightmare.

I began making peace with the idea of putting all my energy into being a mom and being single forever.

As for God, although I'd committed to Him years before, when push came to shove, I'd become like the doubting disciples. *Jesus, it's cool that You can walk on water; just don't ask me to get out of the boat 'cause I'll sink like a brick.* But my doubt wasn't so much about Him as it was about me. My hesitance was code for a deeper truth that I would unlock later: deep down I didn't believe myself worthy of a relationship with God. Why would He want to bother with a failure like me? I'd sided with Frank Sinatra and done it "my way"—and my way had turned out to be a colossal failure.

Summoning every ounce of energy I had, I eventually found a rhythm. When Chloe was visiting her father, I'd work as many hours as possible. When she was home, I was fully Mom. The hardest times came when I was home alone, unable to pick up an extra shift. I'd wander around my beautiful five-bedroom house making decorating checklists—as if by making each room perfect I could make up for all I'd taken from her—or give her all that I'd never had growing up.

To fill those empty hours, I eventually decided to try dating again, but I quickly realized I was far from the savvy player I'd once been. The few dates

I went on veered to conversations of "Mommy and Me," playdates, and nap schedules. My belief that no one would want me was confirmed.

A friend suggested I come out of the dark ages and join an online dating site.

"Sounds risky," I said.

"Dating in any form is risky," she said. "Doing it online just increases your options. You still have to exercise judgment, just as you would with any other guy. But at least it will be entertaining. Think of it as sport dating."

So I tried it—and I learned that sport dating wasn't so bad without Prozac in the driver's seat. As long as I didn't have any expectations, it killed time and kept me out of the empty house. I rarely dated anyone more than a couple of times for fear they might want a commitment or, worse, catch on that I was completely screwed up.

Then one man came along who messed up my plans completely.

He was different, or at least seemed to be—but I had, of course, been wrong before. We traded several e-mails, and something about his intellect intrigued me on a whole new level. Plus, he seemed like a genuinely nice guy. And persistent.

I reminded myself that I'd had the same thought once before, and look at how that had turned out. I was having a hard time trusting my judgment, so I decided to err on the side of caution. *Just agree to meet him for lunch. Nothing more. Start setting the groundwork when you talk to him on the phone.*

He said his name was Daniel.

"What do you do for a living?" I asked.

"Psychiatrist," he said. "Child psychiatrist."

Psychiatrist? Ugh.

"Interesting. I'm a trauma-neurosurgical intensive-care nurse."

"You sound out of breath. Are you okay?"

"Oh, yeah. Sorry. I'm on the treadmill. This is the only time I have before I leave for work."

"Interesting."

He's psychoanalyzing me already!

"Where do you work?"

"I recently moved from Loma Linda to UCI Medical Center."

I'll give him something to analyze—and move him on his way!

"By the way, I'm recently divorced—still doing battle in court. And I have a two-year-old daughter."

"I'd like to hear more. How about lunch?"

"Are you serious?" I asked, laughing. *I knew psychiatrists were weird. And he probably just wants to continue the psychoanalysis.*

Logic told me to end whatever this was before it started. But it was New Year's Day, Chloe was with her dad, and I really didn't want to spend the holiday alone. The man did seem genuine and kind.

But he's a psychiatrist, I reminded myself. *Just like the one who almost ruined my life. Still, it's just lunch. Why not? One and done.*

It was pouring rain when I pulled up to valet parking at the Four Seasons in Newport Beach. We met in the restaurant. The fact that he'd picked a restaurant in a hotel didn't go unnoticed by me. It might have been a few years, but I hadn't forgotten everything.

Memories of my terrible twenties flashed through my mind. There were few games I hadn't seen, and I could spar with the best of them. But those days were long behind me. And I had no intention of playing games with a shrink.

We both ordered salads and made small talk, then I expanded the conversation.

"So you're a child psychiatrist, huh?"

"Yes, a neuropsychiatrist. I specialize in the health of the brain. My clinics do brain scans—imaging—that help us diagnose and treat people better. We look at how the brain functions in relation to behavior. Instead of mental illness, we focus on brain health." He smiled. "After all, no one wants to see a psychiatrist. But everyone wants a better brain."

He had me at "brain." As a neurosurgical ICU nurse, I was intimately familiar with the human body, especially the brain.

"So what can a scan tell about behavior?"

"It's like a window into the hardware of the soul. It shows us good activity, too little activity, and too much activity in the brain. We can tell if someone has had a traumatic brain injury, emotional trauma, or been exposed to toxic substances and if their brain is working too hard or not hard enough. The scans give us a map for targeted treatment. Combined with other components of a thorough assessment, it becomes a very powerful diagnostic tool."

"Fascinating." I was genuinely intrigued by what he was saying. "Why don't all psychiatrists do what you do? Pardon me for saying so, but it seems that, in general, psychiatrists *guess*. Not that I'd, uh, know *personally*."

I cleared my throat playfully and took a sip of water. "Seriously, I know a lot of people who have been hurt by psychiatrists. My own grandmother was given electric shock therapy following a so-called nervous breakdown, which I think was really a hormonal imbalance. She was never really the same afterward. And I know so many stories like that. Yet in psychiatry the professional doesn't seem to be held responsible when the patient doesn't do well. Instead, the patient is the one who gets the label."

He nodded thoughtfully. "I wish I could disagree," he said. "But I can't, which is why I'm trying to create a new paradigm."

I was smitten by the subject—and, frankly, by the man in front of me thoughtfully discussing that subject. Who invites someone out for lunch and goes on about the brain? Daniel was refreshingly different from so many other men I'd known whose favorite subject, it turned out, was themselves. He was clearly smart about this pioneering technology but seemed humble in the process, as if such a discussion were more about healing the patient than boosting his ego.

Daniel and I spent the entire lunch excitedly talking about the brain and our professional experiences. And my plan for a one-and-done lunch quickly went out the window. We went out several more times. The more I got to know him, the better I liked him.

———

Three weeks later Daniel invited me to hear him lecture at an event for teachers. I figured, *Why not?* I expected a small, low-key event. But when we walked into the "conference room" at the Loews Coronado Bay Resort, nearly a thousand people were waiting excitedly. Dozens of people rushed up to him with books for him to sign.

"Oh, Dr. Amen, Dr. Amen, will you sign this? You saved my son's life!"

"Dr. Amen, your work changed how I teach!"

This went on for more than an hour. *What is going on? Did I miss something? Who is this guy?*

Apparently, I wasn't the only person smitten with him. I'd dated successful men, even some who'd written books. But this man seemed to be in another class.

"Who *are* you?" I asked after the commotion died down.

He smiled. "The more important question is, who are you? I love spending time with you, and I'd like to do more of it."

I left the date intrigued, if not befuddled.

———

Two days after that a friend of mine phoned. She and her husband had concerns that their little girl, about Chloe's age, might have some sort of sensory-processing issue.

"We're so excited," she said. "We just got an appointment with this famous psychiatrist. He usually doesn't take new patients, but because of his connection to a friend of ours, we got in. I've been trying to get an appointment for months."

"That's so cool," I said. "I hope he can help."

"So do we."

"Actually, I just started dating a psychiatrist, though I almost cancelled when I realized what he did for a living. But this guy seems different. I like him a lot."

"Oh Tana, that's *exciting.*"

"Yeah. If you'd like me to ask him about Kimmy, I will."

"No thanks. We have been waiting to see this guy forever. He's *the* best in his field. But, so, tell me about the guy you're dating."

"Well, what he does is a little different. He does brain scans."

There was an odd silence. I thought we'd been disconnected.

"Hello?"

"By any chance is his name Daniel?"

"Yeah, why?"

"Daniel *Amen*?"

"Yes. Do you—"

"He's the guy, Tana! He's the psychiatrist who's going to see our daughter!" Her animated voice was so loud, I had to hold the phone at a distance.

"Really?"

"Tana, don't you know who Daniel Amen is? You're dating a freaking rock star! A rock-star psychiatrist."

"Wait. Slow down. Why would I know that? Besides, I'm pretty sure 'rock-star psychiatrist' is an oxymoron."

"The celebs go to him. He's famous!"

If that were true, he had a strange way of showing it. He seemed far less egotistical—and less interested in talking about himself—than the numerous non-rock stars I'd dated. Maybe I'd been too quick to label all psychiatrists because of my own history and the history of several people I cared about. Maybe it was time to let go of the stereotype.

The only thing Daniel loved more than his work, it turned out, was family. And he was excited to introduce me to his *extremely* large Lebanese clan. He didn't seem to have anything to hide. When he took me to his parents' house a week after our first date, I was overwhelmed by the sheer number of people but comforted by the familiarity of the Lebanese culture, especially the home-cooked food.

I instantly took a liking to his parents, especially his mother, the matriarch they all cherished. Her four-foot-eleven-inch frame contradicted the power she exuded and the respect she commanded. She was the only woman I'd ever met who just might be able to give my mother a run for her money.

"Now I know the real reason you pursued me," I said to Daniel after meeting her. "It's my Lebanese heritage. You want your mom's approval."

"Well, it doesn't hurt," he said laughing. "I adore her—and she has a drop-dead gorgeous brain!"

Meanwhile, I'd offer well-guarded responses to his many questions about me—deep enough to appease his intrigue, but not so deep that I'd be shamed.

"Let's just say I have a lot of baggage," I told him once.

"And who doesn't? Baggage is just life experience."

"Seriously, Daniel, let's just keep this light. You seem too smart, too *together* to get mixed up with someone like me."

"Why not let me be the judge of that?"

"Okay, but to be fair, there is one thing you should know."

"What's that?"

"If anyone ever lays a hand on my daughter, I will kill them in their sleep—if they are lucky. Awake, and very slowly, if they aren't."

I was dead serious.

Daniel didn't even blink. "Sounds rational to me."

———

Finally, one night, I felt things were coming to a crescendo. I was sitting on the couch. He sat down with an arm comfortably draped over my shoulder. The lights were low.

"Tana," he said, "I need to ask you something."

I nodded and looked deep into his warm brown eyes. "Ask me anything. I might not answer, but go ahead and ask."

"Will you—?" He stopped as if realizing he might be crossing a line.

"What? Will I what?"

He paused.

"Just say it, Daniel."

He looked away, then back at me with a contemplative look on his face.

"Tana," he said, "will you allow me to scan your brain?"

I laughed. "First time anyone has wanted to see my naked brain. Best line ever."

————

That's how it happened that, just weeks after we started dating, I went to Daniel's clinic and had my brain scanned.

Promptly after the scan, he was able to pull up a cool 3-D image of my brain on the computer screen in his office. "Anything in there?" I asked.

"Lots," said Daniel. "Have you ever had a head injury?"

"No," I said with absolute confidence. To a neurosurgical ICU nurse, the words "head injury" conjure images of missing skull fragments, drains inserted into the brain to relieve pressure, or coma—things I had not experienced.

"Nothing? Ever fall out of a tree? A second-story window? No car accidents?"

"Well, I had one. We were going seventy-five miles an hour and rolled twice. That was many years ago, but I didn't lose consciousness. I walked away from it unharmed."

He just stared at me. "Well, that qualifies. I can see that on the scan. Your brain is soft, and your skull is hard, with many sharp, bony ridges. Imagine it shaking around like Jell-O, then stopping fast. Head injuries ruin people's lives and no one knows it. Think of shaken-baby syndrome."

Wow. An aha moment. I'd sometimes wondered if the minor change in my memory that started after the car accident had been related. But the doctor—yeah, the one in jeans and cowboy boots—had said I hadn't sustained any injuries, so I'd never pursued it. I'd just been grateful to be alive.

"And your frontal lobes seem a bit sleepy—mild ADD. You talked about depression after your cancer—and an antidepressant?"

"Wait, ADD? ADD is nonsense. It's an excuse to fail or not even try. It's crap."

"You said you drink nearly two pots of coffee every day, right? And you do intense workouts for two hours every morning to—I think your words were 'clear the cobwebs and relieve anxiety.' That is a classic example of someone trying to stimulate their brain. You're lucky you found exercise. Some people turn to less healthy options, like drugs."

I knew this guy was psychoanalyzing me all along.

"Back to the antidepressant you took. I'm curious what they gave you."

"Prozac."

He furrowed his brow.

"Hm. Prozac wouldn't have been my choice, based on this scan. But SSRIs—which is what Prozac is—are often the first thing doctors try."

With suspicion I asked, "Why wouldn't you prescribe Prozac to someone with a brain like mine?"

"Prozac increases the availability of serotonin in your brain, which can decrease frontal lobe activity. Your frontal lobes are already sleepy," he said, pointing to what looked like a small dent on one side of my scan. "This dent is actually decreased blood flow. Certain medications—like Prozac—can decrease it further. It's great for a really busy brain, but not so much for a sleepy one.

"Now, that's a pretty simplistic explanation," he added. "But bottom line, for the wrong person, Prozac can increase impulsiveness and decrease judgment. There are medications that probably would have helped—a lot—but I wouldn't suspect Prozac would be one of them. How did *you* feel taking it?"

"Ha! That's a discussion for another time. Let's just say that the quack who put me on it should have lost his license."

He smiled—the same warm smile I was growing a little too fond of. It was reassuring to talk to someone who seemed to understand what I'd gone through.

———

Gradually, as we got to know one another better, I opened up to Daniel about my childhood. By this time the chaos seemed normal to me. I joked about being a member of the "Garden Variety Dysfunctional Club."

Daniel smiled and said, "I think you're amazing. It's impressive that you've done as well as you have with the tools you started with."

I shrugged. "It's not a big deal, really. Everyone goes through *some* trauma. All families are dysfunctional, aren't they?"

The false bravado of the practiced words concealed my secret—I hoped. Though these days I managed to keep my disordered-eating behavior under control, it was clear to me that all I had managed to do with my intense work-outs was to put a Band-Aid over a gaping wound. I hadn't actually dealt with the underlying problem. So every decade or so the bandage would give out, oozing the contents of the infected wound—my soul—everywhere, until I managed to replace the bandage again and get it under control.

Would the cycle ever stop? And what would Daniel think of me if he knew?

I made up my mind. I simply couldn't allow myself to be in a romantic relationship with a man like him. I wasn't worthy. And he was too wise not to eventually see how screwed up I was and move on.

Still I knew that at the very least I'd found a friend.

I began to trust Daniel as I hadn't trusted other men, so much so that I broke my one cardinal rule of dating: don't introduce your daughter to men, unless it becomes a full-blown commitment. I agreed to let him meet Chloe, who was immediately taken with him, and they began creating a bond under my ever-watchful eye.

In January 2006, a couple of days after my visit to the clinic, Daniel invited Chloe and me to a Los Angeles Lakers basketball game, his favorite pastime. We had some fun and decided to leave at halftime for Chloe's benefit. (The Lakers were losing anyhow.) Wearing a little zebra hoodie, Chloe rode on Daniel's shoulders to the car, singing all the way. Just as we approached the car, she stopped, wrapped her arms around his neck, and kissed his bald head.

"I love you, Daniel," she said with a smile, her zebra ears askew.

"I love you, too, Chloe. And guess who else I love?"

"Mommy?" Chloe asked.

"Yes. I love your mommy."

My heart filled with joy and fear at the same time. The moment was so beautiful—my little girl so open and honest with her feelings. How freeing that must have felt. But even as the words were spoken, I felt the sentries mustering to guard my heart. It couldn't be true, could it? He couldn't really love me, could he?

And if he did, how would I possibly handle that?

As we drove home, with the game on the radio, Daniel suddenly pounded the steering wheel.

"No! No! No!" he yelled. "I can't believe we left! What was I *thinking*?"

The Lakers' Kobe Bryant, it turned out, was on a scoring rampage. In fact, he was on his way to scoring a personal-best eighty-one points. Chloe wasn't sure what that meant, but she laughed. She thought Daniel was hilarious.

"Daniel, you're silly."

As we drove home Daniel's words replayed in my head and tugged at my heart. "I love your mommy." Did I deserve to be this happy? Could I accept that someone like Daniel saw value in me that I didn't?

Or, as Daniel said about missing the historic game, "What was I *thinking*?"

Would I walk away, lamenting what I'd chosen to pass up?

CHAPTER 13

THE GIFT

It's not your job to like me. It's mine.

—Byron Katie

For anyone else, it would be simple. But there was nothing simple about me. Daniel Amen clearly cared about me, not just about his own needs, and he adored my daughter. He thought my "baggage" was life experience that gave me depth. It would be great to say ours was a fairy-tale romance, but I'm the girl who never believed in fairy tales, so of course I made sure it wasn't.

I really didn't want to fall in love with Daniel Amen. In fact, I was adamant that I would never get married again—never go through a divorce like I'd just gone through.

Besides, in my experience, nobody could be this earnest. This caring. This nice. So I found myself waiting for the other shoe to fall. My template had been set from birth to believe that men would eventually disappoint me—and that if they didn't, I would disappoint myself. To save myself the pain of ever being left again, I'd almost always left first. And the last time I'd taken a leap of faith and thrown caution to the wind, I'd paid a hefty price.

I was certain it was only a matter of time before something happened to thwart this new relationship, too, so when Daniel started talking marriage, I started looking at the door. If I couldn't trust my own judgment, I certainly couldn't trust his.

"I'm sorry," I said. "I'm not ready to go there. I'm not sure I ever can again."

"I can wait. But Tana, you do know that you deserve to be happy, right?"

Why does he always know what to say to break down my walls? Without planning to, I started regurgitating my entire past. I didn't sugarcoat anything. In fact, I probably made my life sound worse than it was in an attempt to push him away.

For hours he just listened as I matter-of-factly told him my history, sounding more like an ICU nurse giving a shift report about a broken, battered patient than someone who'd actually endured the past I was describing. I left out only one thing. I still couldn't say the ugly word that described the behavior I despised but couldn't stop.

Through it all, Daniel just listened with what seemed to be love and compassion.

Why is he looking at me like that? Whatever possessed me to tell a man the very worst things about me? Well, almost all of them. My typical MO was to keep my facade intact, portray perfection as long as possible, then bail when that didn't work. I couldn't figure out why I was so uncomfortable and yet why I felt compelled to open up to this man. And yet, for the first time in years, I glimpsed light at the end of the tunnel.

The first gift Daniel gave me was ten sessions of EMDR—eye movement desensitization and reprocessing—therapy. (What would you expect from a guy whose first "ask" was for a brain scan?) It was a specialized form of therapy for trauma. When he told me about it, I wondered if I'd been right about him psychoanalyzing me all along—or, worse, trying to fix me. "I'm not interested in being your pet project," I snapped after an inquisitive exchange.

"Tana, we all psychoanalyze each other. You've been interviewing me—interrogating me, in fact—since you met me, and looking for an excuse to move on. It's obvious," he said, with a calm smile. "I think you're amazing just the way you are. It's *you* who's unsure, which is understandable given what you've endured. But enduring and overcoming are very different. Even if it's not with me, you deserve to be happy and loved."

I had never heard words like those from a man I was dating before, and it made an impact on me. "I'll think about it," I said. "Just let me go at my own pace."

And he did.

Several weeks later Daniel said to me, "There's someone I'd like you to meet. She lives several hours north of here. Her work has helped millions of people."

A road trip sounded fun, but I had no idea what I was in for. About two hours after trudging through LA traffic, we turned off the main highway and entered a picturesque little village dotted with quaint art shops. The sun blazed overhead in the touristy valley town. Beyond the three main traffic lights sat an unpretentiously elegant ranch-style home that perfectly suited the unpretentiously elegant silver-haired woman who greeted us from the sprawling wraparound porch. Her lightly lined face, twinkling blue eyes, and tranquil demeanor spoke of a lifetime of wisdom.

"Hello," she said. "I'm Byron Katie."

Later I would learn that Byron Katie's followers saw her as a spiritual guru—not that she liked the label—because of a program she created that had helped millions around the world. She called it The Work. I didn't know it at the time, but she was about to lead me through the four simple questions that made up her program, and they would twist my mind inside out. Daniel loved The Work and thought it was the simplest form of cognitive therapy he'd come across—though Katie, as she's usually called, wasn't a therapist by training.

For a few minutes we made small talk, then sat down to have tea.

"So," she said, before I'd said anything about myself, "how long have you engaged in eating-disorder behavior?"

My face reddened. I prided myself on the fact that *no one* knew, that people thought I was so together. I glared at Daniel.

Shrugging innocently he said, "You *just* told me about the b-word an hour ago, on the drive here. I couldn't have told her."

It was true. I'd finally told him—made him guess, actually, like a game of charades—because I'd been worried about him finding out somehow. But I hadn't anticipated this.

Great. She's like my mom. Can't hide anything from her.

"Since I was a teenager," I stammered uncomfortably, "I mostly control it with exercise."

"What I want to know is what it means to you."

"I don't follow."

"'I have an eating disorder,' and that means what?"

"Oh. I see. I guess it means that I'm weak. That I'm not lovable. That no one would love me if they knew the truth about who I am," I said, biting back tears.

She nodded slightly. "Okay, we're going to be here a while," she said with her kind smile. She glanced over at Daniel. "And it looks to me like someone already does love you."

I squirmed in my seat. With the exception of a couple of friends many years before, I hadn't spoken about this ugly part of myself to anyone. Now I couldn't seem to stop talking about it, like it or not.

"Is it true that no one could love you if they knew the truth?" she asked.

"Yes."

"Can you absolutely know that it's true—know better than God or the universe knows?"

"Well, of course not." I glanced uncomfortably at Daniel.

"How do you feel when you have the thought, *No one would love me if they knew me?*"

"I hate myself for being weak. I get angry. I feel like I must isolate and not get too close to anyone, so I push people away. I'm terrified that I will somehow pass it on to my daughter like the flu."

"I'm curious," she said. "How do you treat yourself and others when you have that thought?"

"I beat the hell out of my body with exercise. Sometimes I purge. I push people away. I guess I've used food and exercise like other people use drugs," I said, feeling tension in my gut increase as I spoke.

"So, Tana, who would you be without that thought?"

"Wow! I'm not sure," I said softly. The gravity of my own toxic thoughts weighed hopelessly on my mind.

"If you could never think that thought again . . ."

I paused for a moment, then said, "Peaceful. Free. Able to love and let people be close to me. Able to allow them *not* to love me and be okay with it. I would just be free."

The minute I said it, I felt the tension lessen. I was lighter, freer. And I began to wonder if what she was suggesting was really possible.

"Right. It's not anyone else's job to love you. It's yours. So can you see a good reason to hold on to the thought? I'm not asking you to let it go. I'm just wondering if you can see a good reason to keep it?"

"No."

"Okay, let's turn it around. What is the opposite of 'No one would love me if they really knew me'?"

"People *would* love me if they knew me. But that doesn't seem right."

"Really? Just sit with it. Give me three examples of how that is true or truer than the first thought—that nobody would love you if they really knew you."

"Hm. I guess Daniel bringing me here is an example. I suppose even my mother freaking out over my eating disorder when I was seventeen—and, later, when learning I had cancer—was because she loved me, even if it wasn't all that helpful. And I'm not sure I'd call it love, but you're here, and you're being kind and helping me."

"Wonderful. Find another turnaround."

I had to think about that. But eventually I looked up.

"I have two. I can't love *others* because I'm afraid they will see the truth about me. And I don't love *me*. That's why I can't accept the truth about me."

That was the heart of the matter. I didn't love me. I hadn't accepted the truth about myself, so I assumed others would judge me as harshly as I'd judged myself.

We continued for a few more hours. By the time we left, my thinking had been cracked open. I wasn't magically fixed, but I was open to new possibilities and ready to begin the healing process.

———————

A short time later Daniel and I were invited to attend a seminar Katie was leading, titled simply "Loving What Is." The setting was beautiful—the Esalen Institute in Big Sur, perched on the cliffs over the Pacific Ocean and surrounded by towering redwoods. A retreat center started in the hippie-oriented sixties, it was still a functioning commune.

I was a little uptight about attending an event where I assumed everyone would happily parade their demons, but I was excited about spending a weekend with Daniel in Big Sur and valued the one-on-one work Katie had done with me. I began to think I might even be ready to start therapy. But being a skeptic by nature, I wasn't about to drink the Kool-Aid at some hippie camp. For now I chose to consider it a fun weekend with my sort-of boyfriend in a spectacular setting, with the added bonus of being "spiritually enriching."

"You should get involved," Daniel had told me from time to time as the weekend unfolded. "Interact."

"When hell freezes over," I said with a plastic smile. "You must be smoking some of the 'herbs' these hippies are growing."

The eclectic group was made up of men and women; professionals, housewives, and addicts. There were no signs announcing, "Alcoholics this way" or "Drug addicts through that door." There were no labels at all. Most people just shared their issues. But though I kept notes in my journal, I had no intention of sharing anything with anybody. For all anyone knew, I was just a guest, not screwed up in the least. A woman as together as my appearance suggested. And for now I was comfortable with that.

Under the giant tent, Daniel and I settled on the floor near the front where Katie was leading the group in a comfy armchair. Several hundred people meandered in, some filling the rows of chairs in the center, others sprawling on the ground.

"What do you hate about your body?" she asked, a question that clearly triggered an avalanche of chaos with the women in attendance, me included. Her smile never wavered. "Write it in your journal."

I was game. After all, I had decided to get help. I knew it would require some work. As long as I could do it privately, I was happy to oblige. But as a few people started sharing aloud I knew I'd never be able to share my problems in a group like they did.

After completing the exercise, I went back to my recumbent position, eyes closed. Feeling peace wash through my body with the sound of each wave crashing against the rocky shoreline below, I felt cradled in a cocoon of pillows—until I was jolted by the deep, strained voice of a woman describing why she hated her body.

"I hate my body because I'm too fat, I'm too old, and I get sick too often. I hate my thighs and my butt. I hate the skin around my eyes . . ."

I couldn't believe it. Her list was almost identical to mine.

The voice suggested the speaker was older than me. I opened my eyes to see who was speaking. She weighed somewhere between 250 and 300 pounds.

How could her list be exactly like mine? I weighed 125 pounds, and we were nothing alike.

I realized I felt anxious and tense, and I didn't understand why. I closed my eyes and focused on my breathing, trying to regain my equilibrium.

Another woman spoke up.

"I hate my body, and sometimes I vomit my food," she said.

I cringed. My heart raced. I couldn't believe she had said that out loud. I looked up to see an average-sized woman with no makeup standing near me. I wouldn't have noticed her in a crowd. *Why would she tell a group of strangers such a vile thing, especially with men present!* I'd started the journey toward healing, but I wasn't about to start waving my personal crap around like a badge of honor. I was embarrassed for the woman—no, I was mortified! I was afraid that her admission would cause people to look around and somehow figure out that I was "one of them." Attempting my best poker face, I closed my eyes again, trying to mentally distance myself from the group. I would have left if I hadn't thought it would have drawn more attention.

The next woman spoke about the horrors of her life because she was fat, dumpy, and middle-aged—and that her husband had left her for a younger woman. This woman was convinced that all her problems stemmed from the fact that she wasn't pretty enough, thin enough, or able to "manipulate men" enough!

"I hate my life," she said. "I know it would be different if I could be skinny, younger, and more beautiful."

"What do you hate about your body?" Byron Katie asked in a serene voice.

"It's too fat, too old, and it sags. If I could be younger and have a hard body, my life would be different. My husband left me for a twenty-six-year-old woman. She's skinny and beautiful. She can have any man she wants. Life is different for women like that."

By now I was sitting up, shaking.

"So you want to be able to have the same control over your husband that the other woman has?"

"Yes. I want to be young and beautiful and have a beautiful body so *I* can manipulate men."

"So you don't necessarily want him to love you because he *does*. You want to be able to manipulate him."

"Yes. I want to be one of those women who are beautiful and able to manipulate men and make them fall in love with me."

My heart was thudding. My head was pounding.

It was the last day of the seminar, and I'd masterfully managed to avoid the share-and-tell sessions. I vacillated between envying the candor of my fellow attendees and considering their gratuitous sharing nothing more than a desperate cry for attention. Besides, I figured that if I was judging them, they were judging me just as harshly. Yet this exchange was suddenly tugging at me in a most disturbing way.

Oh, my God. I wasn't going to—yes, I was. I jumped to my feet, almost against my will. It was as if a voice that wasn't mine began to speak.

"I hate my body because it is not thin enough," I read from my journal. "It is not perfect enough. It got cancer. It betrays me. And it is getting old."

Trembling, I stood there, looking fit in my snug designer jeans, perfectly made up. Though I was thirty-seven at the time, I fit the description of the twenty-six-year-old the woman had described. Though I was a decade older, few people would have guessed my age.

Daniel's initial surprise turned to a slight smile of approval. Swallowing the boulder in my throat, I continued to read from my journal, my voice shaking, eyes pooling with tears.

"I hate the scars I have from cancer treatment and from my C-section. I hate the lines around my eyes. I hate that no matter how hard I work out, I always have a little loose skin on my abdomen from having a baby. I wake up every morning and kick my own butt in the gym regardless of how tired or sick I am, and then I stand in front of the mirror picking myself apart, looking for flaws. It's never good enough."

I paused for a moment before looking directly at the woman who had just spoken. "You think your life would be better if you could be a perfect size 4 and be 'more beautiful'? It wouldn't. You would just have *different* problems. It's never perfect enough. The young woman that 'took' your husband sounds the way I've often been described. But you have *no idea* what it's like to be that woman. You have no idea what it's like to always wonder if men only want you for the way you look . . . and the pressure you feel to always look that way . . . or what it's like when men like your husband 'forget' to tell you they're married when you're on a date.

"You have no idea what it's like to feel valued only for your appearance and build a life based on that, then wake up one day to find that if—*when*—your looks change, your value disappears with them. And as angry as you've been for feeling manipulated, you realize it's a game—survival of the fittest—that you'd better learn to play. God forbid you wake up one day and realize you're *sick* and you can't rely on your appearance any longer.

"I didn't ask for this. I've never thought I was pretty. Sometimes I've hated having so much pressure to look the way I did. There were times I wished I could eat an entire pizza and not have people watching, wondering if I was going to go throw it up. Sometimes I just wanted to blend in and not be seen at all. But then if no one notices you, you go into a funk, wondering what's wrong with you because you're so used to the attention. Either way, you're screwed. You can't be happy. Sometimes I just hate my body for getting older because I'm terrified that people won't love me when I can't keep this up. I'm exhausted."

Nobody said a word. All was still.

"And by the way," I said, "my marriage still fell apart. I still wasn't good enough."

I all but ran from the canopy we'd gathered beneath. But I didn't make it far before being approached by several women, a few who were crying.

"Thank you so much for sharing your story," one said. "You have no idea how much it helps me to hear it coming from someone like you."

"If someone who looks like you isn't happy with her body, then I realize I'd better start looking for a different answer to happiness," another woman said as she hugged me. "I have been suffering with an eating disorder for twenty years, thinking if only I could be a size 4 it would magically go away. Now I realize my problem has nothing to do with that."

The responses kept coming. I had never considered sharing my story for fear that people would reject me, shun me, judge me, ridicule me, think I was a freak, hate me, or think I was superficial and spoiled, disgusting and weak. It had never occurred to me that sharing might actually bring them closer. That we suffer from the same thoughts.

This was the beginning of an arduous and beautiful journey of healing—the journey to know and love myself for the first time.

CHAPTER 14

FIVE-CARD DRAW

Your flaws are perfect for the heart
that is meant to love you.

—Unknown

Understanding myself wasn't just for me. It was for Chloe. Seeing so many damaged, hurting women at Katie's seminar made it clear that to be the best mother, I had to be the best *me*. And I was finally beginning to see that being my best me might require some professional help.

Despite three decades of trauma, I'd never *really* allowed a professional to try and help me make sense of my imperfect self. I just hadn't trusted anyone or believed there was hope—especially after my failed attempt at working with a psychiatrist.

So I decided it was time to redeem the gift Daniel had given me. I'd try EMDR. If it didn't work, I wouldn't have lost anything.

I was pleasantly surprised to discover that EMDR therapy doesn't require ongoing talk discussions about the past. Instead, the goal is to reprocess traumatic memories that get stored in a maladaptive way, leaving the neural networks in the brain less able to process traumatic stress. My therapist Lisa explained it like trying to play a scratched record. The section where the scratch is located will keep looping until the needle is moved.

Lisa then asked me to recall a traumatic event while moving her fingers back and forth in front of my face as I followed them with my eyes. There are a number of theories as to why it is so effective, but ultimately it's supposed to help the brain reprocess the trauma, while reducing the vividness and emotional intensity of a memory.

It wasn't magic. It was often painful. And it got worse before it got better.

When I first started therapy I hated myself. My body and my relationships paid the price. My weight dropped to an alarming level as, for the first time, I tackled my eating disorder.

Once I started it was clear to me that I needed more than ten sessions. So I continued. For the next six months, I hated my ex-husband, my family, and my past circumstances.

Finally, when there was nobody left to hate, I realized that hate was the wrong strategy. Hate was destroying my life.

Since I obviously couldn't change the people around me, I decided I would concentrate on changing myself. I was angry that I hadn't been the person I'd aspired to be, that I had violated my own values and not lived up to my potential. But it was time to move forward. I recalled something I'd heard in church, a place I hadn't been for a long time: "It's arrogance when you choose to hold on to what God has chosen to forgive." Lord knows I had been arrogant. But maybe now, at last, I was ready to let go.

I'm not sure if it was the EMDR, the amazing therapist, or the timing, but I could tell that something was beginning to change. I quickly realized getting well was a process and I'd need more than the ten-session gift, which had barely exposed the tip of the iceberg. For the next eighteen months I wholeheartedly threw myself into therapy, which included a combination of EMDR and talk therapy. I'd finally gotten over my aversion to talking about the painful memories and decided it was time to heal the past trauma in my life.

Trauma was a word I couldn't even acknowledge until I started therapy. It sounded so, well, dramatic. I could not acknowledge that I'd been molested, couldn't use the word. It had only been a close call, hadn't it? Then my therapist turned it around and asked, "What would you do if someone did the same things to Chloe?"

"Rip his beating heart out of his chest and feed it to my dog," I said without hesitation.

"Why would you do that to someone who didn't really hurt her, to someone who *almost* molested her?"

I couldn't reconcile these thoughts for months. To do so would be to acknowledge the one thing I couldn't fathom: I had been a *victim*. But I had survived by *never* being a victim—at least not in my own mind. Or had I? Maybe I had been hurting myself, even victimizing myself, in my attempt to bury the truth. Maybe the little girl who had been violated needed to finally be validated so she could let it heal.

I had found being a victim so distasteful that I'd replaced that word with "b*tch," as if it had to be one or the other. Was it possible that having once been a victim didn't mean I was sentenced to remain a victim? Was it possible that the bite I'd developed had been a protective reflex, that I wasn't actually a *b*tch*? Not that I thought there was anything wrong with playing the b*tch card when necessary, but maybe it was becoming less necessary.

One of the best ways I discovered to avoid the victim/b*tch trap was martial arts. I discovered it after a chance encounter. I was in a parking lot, putting Chloe into her car seat. As I bent over, struggling with the toddler, the hair on the back of my neck stood up. I felt him before I saw him—a man standing behind me. Though he was simply getting into his car, I had a flashback to when I was fifteen and attacked from behind. Realizing there would be nothing I could do to defend myself with a baby in my arms, I panicked. And the next week I signed up for those lessons Joe had wanted me to take so many years earlier.

I'd taken a few self-defense classes over the years, and of course I'd worked out to stay strong. Until that day I had thought I could take care of myself—*myself* being the operative word. But not myself *and* a baby. Besides, I figured, if I took lessons it might motivate Chloe to do the same when she got a little older.

I never anticipated falling in love with martial arts. I was mesmerized by the feel of flesh hitting pads, by the intensity of the training. It made me feel empowered. Working out was no longer just about exercise, though the workout was intense. It was my newfound passion. And it was the perfect companion to the self-improvement work I was doing in therapy.

As for my relationship with Daniel, I'd love to say that some romantic miracle happened overnight and that I was suddenly itching to be swept off my feet in a fairy-tale romance. It wasn't and I didn't. It took a couple of years of hard work. As Katie said, "I don't call it The Work for nothing."

Daniel did propose, not long after we went to Katie's seminar. And I said yes. But I wasn't ready to get married. I soon called off the engagement and broke his heart. I said we should take a break from each other. I was finally beginning to believe that I deserved someone as kind as Daniel, but I was fully aware that I had a lot of work to do lest I repeat the past. And I was committed to taking the necessary time to heal before committing my life to another person, no matter how much I loved him.

"Before you take this *break*," he said, "meet me for lunch."

Here we go. I knew it was too good to be true. The control freak is coming out. Why do men always resort to control and screw things up? I was sure he was going to either beg or give me an ultimatum.

"Okay, but—"

"Tana, just trust me."

"Fine."

I did my usual speed rationalization: if he gave me an ultimatum it would just make breaking up with him easier.

As usual, we met at a lovely beachside restaurant. As always, it was easy for me to be with him. We laughed and joked. I was really hoping he wouldn't screw this up. He had become my best friend. I just wasn't ready to walk down the aisle.

Daniel finished his lunch, dabbed the corner of his mouth with his napkin, then reached into his jacket and produced five greeting cards, fanning them out like a poker dealer.

"For you," he said.

A look of puzzlement creased my face.

"I'm offering you five choices for our future," he said. "You don't need to decide now. Take your time as we take a break from each other. And let me know which of the five you want."

I was frozen in bewilderment. *What is he up to?*

"Go ahead. Open them."

A bit suspicious, I did so. The first one was a sympathy card. It read, "I'm sorry for your loss. We're like two ships passing in the night. We were never meant to be, but I will cherish the time we had."

I smiled suspiciously, wondering if he was playing a clever game of reverse psychology.

The second was a friendship card. It read, "I love having you in my life, and if 'friends' is all it can be, I will be grateful."

The third, also a friendship card, read, "Let's be friends—with benefits." I laughed. That was the fun personality I'd come to know.

The fourth read, "Let's commit to be together for the future, with no pressure to set a date."

And finally, an engagement card: "Let's commit, with plans of marriage."

I laughed, relaxing as we finished lunch. *How does he always do the opposite of what I expect? Must be a shrink thing.* If I were ready, he would be the one. But I wasn't ready.

I will admit that Daniel's behavior over the next couple of months had me reconsidering. His decision to not force my hand, his willingness to risk losing me if our staying together wasn't what I wanted, his respecting me enough to let me decide for myself—these offerings proved his integrity.

While taking a break was not the choice he wanted, he accepted it and supported me. He knew it's what I needed. He, too, had been through a divorce and understood what it was like not to trust your own judgment. Rather than making me feel broken or defective, as I did with myself, he acted as if it was a perfectly normal, even rational, reaction.

During our break we got to know each other on a totally different level. In short, I fell deeply in love with my best friend. Daniel was the only man I could tell anything and everything to—the good, the bad, and the ugly. And the more I told him, the more he loved me.

How could I help but love him in return? I was truly in love for the first time.

Soon Daniel and I were officially dating again, with hopes of making the relationship permanent.

CHAPTER 15

RETURN OF THE PRODIGAL FATHER

When we forgive, we set a prisoner free and then
discover that the prisoner we set free was us.

—Lewis B. Smedes

My father was dying—or at least that's what my sisters were telling me. I was now thirty-seven and I had only spoken to him a few times over the past several years. Tamara described his condition to me over the phone. This was the first news I'd heard from either of my sisters for years. Since the car accident with Tamara more than a decade before, we'd rarely spoken. Drinking beer and smoking pot with Dad during her teen years had progressed to harder substances. She'd lived in her van for two years, moving around like a gypsy, until she discovered she was pregnant and decided to clean up and settle down. Jenny and I had never been close. I was curious why they decided I was the person to seek advice from.

"Sounds like dementia, not an acute illness," I said. "I don't think he's dying right away, but you should take him in and have him assessed."

"He's been diagnosed with Alzheimer's disease. But Dad thinks he's dying."

"Dad always thinks he's dying. He's been collecting disability for a decade—as though."

I tried to conceal my cynicism, but for as long as I'd been alive my father had conveniently been "sick"—his way, I'd come to believe, to take a pass on the responsibilities of life.

"But if he does have dementia," I said, "it's serious, and you need to start planning."

I didn't cry as Tamara delivered the news. I didn't do anything. I couldn't.

How do you care about someone being gone when, while they were present, they already *seemed* gone?

You could fit my memories of Dad as a father in a teacup, the good memories in a thimble. I remember a friend telling me of the way her father would come into her bedroom each night and snuggle with her, pray with her, and say good night. I had no idea what she was talking about, though it sounded nice.

How do you grieve for someone whose death will end a relationship that never really began?

It's like that tree-in-the-forest conundrum; if it falls and nobody's around to hear it, did it make any sound when it fell? Likewise, if a father dies and nobody had ever noticed him actually *being* a father—defending you, teaching you, encouraging you—did your father really die or was it just some random guy?

How do you come alongside someone who only came alongside you when he ran out of tricks in his bag?

I wanted to say, *Where were you* when I needed you *to tell me not to worry about the monster under the bed, to snuggle with me and tuck me in? Where were you when I was six and already a latchkey kid? Where were you when I graduated from high school and struggled to make a start in life? When I had cancer or was zapped out on Prozac? When I just wanted it all to end and prayed that God would let me die?*

The reality was that Dad had never been there for me. And now my sisters were suggesting that I was the wisest choice—the only choice—to be his caretaker.

"Sorry," I said. One word. That's all.

After so many years, I was finally getting my own life back together. I was taking care of a toddler, focusing on a new relationship, and working hard to heal my past. My therapist was good but not a miracle worker. And having my dad live with me in peace and harmony would truly take a miracle.

Bringing an ailing father that I didn't know into my home didn't make sense in any way. According to Tamara, the man had become a virtual recluse and seldom even showered. And who knew if he was still using drugs? He'd done drugs with my uncle when he was supposed to be babysitting me. He'd smoked pot and drank with Tamara when she was a teenager. And she claimed he had a problem with opiates during the time I'd visited him in Texas, later telling me she'd been hospitalized from overdosing on his pills. I had no reason to think he'd changed in any way.

My life finally had a sense of security I'd fought hard for. Why would I risk it for a guy who notoriously left trouble in his wake? My father had never taken responsibility for his actions. Why should I now rise up to take responsibility for him?

Yes, I'd forgiven my father. But forgiving didn't constitute obligation.

And why was his problem suddenly my problem? I was finally with an amazing man who had a faith in me that I didn't yet have in myself. And in the wake of all this, my reaction to my father's impending death was, well, no reaction at all. I felt vaguely sorry for him, the way I might feel sorry for a stranger on the street you see screaming at people passing by. I might hope that screaming stranger gets the help he needs, but getting too close could be unpredictable and dangerous. It's best to make a few phone calls, maybe drop a few bucks, and leave it to the professionals, not invite the guy in for a sleepover and risk the potential consequences.

My sisters had targeted me for Dad duty because I was the oldest, the most financially set, and the best educated.

My response? "So what? Not my monkey, not my circus."

I went to Daniel for support, sure he'd nix the idea in a nanosecond and relieve me of any lingering guilt. He listened, furrowed his brow, and nodded ever so slightly, indicating that he was thinking about this on a level far deeper than I expected—or wanted. *Just agree that I'm justified in washing my hands of the guy.*

"Tana, I need to assess your father—and scan him," he said. "I need to see him. To confirm the diagnosis."

"Oh, *really?*" I said. "And just where is he going to stay while you're doing this diagnosing?"

"With you," he said simply. "Eventually with us."

I recoiled. "Abso-freaking-lutely not! You don't know what you're asking. Maybe you're the one with dementia. Do you recall any of the crap I've told you about my 'dear old dad'?"

"Of course. But how awesome would it be to understand him on a deeper level?"

"Um, not awesome at all. My family isn't like your family, Daniel. We have baggage. Actually, we have crates—massive crates—full of wormy skeletons. This is Jerry Springer material."

"The operative word is *family*," he said. "He's your father, which makes him my family. And members of a family take care of each other. Tana, we need to take care of your dad. And you'll have no idea what motivated his past behavior if I don't look at his brain."

I loved Daniel's generosity, even if I hated the idea of us trying to cope with a man I'd never been close to, who had wasted much of his life, and who was now in failing health.

Daniel insisted, and I gave in. Daniel assessed my dad and scanned his brain. And to everyone's surprise but Daniel's, my father had been misdiagnosed. He didn't have Alzheimer's; he had pseudodementia, severe depression that masquerades as Alzheimer's disease. It's typically triggered by a toxic combination of medications that should have never been prescribed, medications that made him worse, not better.

My sisters were beyond relieved. And I was happy that Dad would be able to go home soon, wherever *home* was. But again, Daniel had other ideas.

"My gosh, I haven't seen this drug combination since the seventies," he said. "We need to get your dad off all this stuff and get him well. And the only way to do that is to have him move in with you. It's going to take time."

"I'm sorry. Say that again? Now I *know* you've lost your mind!"

But Daniel could be very convincing. I reluctantly had my dad move in with me, and Daniel and I started working on his treatment plan immediately. We got him exercising, eating clean, and taking the right medicines and supplements. The process was tedious at first, but as he felt better, his progress picked up pace.

Even though he occasionally succumbed to his Taco Bell cravings, he still lost twenty pounds. He'd battled with depression all his life, but now his mind was bright and focused, he said, like never before. Even his self-righteousness began to evaporate, replaced by a renewed faith, a repentant attitude regarding his shortcomings, and a renewed sense of purpose. Soon he started attending a church not far from our house.

One day he came out from his bedroom dressed in slacks and a sports coat he'd taken out of storage.

"What's up, Dad?" I asked.

"I've been invited to lead a Bible study at the church I'm attending."

"You?" I was surprised he was up to it.

He nodded. "Me."

I confess that I glowed inside with a sense of pride, though I didn't dare show it. Instead I stammered for what to say. This, after all, was the guy who'd gone from being deeply spiritual to partying with his daughter, from delivering rich sermons to allegedly stealing his congregation's money. So yeah, I was wary.

I cleared my throat. "You're serious?"

"Yes."

What could I say? "Well, that's nice, Dad. I'm happy for you."

He pursed his lips and nodded to seal one of the rarest moments we had ever experienced together. His eyes were a touch misty. "Thank you for helping me."

Soon Dad was leading Bible studies right in our house. He even conducted a full-blown seminar at his church—a seven-hour event with a packed room. He'd gone from Alzheimer's recluse to seminar leader in six months. He was the second coming of Robert Duvall's character in *The Apostle,* the movie about a small-town Texas pastor whose life spins out of control and who then moves to Louisiana and reinvents himself.

When Daniel and I bumped into a friend of ours who had attended the seminar, the guy said, "Where've you been hiding your father? He's wonderful. He's been mentoring me."

My father? Wonderful? *Mentoring?*

Yes, apparently. All I could do was shake my head.

———

Over the next year and a half, Dad's mental health improved as I grew emotionally stronger, healing the past day by day. Then one beautiful morning, when Daniel and I were walking on the beach with Chloe, I surprised him.

"I'm ready," I said.

"Ready for what?"

"Ready to marry you. I *want* to marry you. You still have my ring, right?"

Stopping and raising his eyebrows, he said, *"Reeaally?"*

I laughed. "Why are you looking at me like that? I told you before that I wasn't ready, and I wasn't. Now I'm telling you that I'm ready, and I am. Your patience gave me the space I needed to heal. Now I actually have something worthwhile to offer, the ability to be the partner you deserve."

"How fast can you plan the wedding?" Daniel asked, grabbing me in a tight embrace as Chloe wiggled her way between us.

As I made plans for my new future, which included moving in with Daniel permanently, I realized I needed to make plans for Dad too. Daniel and I found him a roommate (a Christian man), bought him a car, and helped him move to a lovely house near us.

Dad wasn't exactly thrilled with the change. In fact, he acted a bit petulant. But I was determined to allow myself the joy of preparing for my marriage. I refused to allow the demons from the past to resurface, so I simply told Dad I'd be ready to talk when he was.

The day I married Daniel Amen marked one of the two best days of my life—minus the labor pains. The only thing missing was Dad, who failed to show up as promised. Still, I was joyful. My focus was on the amazing man who was now my husband and the new life we would create together. Without a shadow of a doubt I knew I was starting a new chapter in my life. And I was a better version of myself—a hard-won, healthier version.

I wasn't damaged; I was resilient, as if I'd been forged in fire. I wasn't defective; I was wise. As a result, I would be a better wife, a better mother, a better role model.

The work of the past two years had been painful, and it had left its mark, but I was stronger as a result. Stronger for the trials. Stronger for the scars. For the first time I really felt *whole*, a word I used to find ridiculous. Instead of hiding, I was able to shed light in the darkest corners of my past. And for the first time in my life, I actually loved myself.

Moreover, I had a husband who was my best friend, lover, and partner in life. As we sailed around Balboa Bay following the ceremony, I said a quick prayer, thanking God for putting this man in my life and allowing him to be patient while I healed.

I thanked God, too, for His patience and mercy toward me on my shaky faith journey. For several years my faith had been tepid at best. In fact, it had been downright questionable at times. I had searched for answers in all sorts of bizarre places, taken many detours, and come up empty. But now I was vividly aware that God had never abandoned me. It was me who had strayed. It was always me. And I was ready to come home to Him.

I was not worried that a vengeful God would punish me, as I might have been in the past. I knew He would welcome me back. There was no fear of returning. So return I did.

Having lived too much life to believe that I'd finally "arrived" or that my challenges were over, I saw myself in a new light. I was a warrior—armed, aware, and prepared. Rather than believing I needed to find a world without challenges, I simply needed tools and strategies for meeting those challenges as they arose.

That's basically what I had been doing for the past year, arming myself with tools and strategies. And oh, how I needed them, because like all warriors I was about to be tested—repeatedly.

———————

While on my honeymoon, I learned that Dad had convinced Tamara to come and move him to Reno to live with her. He'd packed up the new car Daniel had bought for him and taken off before Daniel and I returned.

Sadly, Dad had been diagnosed with a blood disorder prior to our wedding. The doctor had told us that his health would eventually deteriorate but had assured us that he'd likely have a decent quality of life for a couple of years and would be able to live independently. Having Dad attend my wedding would have been extra special in light of all we'd been through together. But he didn't. And I hadn't been able to figure out why.

When we returned from our honeymoon, Tamara called to say she was going to take care of him.

"He's sick," she said, "and I want him with me."

"How touching." I didn't even try to hide my sarcasm. "You call me to clean up the mess, then welcome him home when the dirty work is done. And you do this while I'm on my honeymoon—without even discussing it with me?" I couldn't resist a little jab. "Could it be because you need to use his new car—the one Daniel bought him?"

"Tana, he is sick. Eventually he will have leukemia."

"No sh*t! Who do you think has been taking care of him?"

"I want him here, and he wants to be here. Of the three of us, I've been the closest to him."

Of course. You two partied together. "I wish you would have had that revelation two years ago. It would have saved me a lot of time and money." *And heartache.* But I'd never admit to that.

Once again, I had no idea how I was supposed to feel, let alone how I should respond. I didn't feel hate. But I felt a lot of anger—toward my sister as well as my father. After nearly two years of working to get Dad healthy and helping support him financially, I felt I should have been consulted about what happened next. I was peeved with my dad for using me and then abandoning me—again. I was sad that he was sick. And I felt guilty for being angry during this time when Daniel and Chloe deserved my best.

But I didn't disconnect in the way I once would have. Instead I did something I wasn't used to: I acknowledged the pain and I prayed for forgiveness. I prayed for Dad. For Tamara. For me. And after I prayed, I made a point to check on Dad regularly.

I was making progress. And I have to admit I was proud of me.

————

And then, at the start of my new life, I got some bad news: my thyroid cancer had returned.

Initially the plan was to do a third surgery. But I was informed that I wasn't a good surgical candidate due to the scar tissue that had accumulated in my neck from the first two surgeries. So my thyroid medication was increased to induce hyperthyroidism and suppress the cancer.

The meds made me miserable—wired and tired. I couldn't sleep at night but was exhausted all day. My heart raced. I felt anxious. I became fearful that the depression I'd spent sixteen years running from would hunt me down and drag me through the dark alley once again.

When I spoke to my doctor about my concerns, he flippantly told me that I should probably talk to a psychiatrist. That was the second time he had said those words to me, and it would be the last. I was fed up with being treated like I was mentally ill because of a medical condition that affected my hormones and mood. By this time I'd had enough medical training and life experience to know that MD didn't stand for "minor deity." The man in front of me wasn't a god whose word was gospel. Neither was he my parent, who could diminish me for being "naughty" and not behaving as I should.

"You're going to need to remain on this medication at this level for the rest of your life," he said. "In essence, it's your chemotherapy. There are side effects like rapid heart rate and anxiety—also thinning hair and bone- and muscle-wasting over time. You'll need regular bone scans, and you may need medication for osteoporosis in the future. In the meantime you should stop practicing martial arts and take it easy in your workouts, maybe practice yoga instead. And I'm serious about talking to a psychiatrist. The sooner you accept the situation and stop fighting it, the sooner you will find peace."

"Seriously? You just told me I'm going to feel like crap indefinitely, take a laundry list of medications, and have to quit doing the things I love most in the world—and I should just accept it? Why don't you just put me out to pasture and let me die?"

I was put on several *more* medications, nine to be exact—some to manage my heart rate, some to help the anxiety, some to manage the side effects of the other medications. Once again, I wondered why I was even alive. What was my purpose for being here?

Then I learned I qualified for an experimental treatment developed by the Mayo Clinic. While my doctor wasn't sure how effective it would be, it was less risky than the surgery he'd originally suggested. It would be administered in a sixty-minute office visit, was painless, and seemed to be effective. I wondered why the doctor hadn't offered that as the first option, and I agreed to do it.

Once done with the treatment, I found a new doctor who actually listened to me, and I went on an all-out mission to learn about the healing properties of food, exercise, and supplements. I was determined to be my own advocate and to do my part in healing my body.

Within a year of radically changing my diet and supplement routine, I felt healthier, sharper, and stronger than I ever had. I listened to my body—really listened—in regard to what I was eating. I listened to others who knew more than I did, taking more than three hundred hours of training in metabolic medicine and nutrition over the next couple of years. (This new passion would eventually manifest itself in my *New York Times* bestselling book *The Omni Diet*.)

In helping myself learn to use food as medicine, I had discovered my true purpose—to help others heal with food. More important, I knew I'd never crumble or give up because of my health ever again. Just as I'd done with the predator on the street—if not given the choice to run, I'd fight to the death.

The most enlightening thing I learned about food is how it affects hormones and mood, how food is instrumental in treating anxiety, depression, ADHD—even eating disorders. *Where was this information twenty-five years ago when I first needed it?* I felt robbed of information that could have helped me avoid the soul-crushing pain of my past. As a result, teaching people about the connection between food, mood, and brain health became my mission.

What started as a personal odyssey to heal myself organically morphed into a new career. Daniel was working on a book that he would feature on a public television show of the same name: *Change Your Brain, Change Your Body*. He asked me to create a companion cookbook for it, and I welcomed the opportunity to share what I'd learned.

A week after the show aired, we received a call from the bookstore chain Barnes & Noble. An extraordinary number of people were asking where they could purchase the cookbook. That's how my career as an author, coach, and speaker was born.

Sadly, I wasn't able to share my newfound success with Dad.

Since he moved, our conversations had become more superficial. Then the call came—the one I had been expecting. Fourteen months after he moved to Reno, my sister Tamara phoned to tell me that Dad had leukemia and that she could no longer take care of him and her two small children.

I could have told you that. When the hell will you guys grow up and be responsible? Once again, I get the call to clean up the mess you made. Not that I said any of this to her. I spoke with Dad's doctor and made arrangements to accompany him to LA by plane. Dad's doctor authorized the flight only because of my ICU nursing background, but he spoke words of caution to me.

"Your father is in bad shape," he said. "He is confused and weak. Today he ripped his IV out of his arm, got out of bed, and hid from the nurses. The lack of oxygen in his blood is making him act this way. He could code—you need to know that."

The next day I was in Reno to pack Dad's things once again and take him to the airport. He wouldn't need much to take his final trip to my house, where hospice would be waiting.

As I wheeled him to the gate, my niece took one last ride on his wheelchair. My sisters followed on either side of the chair, one carrying his oxygen tank and the other a small carry-on. His well-worn Bible was tucked into the side pocket. He smiled down at it and said, "It's the only thing I really need on the trip to where I'm going."

We said a tearful goodbye as the flight staff helped Dad and me onto the plane.

During the flight, Dad experienced chest pain and occasionally acted confused, but he also flirted shamelessly with the flight attendants. I struggled to keep him from wandering down the aisle, dragging his oxygen tank. But under the circumstances it was a successful flight—medically speaking.

By the time Dad walked into his new digs—the downstairs bedroom in the house Daniel and I had moved into a few months after we married—they had been converted to a five-star hospital room with a view. We had already rented a hospital bed and all the medical devices we would need to make him comfortable.

Over the next several weeks his mood and memory improved so much, I wondered if he would continue to qualify for hospice. The hospice physician was quick to tell me not to hold on to false hope.

"He's likely improving because of the change in altitude. And it's not uncommon for people to have a burst of energy at the end. We call it terminal lucidity. Enjoy this time. He is in pretty good shape under the circumstances. If I had to estimate, I'd say he has a few more weeks."

As the end neared for my father, our relationship continued to improve, but that didn't mean the past didn't occasionally return to ruffle the waters. I was still resentful that he had disappeared the day I married Daniel, and that resentment occasionally leaked out. We had planned to have him read some Scripture during the ceremony, but he hadn't shown up. And the only explanation he had offered was that he'd "gotten sick."

One day as Dad basically waited to die while living with us, I went into his room and opened the doors so he could get some fresh spring air. He smiled at the sound of birds splashing in the fountain outside his door and patted the bed, motioning for me to sit.

We sat together quietly for a while, watching sailboats ply the Pacific Ocean.

"Beautiful," Dad said sweetly, looking at me. "And the view isn't bad either."

I smiled.

"I'm sorry I've been such a disappointment," he said. "And so much work. For so long."

I squeezed his hand, thinking of what to say. It's never been my style to flatter or to make people feel better with false truths.

"I'm glad you're here, Dad."

It was the truth. I was glad. And I was thinking this might be a good time to clear up the issue that was bothering me.

"Dad, how come you didn't come to our wedding? I talked to your doctor. He said you were still well enough to come if you'd wanted to. And you were at least well enough to let me know if you didn't feel like coming. Instead you just didn't show. There has to be more to the story than what you told me."

He looked away, sadness clouding his eyes.

"I didn't think . . ." He teared up, the words stuck in his throat. "I didn't think I deserved to be there, not after the kind of father I'd been for you." He sniffed and rubbed his eyes with his fingers. "I was ashamed to come. I wanted your mother to give you away without feeling bad for me. But that would have magnified my shame."

I put my hand on his. Our eyes met ever so briefly in a wisp of understanding. For the first time I saw the depth of his pain, the burden of shame and guilt he had carried for half a century.

For me, that was enough. I was able to release my pain from the past, knowing it wasn't nearly as bad as the pain, shame, and guilt my father carried from a lifetime of bad decisions.

Within a couple of weeks it was clear that the doctor had been right. Dad's energy level dropped. He was unsteady on his feet, and his appetite all but vanished.

It was March 2010. Dad was sixty-four. And dying.

The hospice nurse was a saint. I don't think I've ever seen someone so grace filled. She taught me what it meant to help someone you love die with dignity.

During that time I realized I sucked at doing nothing. I was a trauma nurse. We reacted to horrific accidents every single day. *Protect the airway! Monitor the heart! Stop the bleeding! Get the fluids going! Do this. Do that. Action. Stat. Stat. Stat.* In the ICU we didn't let people die with dignity; we busted our tails to save them.

What was happening with Dad, on the other hand, required little action and lots of attention. Lots of patience and a serene environment. In the trauma unit, the fight was to keep someone alive. In our house, the struggle was to let someone go, which grated against me.

My head knew I needed to let go. My heart wanted to *do something* to save him—or at least to help him transition more easily. But every time I tried to *do* something for Dad, he just wanted me to let him sleep. So I paced—nervous, anxious, unsettled. I developed terrible migraine headaches.

But in the quiet, in the waiting, my perspective on my father slowly began to change, my disposition to soften, my eyes to widen. I realized that all my life, I'd seen only my father's failures, his shortcomings, his sin. I hadn't seen him as a whole person—a flawed person, but created by God and forgiven by God.

I thought once again of another David, King David in the Bible: how flawed he was. The affair with Bathsheba. The sending of her husband, the warrior, to the front lines in battle so he'd be killed. The utter sense of selfishness at the expense of others. Just like my father. And if I was honest, just like myself. And yet God had not only forgiven David but used him mightily.

I took comfort in that as I paced the room, waiting for my dad's time to come.

————

Realizing I was best with action after all, I decided to fly my sisters and my nieces, Tamara's daughters, to my house for a final family reunion. I was hopeful that under the circumstances there would be no personal drama.

Dad was weak but thrilled to see his family together, rallying around him. He spent what little energy he had sitting with us and holding his granddaughters. I had an enjoyable visit with my sisters under the circumstances. And Chloe enjoyed bonding with her little cousins, Alize (Tamara's daughter) and Aurora (Jenny's daughter), who didn't fully grasp that their grandfather was dying. For them it was an extended sleepover. I even took the kids to Disneyland to give them a break from the sadness that permeated the house.

When my sisters and all the children left, the quiet of the house was overwhelming. Once again I was left alone to process my feelings about my father's impending death.

At Dad's request, I called one of the pastors of the church where he attended. The pastor spent hours with Dad, talking and praying. While I can't be sure of the details, I knew my father was seeking forgiveness and peace before he passed. He wanted his friend to pray with him as he asked for God's grace. After that conversation, my father was the most peaceful I'd seen him, maybe ever.

Ever so slightly, guided by a reinvigorated faith, I had begun putting the man into context. His stepfather had been abusive, his mother depressed. No one grows up in a vacuum, I'd come to realize, and he was no exception. How do you become a good father when you've never seen a good father modeled?

Well, for starters, my evil side sneered, *you take responsibility for your actions and, if you can't be a great father, at least use whatever tools you do have to be a good father, or at least an okay father.*

Cut him some slack, the revised-standard version of myself countered. *We're all flawed, yourself included, Tana.*

But wait. There are basic flaws—like forgetting to put the toilet seat down—and there are you-gotta-be-kidding-me flaws—like abandoning your first child and doping the others.

Psalm 103:12 popped into my mind: "As far as the east is from the west, so far hath he removed our transgressions from us." Oh, how I hated the conviction that Scripture confronted me with, especially when it involved looking at myself in the mirror.

Sitting next to my father's bed, I held his hand. Though I couldn't reminisce about the good ol' days—I couldn't think of any—I could focus on now, on the gift of healing God had given me as I reluctantly became Dad's caretaker. Somewhere deep inside, I let it go. Let it all go. Okay, most of it. I'd like to say the impetus was my integrity, my big-heartedness, my faith-in-action commitment. But I'm not that big of a person, or that strong. Much bigger things were at work in that time of our lives.

Daniel had taken time to be there with my father and to support me, despite the fact that his new TV series about brain health had started on PBS and he was in demand for numerous media requests. While he sat with Dad, I stepped outside with Eric, the pastor, and told him about the history between my father and me.

"Have you forgiven him?" Eric asked. "Totally, 100 percent, forgiven him?"

"For the most part, yes."

"And what about the other part?"

I dragged out my usual laundry list of the ways my father had hurt me, disappointed me, shamed me—the unspoken answer being no, I hadn't *totally* forgiven him.

"Tana," he said, "why are you holding on to what God has chosen to forgive?" Those words really hit home—again. *Why do I keep getting beat up with that question?* Apparently forgiving myself and others wasn't a natural tendency for me.

I had no answer for the familiar question. I knew it was spot-on. What right did I have not to forgive when God had not only forgiven my father but had forgiven me?

Before my father came to live with us, guilt and shame on both sides had mortared the wall between us higher and higher. Now grace was breaking that same wall down. When I'd sit with my father—yes, I had gradually learned to relax and just *be* instead of trying to fix everything—the pain that had defined our relationship had been replaced by peace. And my migraines were gone.

One quiet morning as I sat holding my father's hand, I was overcome with a childhood memory of him. A sweet memory. A final gift.

I was six. I was in a warm tub. It was a baptismal—my dad was baptizing me! How had I forgotten that? For years I hadn't been able to recall *any* good memories of my dad. Now, as I allowed my anger to dissipate, allowed love for this man to fill my heart, God gave me this parting gift, this memory of a little girl smiling up at her father as he dunked her under water, holding her nose.

Tears filled my eyes. I continued holding Dad's hand, love filling my heart. We said little. But what we said was big.

"I'm sorry for the pain I've caused you," he told me once in a halting voice. "And I'm blessed by God's forgiveness, even though I know I don't deserve it."

"Well, your daughter can be a little arrogant, you know."

He laughed.

"I love you," I said. "You know that, right? I've totally forgiven you, and I hope you will forgive my stubborn pride. Please let go and just be peaceful now."

He nodded yes, his eyes getting a little glassy.

"Just one more thing," he said. "One more thing before I die."

"What's that, Dad?"

"I'd love just one . . . more . . . enchirito from Taco Bell."

I laughed, even as the tears rolled down my cheeks. Daniel smiled nervously and nodded me over to the corner of the bedroom, out of Dad's earshot. In these pre-Door-Dash days, he was the one who would need to make the Taco Bell run because I certainly wasn't leaving my father's side. But Daniel's PBS special, much of which involved eating healthy, was airing this week.

"No way can I be seen at a Taco Bell," he whispered. "One shot of me on the Internet with an enchirito, and PBS will drop me like a hot potato."

Ultimately Daniel did make the cloak-and-dagger trip to Taco Bell. Basically, he used the drive-through and picked up the order wearing a hoodie and dark glasses.

Dad got his enchirito and enjoyed it thoroughly. An hour later he passed away. To this day Daniel swears the enchirito killed him.

As my father was breathing his last breaths, Daniel held his hand, and I crawled into the bed with him. As I held him in my arms and softly prayed for him, I did something I'd waited a lifetime to do. I snuggled peacefully with my father for the first time ever—and the last.

CHAPTER 16

NOT MY SISTER'S KEEPER

I am not my sister's keeper. I am my sister.

—IYANLA VANZANT

It was one of those mother-daughter mornings that you'd like to use as your life's screen saver so it would come up over and over again. Chloe and I were enjoying our morning ritual: girl talk, drinking warm ginger tea, and making breakfast together before school.

It was a picture-perfect day. The sun was up. The sky was blue. The birds were fluttering outside.

In retrospect, I should have paid closer attention to the fluttering fowl and realized they were straight from Alfred Hitchcock's *The Birds*—the ones ruffling their feathers on the school playground, a foreshadowing of impending doom. But I was too immersed in my personal bliss to notice.

I was forty-seven and had been married to Daniel for eight years. Eight very happy, very peaceful years. That peace was hard-won. It had come with a price—keeping anyone and anything that threatened the sanctity of my nest—namely many of my well-meaning but drama-seeking family members—at a safe distance.

I hadn't seen either of my sisters in the seven years since my father died, for good reason. It had been four years since I'd spoken to Tamara, after another relapse—opiates on that particular ride. She'd raged, lied, and hung up on me. I'd done what I do best—disconnect. And frankly, I was fine with the situation. Better than fine. I was happy.

After beginning life as a married couple, Daniel and I had had a resurgence of faith. We'd both sunk roots deep in the Christian faith. Long before we'd both attended Christian colleges, but we'd both drifted. So it felt good that we had recommitted and started attending church together.

We ultimately ended up attending Saddleback Church after Pastor Rick Warren asked Daniel to be involved in creating a program called the Daniel Plan, designed to get the congregation healthy. (It was named for the Old Testament prophet, not my Daniel). I experienced a full-circle moment when I walked through the doors of the church I had first gone to with Krissy—a church that was now one of the largest churches on the planet.

Channeling my mother's tenacity, I had also transformed my health and my life, reaping success and joy along the way—in stark contrast to many of my family members, who remained entrenched in a life of chaos and substance abuse. An occasional twinge of guilt pulled at my heart for all the blessings I'd reaped and the contrast of my life with the lives of those family members, especially my sisters. After a lifetime of struggle, leave it to me to feel guilty for being happy.

By now I had been working with the recovering addicts at Leslie's rehab facility for several years, and I'd learned life-changing lessons from them. And yes, God had healed my heart when I'd agreed to caring for Dad in his final days. And I'd been successfully converted—okay, *almost* converted—from judgmental witch to empathetic healer. I was excited to test my new skills and help anyone and everyone.

Well, maybe not *everyone*. When it came to my sisters, I preferred to keep my distance when I could. I was very bonded to my immediate family: Daniel, Chloe, and Mom. Joe had passed away when Chloe was nine months old. Not that I was happy Joe wasn't in the picture any longer—we had finally become friends before he died—but Mom and I were closer than ever now that there was no family drama, which had seemed to focus around Joe.

Remaining committed to not starting Chloe's days with the same chronic stress of screaming and chaos I had grown up with, I'd deemed mornings in the Amen home sacred. Off limits. *Everyone* in my family knew my inviolable rule: *Do not call my house with drama before nine in the morning unless you are bleeding out or you are on fire. And I mean you personally are on fire, not your house!*

So now, on this perfect California morning, Chloe and I were talking about her week: schedule, necessary rides, homework, and social events. It was just after seven in the morning. And the phone rang.

It was Tamara. She was screaming about "them" following her again. But this time she claimed they had taken her children. *She's screaming, so she's obviously not bleeding out. She had better be on fire!*

It was the third such bizarre call in as many weeks. After four quiet years, Tamara seemed to be embroiled in some delusion about people being after her, using electronic devices to control her mind and take her kids. In a previous call I'd learned that in the Pacific Northwest coastal town where she'd moved, her significant other had covered the windows with aluminum foil and dug massive holes in the backyard, looking for the buried electronic devices he was sure were causing harm to the family. The kids had been given foil hats to reflect the microwaves that were believed to be "cooking" them.

Okay . . .

As chaotic as my life had been in childhood, I knew Tamara's had been just as hard. She hadn't been around for the early years of chaos and trauma that marked my life. But I hadn't been around a decade later, when she was coping with a partying mother and doing drugs with our father. Since then, our age difference and wildly differing values and personalities had created more distance than the geography that had separated us as children.

I liked order and rules, especially since becoming a mother. Tamara was like a gypsy, and she saw rules as an inconvenient suggestion.

After the long, arduous journey I had taken to radically change my life,

Daniel and I had helped Tamara take serious steps to change hers. That was the closest we had been. She'd started eating right and lost sixty pounds. But after our father died, Tamara had relapsed, and our short-lived intimacy had relapsed with it.

"What do you mean the kids are *gone?*" I said now into the phone.

"They're gone!" she screamed. "The bastards came and took them!"

She choked through her sobs. For the first time, her plight was starting to sound real, not imagined. I wanted to disconnect and get back to my regularly scheduled program—my serene, thoughtfully-laid-out life. But something in my gut told me not to, even if the trailer on this show smacked of a Hitchcock horror.

"Listen to me," I said, shifting into kick-butt gear. "Get yourself together. Figure out who took them. If it was Child Protective Services, we need to know why." Cringing inwardly, I said, "You should probably make a trip to my house so we can assess you and the situation. Something is very wrong."

After hanging up the phone and making a few more calls, a deep dread began to settle in my bones. Tamara's story wasn't a hysterical delusion. My nieces were indeed official wards of the state, and we had no idea who they were with or exactly why they had been taken. I surmised that neighbors had seen Tamara and her significant other ranting or driving recklessly— endangering the children, in other words—and reported her, triggering the visit from authorities. But that didn't explain the story of "electronic harassment."

I'm not proud to admit it, but had it not been for my nieces being missing in action, I probably would have sent her packing when I saw an unkempt, crazy-eyed, manic Tamara on my doorstep. I didn't believe Daniel, who thought the problem was more complicated—that Tamara's brain health (he refused to call it mental illness) was partially to blame for her behavior. My mind screamed, *Fricking drug addict! Why do so many of my family members seem hell-bent on destroying the lives of everyone around them and not taking responsibility for their own lives?* My bitter thoughts were a reflection of my worst childhood fears. *Don't let "them" get too close, or they will take you down with them.*

But my nieces—Alize was now eleven and Amelie six—*had* been taken.

As I evaluated the situation and made calls to the Department of Human Services, Tamara found as many opportunities as possible to leave the house and get plastered. When she wasn't drinking, she was manically pacing or raging. The very thing I'd worked so hard to protect Chloe from had taken up temporary residence in our guest room.

To make the challenge increasingly difficult, Chloe, now an eighth grader, had recently transitioned to being homeschooled. She had tired of the distractions of a large school—toxic social media, continual social climbing, and the class disruptions that got in the way of learning.

I'd been so proud of her decision. It was classic Chloe. Often referred to as an old soul, she would almost always choose the wise but less obvious path. But with her being home during the day, while Tamara was ranting and pacing, I needed to explain the situation and reassure her that it was safe—and temporary.

Daniel did his best to understand my annoyance, but naturally he had a different perspective. This wasn't his first rodeo helping Tamara with her addiction. Still, he suspected she was suffering from more than just substance abuse, and he refused to condemn her with labels that seemed obvious to me: bipolar, delusional, or my personal favorite, "irresponsible pain in the a**."

After a thorough assessment and brain scan with one of our doctors at Amen Clinic, Daniel told me that the emotional centers in Tamara's brain were on fire. Her limbic system—which can be triggered during traumatic events—was overreactive. She was struggling to sleep and think rationally.

"It's a pattern that indicates trauma," he said. "She clearly has a problem with addiction, but right now we need to focus on settling her brain down and getting her to sleep. If we don't do that, her urge to self-medicate will be greater."

But why was this my problem? *Because your nieces don't deserve what's happening to them.*

My mind was a tornado of conflicting emotions. During the next few days, I frequently dragged Tamara to the dojo with me—I didn't trust her at home alone or with Chloe—where I'd pound pads until I could think straight. It was the one outing Tamara didn't complain about. She was genuinely enthralled that a woman could learn to fight.

I'd been practicing martial arts consistently for ten years and hadn't found a better form of stress relief. My karate master, Bob White, had taught me valuable lessons that applied to life as much as to self-defense. He taught me that it's better to be prepared and aware so you can avoid fights. He also taught me that getting hit and falling isn't failing; it's a normal part of learning. *Why didn't someone tell me that twenty years ago?*

"As long as you always get up, you're not a failure," he'd say. "While it's better to give than to receive, there is a gift in getting hit and in falling—the gift of knowing how not to do it next time." I tried to impart these bits of wisdom to Tamara, but her anxiety overrode her ability to listen. She just liked watching me hit things.

After a particularly grueling and mind-clearing lesson, I tried to imagine losing my daughter and having no idea where she had been taken. Regardless of the preemptive circumstances, I began to feel more empathy for Tamara's wacky behavior—until I'd discover that she'd polished off a bottle of vodka and left her car on the side of the road with no memory of its location or called me singing some pop song and fallen asleep in midchorus. On those days I felt only contempt for her.

I struggled to keep my anger in check, knowing it wouldn't help. But eventually the dam always burst.

"Tamara, what the hell is wrong with you?" I snapped. "I know you're in pain, but you lost the right to lose your sh*t in a crisis the day you became a mother. Your children are counting on you."

"I know, Tana. But I feel so hopeless. I'm never getting them back. I can't handle thinking about what might be happening to them." Her whining grated on my nerves. I wanted her to man the hell up.

"This isn't about you. You don't get to give in to fear. Imagine how scared those little girls are. Get your a** in gear and fight!"

In my mind, giving up was not an option. The only language I knew was "fight to win." As anger and empathy warred in my head, I made more calls to the Lane County Department of Health and Human Services. Someone there knew where my nieces were, and I intended to find out who.

After two weeks of messages and one thinly veiled threat of arriving with a lawyer to help me understand why DHS had taken the children, I learned from a supervisor named Ms. Smith that the girls were safe—"Happy," she said—with a foster family.

Ms. Smith turned out to be incredibly helpful. "Let's set up a phone visit," she suggested. "But there *are* ground rules, and the call will have a bearing on future visits."

"Oh, trust me. She *will* follow the rules. You have *my* word."

Not that I believed for two seconds that Tamara could step out of her own pain long enough to be strong and present for her kids. Frankly, I wasn't convinced she was fit to be a mother. My efforts were more focused on figuring out how to get my nieces home, not necessarily on reuniting them with their mom. Meanwhile I'd do what I could to keep Tamara on a short leash so she could talk to her girls.

Nearly three weeks after the girls were taken, and after much intense coaching and role playing with me, Tamara had her first phone visit. The massive sense of relief Tamara felt when she made it through her first phone call and heard the voices of her babies made dealing with me worth it.

————

The more Daniel and I learned about the precipitating circumstance that had landed my nieces in foster care, the more our hope diminished. The story about the girls' parents believing they had been electronically harassed was so convoluted that drug abuse or significant mental-health issues were strongly suspected, though no one knew for sure at the time.

As we contemplated our options, the most obvious one was for us to adopt the girls. Besides the story that grew more and more bizarre, sobriety didn't appear to be in Tamara's future any time soon. As more of the story was revealed, however, I also felt less confident that adopting the girls was going to be the "easy way" to handle things—or safe for us as a family. But what other choice was there?

What had originally appeared as my sister playing with matches—bad decision after bad decision—now looked like a full-blown wildfire headed for my house. Adding to the heat was my growing sense of annoyance that my usually understanding husband wasn't listening to me.

———

"We're their family, and they need us," said Daniel. "We need to bring the children into our home."

"Daniel, slow down. I'm worried about the consequences of jumping in without all the information. All we have is a crazy story and not all the details. I love you for wanting to rescue them. But those girls have *parents* who are not going to just accept us adopting their kids and let us live happily ever after. They also have other family who are not just going to go away. And their father struggled with drugs and the law, and that's trouble I don't need or want on my doorstep. Besides, I'm guessing that the girls have been traumatized from being taken from their parents. I'm worried about the effect those dynamics could have on Chloe."

I was torn between admiration for the man who wanted to swoop in and save two innocent little girls and frustration that he wouldn't listen when I voiced my fear about this plan putting our family in danger. Where I saw hell, Daniel saw Hallmark. It was like he had Mickey and Minnie in his head doing the waltz, as if nothing bad could happen. His head was the happiest place on earth. But I knew better.

Daniel believed that Chloe's world of privilege would be broadened if we adopted the girls and possibly even had Tamara stay with us for a while. Chloe would have an up-close view of someone in need and family members helping fill that need.

"This is how families work," he liked to say. "They help each other out." For him it could be one big, happy "teachable moment."

I might have agreed if I'd had any evidence of my sister being the least bit teachable—or if she'd had a track record of learning from her mistakes and making better choices. Such was not the case. The idea that Chloe would somehow wind up the beneficiary of having all this drama unfold in our home seemed incredibly naive to me. My deepest instincts were about protecting my daughter, and my version of the narrative didn't have the happy ending that Daniel's did.

For the first time in eight years, my nest didn't feel safe and secure or even happy. Daniel and I were arguing more, always about the same topic, his righteous stance serving only to annoy me further and make me dig in my heels.

"Why do you believe you're right or justified just because you see your actions as noble?" I'd ask. "That doesn't make those actions safe, or even smart."

"I am a trained professional," he'd answer. "I know what I'm doing. I am confident I can handle any problems that come up."

"Well, good for you. But the fact that you're trained to handle 'crazy' in a clinical setting doesn't make you more of an expert than me where *my* family is involved. I have forty-eight years of experience in handling my family's kind of crazy; with them I am the expert. I love your *Big Fat Lebanese Family*, but mine is the *Nightmare on Elm Street*. And you don't get to diminish my feelings, fears, or experience in the name of a noble cause."

"Tana, I realize you still have unresolved childhood trauma," he said, "but it doesn't mean your thoughts are true."

"Don't you dare 'shrink' me," I snapped. "Therapy heals the past, but it doesn't make you blind to future threats and bullsh*t."

"I just can't let the girls stay in foster care," he said sharply. "We have a chance to make a difference, Tana."

"And a chance to traumatize my daughter for the rest of her life, Daniel. I absolutely know that we must get the girls out of foster care; they're the only innocent ones in this mess. And if I thought that adopting them was that simple it would be a no-brainer. But it's not."

I couldn't sit still; I had to pace. "You weren't around for all the craziness over the past four decades. For our 'fun' family reunion when I had to buy a plane ticket and send Tamara packing because of her raging and screaming all night. Or for all the times she's called me because she was fighting with her mother or sister and they're calling the police on one another and throwing each other's belongings into the middle of the street, screaming and threatening at all hours of the night."

I stopped and gazed at him, pleading. "Daniel, you're my best friend. I need to be able to talk this through and not feel bullied about something that feels unsafe, even for a noble cause. Otherwise I will put my foot down, and we'll be at a standoff."

"Tana, you are one of the strongest people I know. You survived your past, and you're better for it. Why is this so hard for you?"

"Most Holocaust survivors are stronger for their nightmare also. That doesn't mean they want to go to back Auschwitz for a camping trip. The whole point of surviving a traumatic past is *leaving* it in the past."

We were at an impasse, with no solution on the horizon.

That night I went to bed and had one of the most vivid and horrific nightmares I've ever had. There were three snakes representing chaos, division, and drama, and they brought to light my innermost fears. Daniel and I were fighting to get the neon-colored serpents under control.

I grabbed the largest one by the head, squeezing until it spewed green venom at me. It had horns and was hissing and thrashing. The two smaller snakes rapidly slithered around the house as Daniel chased them. He grabbed one, and as he struggled to subdue it, I took the one I was wrestling with and slammed its head on the counter. Grabbing a nearby ax, I held it over the snake's head.

Just as I swung, severing the snake's head from its body, Daniel screamed, "No! Don't! I was handling it. I was protecting us." He was furious with me. Disappointment clouded his eyes. But Daniel was not nearly as angry or disappointed as I was. In my dream, I had lost respect for him.

"You did *not* protect us!" I yelled. "*I* protected us. This is how you protect us from snakes. [I pointed at the headless body.] You *kill* them! You chop their fricking heads off. End of story!"

Green ooze covered the floor, trapping our feet in sticky goo. As we struggled to get free of the gelatinous slime, I could see Chloe's face, close at first, then drifting off into the background until she disappeared. I was unable to reach her. I screamed in anguish as tears streamed down my face. I had failed at the one goal that mattered most: protecting my daughter.

———

Waking from the nightmare, my heart pounded fiercely as I lay in a pool of sweat. The vivid dream had brought my fears into sharp focus. I knew why I had been resistant to moving my nieces in. Sadly, they were innocent bystanders, scared little girls trapped in a situation not of their making. My resistance was due to a lifetime of family drama—and the potential for it to swallow my family up if we let it into our home.

The issue was my family history—the drugs, the fights, the police and murder and multiple suicides, the mental illness and just plain insanity. It was a risk I wasn't willing to take with Chloe. If I let part of the family in, eventually the rest would come slithering in, scrambling to find a safehold, oblivious and indifferent to the chaos they left in their wakes.

The most ominous message of the snake-filled dream concerned Tamara. It became clear to me that if she lost her girls to me, she would not survive. To her it would be an epic failure to lose them to the "perfect," self-righteous sister, the sister who had cut her off because of her out-of-control addiction and related behavior.

She knew little of my past struggles. She saw only my success, and she resented me for it. And if she knew that her daughters were safe and cared for with Daniel and me, I was convinced she'd be free to give in completely to her addictions. Most likely she would end up dead.

I shook Daniel out of a dead sleep. I was no longer the least bit wishy-washy about my position, nor feeling any remnant of guilt.

"I am *not* ready to adopt the girls," I said breathlessly. "Not yet. I need you to let me go at my own pace with this decision. I need to feel safe. You can either help me solve this another way or not. If you insist on doing this, I will still love you, and I will miss you. I will send you a postcard from Hawaii. I hear it's nice there this time of year."

I told Daniel the details of my dream and what they meant to me. I was ready for a fight; there was no backing down. Instead, he gently took me in his arms.

"I don't want you to be scared. God gave us both big brains for a reason," he said. "And you might be right about Tamara. Getting her well so she can be a good mother is probably the better solution, even if it is the harder option. But we must get the girls out of foster care and into a stable environment."

"I agree. But how—?"

"There is another way. Are you ready for the fight ahead? Because it's going to be you on the front lines going to see her regularly. I'm here to do all I can for Tamara's medical care, and the finances, of course. But you will have to be present. You'll have to work with her."

I felt myself relax for the first time in weeks. "As long as you're my partner I can do it," I said, then swallowed. "I think."

—————

Comforted by Daniel's smile, I settled into his warm embrace, still skeptical but not terrified, and relieved to feel like we were finally a team again. And we soon realized we needed to expand the team. Chloe had all but gotten lost in the drama, just as I'd feared. My mama-bear nature may have caused me to overprotect her in the past. Now we realized that if this were to be a teachable moment, she needed to be more involved in the situation.

Up to this point I'd been proud, elated even, that my daughter had no concept of the life I'd lived as a child—that she really couldn't relate. Yet now I realized it was time to start preparing her rather than sheltering her. So, in an age-appropriate way, I began telling her about my life. All of my life.

"Mom!" she said when I told her about my Prozac antics.

"Sweetheart, I'm telling you the truth. I didn't say that what I did was smart. A wise woman learns from her own mistakes. A wiser woman learns from someone else's. Be wiser than I was."

The next morning the three of us discussed plans to get our nieces—Chloe's cousins—out of foster care. And two days later Tamara and I were on a plane to begin our mission.

Our lives were about to change like never before.

CHAPTER 17

PUT ON YOUR
BIG-GIRL PANTIES

Fate whispers to the warrior, "You cannot withstand the
storm." The warrior whispers back, "I am the storm."

—Unknown

I hadn't prepared for what demons the trip to her home town would resurrect for Tamara. As we crossed the jetway into the airport, she began to tremble and sob, essentially shutting down.

I wanted to comfort her, but I had little time for tears. We were on a mission. We needed answers, and we needed them before we could hope to accomplish the almost insurmountable goal before us. As Tamara's fear and my impatience clashed, I all but dragged her around town, checking off items on my to-do list. We found her an apartment, set her up with a therapist, and arranged for her to attend weekly AA and Celebrate Recovery meetings. We even looked for potential jobs, though she was in no condition to interview.

I decided that the last meeting scheduled on our whirlwind trip was best left as a surprise. If Tamara had known where we were going, she likely would have bolted to the nearest liquor store for a pint of vodka.

"Tamara, this is the most important meeting we have," I said as we approached our destination. "This is when we get to dance with the devil."

"Tana, *please* tell me you're not taking me to the DHS office. I just can't." The tears started again. I handed her a tissue and kept walking. "Can't we just make phone calls?"

"No, we need to show them you are fit to be a mother. And that you have support." Not that I believed it, but I needed Tamara to start believing it.

"But there are people there who are out to get me," she wailed.

"Get over it. It doesn't matter. If you are scared now, imagine how scared your girls are, all alone in this."

"But what if they come after me?"

"Then become a counterpredator! Do anything—except curl up and cry. If someone came after my kid, I'd be trying to rip their face off, not run and hide. You need to start acting like a mom who gives a damn and *fight* for your kids! End of story! If you ever want to see them again, suck it up and put on your big-girl panties!"

She stopped crying and stared at me.

"Did you just tell me to put on my *big-girl panties*?" For a brief moment Tamara smiled. "You are the scariest b*tch I know."

"Thank you, but this is me being *nice*. Now let's go."

All in all, the meetings with DHS were successful. We met with two supervisors who had the "good cop, bad cop" act down to perfection. Fortunately I liked cops. And after years of working with surgeons in a trauma unit—not to mention living with Joe—I was not easily intimidated.

"We have plenty of evidence showing that it's not safe for the kids to be with Tamara," Bad Cop said in a cold, calculating way. "Regardless of the reason, it wasn't the calm and predictable environment kids need to thrive."

"I agree," I said. "I'm not here to determine whether Tamara will be able to succeed with the very intricate plan we've already put in place. I'm here to figure out what it's going to take to get my nieces out of foster care."

I kept my eyes laser-focused on his face.

"You and I both know that foster care isn't the safest or most 'calm and predictable' place for two young girls, especially if those young girls have family with the means and desire to help them."

Bad Cop offered an almost imperceptible nod of approval, which I could only hope was respect. Good Cop then lined us up with all the services Tamara qualified for to help her get healthy again. Best of all, I had a guarantee that Tamara would have an in-person visit with her girls within a couple of weeks.

Feeling the first sign of hope since the nightmare had begun, Tamara cried tears of relief as we left the DHS office.

"How do you always know what to do? How come you aren't scared?" Tamara grabbed me in a tight hug. "I can't believe that just happened—and I survived!"

"Yeah, I'm proud of you. I only had to kick you once." I smiled. "Seriously, I don't always know what to do. But I do know really smart people I can call for help when I'm lost. That's what you're going to need to do: surround yourself with smart, healthy people."

She nodded sadly. "I'm sorry for being such a burden, Tana," she said. "I just feel so powerless. Like everyone is in control of decisions that affect my life except me."

I refrained from telling her that others had taken control because she'd careened out of control.

"I know what you are," she said. "You're my *momster*. You know, my mom and my sister, my momster. You sort of parent and help me in a way my mom didn't—or maybe she couldn't."

"Uh-huh," I said laughing. "That's just a nice way to call me a monster."

"But, hey, you're *my* monster. Everyone should have one."

Less than a month later, when Tamara's first court date arrived, she was already moved into a cute little apartment and had begun supervised visitation with her children. With Daniel and me there for support, Tamara showed up to court looking fresh and pretty. I hadn't seen her look that vibrant for years. The judge voiced approval of the plan we'd set up and our support for Tamara and said we'd likely have the girls out of foster care within a couple of months—record time, we were told.

And then the snakes began slithering toward my door.

After Daniel and I supported Tamara in court, she thanked us, dropped us off at the airport, then drove off to celebrate—by getting drunk and totaling the car we had just spent thousands of dollars having rebuilt.

Back in California, I didn't know who I was angriest at: Tamara for relapsing or me for believing she somehow wouldn't.

"Tana, it's not going to be perfect," Daniel said. "We have to expect a few setbacks."

"This isn't a mere setback. It's more evidence that it's a lost cause."

"You don't mean that. You're just hurt and angry."

"Yes, I am hurt and angry. And I'm feeling pretty hopeless."

Meanwhile, Tamara sank into a deep depression—not her first such rodeo. As a result of the DUI, we learned, it would now take as long as a year to get the girls back, provided Tamara could actually get back on track. She responded to the news by—wait for it—drinking. Soon she became suicidal. Her mother—my stepmother—Kathy, had to move in and watch her around the clock.

I told the supervisors at DHS that we should shift to plan B, having the girls move in with us. But surprisingly Good Cop had more faith in Tamara than I did and encouraged me to hang in there. And eventually Tamara did start plodding along, focused on the task of getting her kids back. Her progress was marked with volatile rises and dips—steps forward, steps backward—as she struggled to break down the long-abandoned barriers in the shadow-ridden corners of her mind.

When we talked, which was often, I couldn't restrain my iron-fist temperament or refrain from preemptively kicking her butt. I was terrified that she'd relapse and thwart our rescue-the-kids plan yet again. Imagine my surprise when the DHS supervisor asked me to "ease up" on Tamara. Apparently my sister was more afraid of me than of the DHS team. But the plan was working, so I stayed firm.

After several months of voluntary weekly drug-and-alcohol testing, intensive therapy, and completing a rehab program, Tamara got the good word: on Easter weekend, 2017, the children could have their first overnight supervised visit with their mother—in California, with me as the responsible, supervising adult. It seemed too good to be true.

The raw, emotional reunion quickly settled into a fun-filled day at the beach. After unloading a car full of happy, sandy kids at home, I took a moment to be thankful. Despite some obvious emotional scars, my nieces were sweet, well-behaved children.

Tamara took the girls into the guest room, reveling in the maternal bedtime rituals she'd felt robbed of for the prior six months—until twenty minutes later, when she emerged from the room, urgently whispering for me to follow her. And there it was on her finger: a tiny insect—specifically, a louse.

"Calmly tell me what's happening," I said. "*Calmly.* Your kids will feed off your energy."

"They have f***ing lice! The foster parents sent them here with lice! And *I'm* supposed to be unfit?"

Daniel, cool as ever, reassured Tamara and went to get a solution to kill the pests while I went into the bedroom to do damage control with the kids. Alize was curled up in a ball in the corner of the attached bathroom, crying.

"I'm a dirty little foster kid," she kept repeating. My heart broke.

"Honey, they are just pathetic little bugs," I said. "They'll be gone in a few hours. It's not a big deal."

"But I brought lice into your beautiful house," she whimpered.

"Is that what you're worried about? The house isn't important. *You* are. Little bugs can't do anything to hurt my house."

"My foster mom was notified that lice were going around school and that Amelie and I needed to be checked. We've been telling her our heads itch for the last couple of weeks. She said, 'Let your aunt worry about it.' She said the same thing when I told her I needed a bra." The tears wouldn't stop.

My blood boiled, but I took a deep breath. "It's better this way," I said. "Wouldn't you rather be with family for something like this? We certainly feel better that you're going through it with us instead of someone else."

My anger only increased as I learned the disturbing truth about their foster parents. Alize was quick to relieve my fear that there had been sexual abuse. (I could only hope she was telling the truth.) But as she described her foster parents yelling and throwing things, her foster father telling her she was ugly, and the same foster dad picking her up and dumping her in a trash can in front of her friends at a school dance, saying, "That's where you belong," I was horrified.

So was Tamara, but this time she did not react by getting drunk and smashing a car. Instead she became a star for DHS, fueled as much by the joy of the weekend visit as by her anger over stories of their mistreatment.

On Mother's Day 2017, Tamara was reunited with her children as their legal guardian but would need to remain under the supervision of DHS until it was determined she could consistently create a stable environment. Until then DHS would maintain legal custody of the girls and require Tamara to report to their office weekly.

On September 26, 2017, Daniel and I appeared in family court with Tamara for the last time. Following the nightmare that had lasted over a year, my sister was awarded full custody and informed that she would finally be allowed to move out of state to be near us. DHS was withdrawing from the case.

The battle was over. For now.

My sister had done it. I was impressed. And proud. And sickened when Tamara called to tell me about the foster parents' parting gift. Inside the box of children's clothes they'd packed was a pile of feces.

That final act of malice shook Tamara to the core. Though she kept moving forward, she lost her zest after that. She seemed sad and wounded.

We moved my sister and the girls to an apartment near us in California in October 2017. I would love to say joy abounded after that—and it did at times—but it was also stressful for everyone involved. We would provide the structure they needed and help Tamara financially. Tamara and the girls would go to church with us. She would go to weekly AA or Celebrate Recovery meetings, weekly therapy, and psychiatric appointments. She would work full-time at a job we helped arrange. It would be challenging, and we knew Tamara wasn't yet out of the woods.

We'd succeeded. Still, I couldn't relax and fully enjoy the moment. History was stalking me like a vulture, waiting for a vulnerable moment to swoop in and prey on wounds from the past. At Daniel's urging to "focus on the progress instead of the pain," I tucked the thought away and got to work.

Daniel and I were committed to loving and supporting the girls from that point forward, regardless of my sister's success or failure. Even though I dealt with my own demons, dressed as family coming to haunt me, I remained steadfast about maintaining healthy boundaries. I came to appreciate Daniel's experience in dealing with addiction up close and personal. While I had loads of experience dealing with the fallout, drama, and pain of family disappointment, I didn't fully comprehend what he knew so well, that recovery isn't clean and simple. As in martial arts, he saw the falling down as an expected part of the process.

Even though by now I had experience working with recovering addicts, I still wasn't hardwired to offer grace and mercy to them—especially when they shared my DNA. Helping to educate people with addiction who weren't related to me felt noble. Helping family members still in the stranglehold of addiction felt, well, a little too close to home.

Less than a week after her move to California, Tamara relapsed again— and then again after that.

I reached my limit in July when my niece Alize was baptized. Tamara had gotten drunk the night before, so she fought with her daughter. Seeing Alize's devastation on a day that should have been one of her happiest was the final act that zapped my already waning tolerance.

God, why? Haven't I already proven myself? Why do You confront me with the one thing I hate—addicts? What is it that You want me to learn?

Daniel called an emergency family meeting the following day—a meeting I only reluctantly attended. Truth is, I wanted no part of an intervention. I was at the point that I wanted no part of Tamara. But I went. I listened to Tamara's lies and excuses again and burst into tears. I had failed, and I didn't want to try again.

"Tamara," I told her, "I love you. It breaks my heart that I'm not strong enough or smart enough to help you, but I'm not. I can't fix you. I've done everything I can. This is above my pay grade."

Tamara cried, too, her anxiety heightened by my look of defeat.

"Tana, please. I will do better."

"I wish I could trust you, but I can't. Look, your kids will be fine. They're part of my life forever. You, on the other hand, need to figure out what you're going to do, because I am finished. I can understand the struggle. It's the lies and deception and the rage I can't take any longer. And it's not actually me you're lying to and hurting. It's yourself. And your kids—but I can still help *them*."

The devastation in Tamara's eyes added to my own pain. Other than the day she lost her kids, I had never seen her look so sad or scared.

Then a sweet memory of our first encounter flooded my mind—a memory of a time before life had gone so completely off track. It was my annual summer visit with my dad. Tamara was nine months old and I was nine years old; it was the first time we'd met.

She was the fattest, baldest baby I'd ever seen, and she wanted nothing to do with me. It was the summer Dad and Kathy were moving from Texas to Oregon. Tamara and I were packed into the back of my dad's old jalopy of a truck, inside the rusty old camper shell, with only a camping pad and a few blankets. The night wind howled through the cracked Plexiglas windows that were held together with duct tape. I had no way to communicate with my dad and stepmom in the cab—no way to tell them that we were cold or that the baby was curled up in the corner screaming and wouldn't let me touch her.

As I lay there shivering, listening to the incessant wailing, I felt a tiny hand reach for me under the blanket. Tamara had wormed her way under my covers, pressing her body next to me for warmth, burying her face against my neck. The crying stopped. Wrapping my arms around her, we drifted to sleep for the remainder of the night.

From that day forward—until our parents' divorce—Tamara rarely left my side whenever I'd visit. It had never occurred to me until now that she might have been seeking shelter from the chaos of her life.

Now, looking at Tamara's tearstained face, I was at a loss for words. A lifetime of pain and disappointment stood between us.

"Tana, please . . ." She choked on her sobs. "Please don't abandon me." Her words felt like a hot blade slicing through my heart. "You're the only person I've ever really been able to count on. Not one other person has ever made me feel safe the way you do." Her voice got small and quiet. "I can't do this without you."

Feeling trapped, confused, and sad, I said nothing. I had no words left, no faith that I could do anything to help Tamara. But was it Tamara that I was disappointed and angry with—or was my fear-filled childhood haunting me?

"Tamara, I desperately want to be here for you. But I have a painful history you're not aware of. So even though my love for you is unconditional, my boundaries aren't. As protective as I've been of you, it's a fraction of how protective I am of Chloe. She is my primary responsibility. Addiction, violence, lies, screaming, and incessant drama are not things I'm willing to chronically expose her to."

"But I don't want—"

I held up my hand, palm out. "I love you and I will help you, but *you* have to love yourself enough to do the work. I won't abandon you, but you can't abandon yourself. You need to take responsibility. I won't be more invested than you are."

The realization of my limits—and of the pain she'd caused her family—finally broke Tamara's stubborn pride. In the past she'd gotten clean temporarily when circumstances dictated, but never because she *wanted* to.

She had never addressed her trauma or trusted anyone enough to be honest while going through the custody battle with DHS.

Several months later, Tamara called, excited to tell me about an AA meeting she'd been attending. "I'd like you to come to an event with me," she said. "Crackhead Family Feud."

"You're joking, right? Sounds like my worst nightmare." I wasn't that far into my own recovery from judgmental witch to be comfortable with the idea of people making light of addiction.

Maybe someday, but not yet.

Tamara threw herself into therapy and began attending several AA meetings each week with "her people," as she called them. There was a new bounce in her step I hadn't seen before. As her ownership of her addiction increased, her shame decreased. And slowly she and I began to mend our bond, though I kept my heart guarded.

As Tamara worked her steps in AA, she became raw and vulnerable, yet stronger somehow. One day she sat next to me, crying. "I'm such a selfish b*tch," she said. "I've been drowning my own pain instead of tending to the pain my daughters have endured."

I thought back to a time when I'd also been terrified to seek help for fear of being labeled an "unfit mother." A time in my own journey when my words had been nearly identical to hers. My drugs of choice—food, exercise, and attention—hadn't involved illegal substances or even alcohol really. And my addiction hadn't left me cognitively impaired, just emotionally disabled. Was I better than Tamara because I had the sophistication to conceal my brokenness? Or was I just a better liar?

These were hard questions with painful answers. But as she softened her heart, I felt mine softening toward her. As her understanding of herself grew clearer, my self-understanding grew too.

"Tamara, I'm not certain if I will ever fully understand chemical addiction," I said. "But I'm doing my best to see you as a person who *suffered* with addiction instead of seeing the drugs that I hate. Much of my anger has nothing to do with you, but you are paying the price. It's the tax that the previous generation left for us to pay. You're going to need to be patient with me also."

"I know," she said. "There is still so much pain, especially knowing how much I've hurt the people I love. But I'm learning I must forgive *myself* even when others don't. I have to if I want to stay sober. It's okay for me to sit with the painful memories of the past and not numb them with booze or pills. The pain won't kill me."

With a sad look, she continued. "I promise I wasn't doing drugs when DHS took the girls. I was struggling with mental-health issues I needed help with, but I didn't know how to ask for it. DHS said I was neglecting to address my mental health." Wiping tears from her cheeks, she continued, "I was drinking though. I've been an alcoholic for years, even after kicking the drugs, and I don't think I realized it. Since I was a teenager, alcohol and drugs were part of the culture of my family. Dad was the first person I got high with. It seemed normal. But I'm so much more than my addiction. I want a life I can be proud of."

In this simple but profound exchange, I'd finally fully understood the adage Daniel often used: *It's easy to call people bad, harder to ask why.* If Daniel had judged me on my past as harshly as I'd judged myself and now Tamara, we likely wouldn't have had a second date. But he was more interested in the difficult journey I had overcome and the potential he saw in me.

I wanted to see others the same way, and maybe Tamara was proof that I was beginning to. I'd been tough on her, yes, but I'd also given her chance after chance until finally she *got it.*

In short, normal is a myth. Normal is the setting on a dryer. Normal is overrated.

It was as if in this heart-to-heart with Tamara, God broke my own heart wide open. And maybe that's just what we both needed.

———

When that phone call first came two years prior, I was the epitome of the "reluctant healer." *Don't get involved. Take care of yourself.* I could have turned my back on my sister. I *wanted* to turn my back. And God knows the episode took an emotional toll on me, on all of us. But God knows what He's doing, and He has a plan.

Tamara and I continued making progress. She even started looking forward to going to church with us—and reached a point where she didn't cry through the entire service. I wasn't insisting Tamara go to church because I believed she'd magically be healed by attending. I know that healing and a relationship with God were personal choices that only she could make. I was adamant about her going because she needed a new community of healthy people and structure to replace the chaotic life she was leaving behind. People are contagious, and if she was going to "catch" the ideas and thoughts of others, I wanted her to catch something positive. Recalling the positive benefits I'd received at church, I wanted her to give it a chance. Lord knew she had tried every unhealthy option.

Meanwhile, as my own values about control began to shift, I began to trust God more and more to guide me. Tamara was surprised by my spiritual commitment, considering our heritage. She was still traumatized by the hypocritical actions of our father the minister.

"It's a process," I told her. "It's not about Dad. It's about *your* journey. Your peace. When you're ready, God will be there for you."

"Do you really believe all this?" she asked. "The whole Christ-as-Savior stuff? Heaven and the pearly gates?"

"I know. It sounds crazy to hear me talking about God. I'm the last person who should preach to anyone. And I know I still have a tough exterior, but my heart has been softened."

I snickered. "Tell anyone I said that, and I *will* hurt you. But I do believe in that stuff, and I'll tell you why. I was in such a deep, dark hole, and I kept looking for ways to get out—*people* to get me out. But I just kept sinking deeper and deeper—so deep that I knew it would take a literal miracle to get me out. Finally everything caved in at once—my health, my finances, my past that I couldn't elude, my eating disorder, even my facade of having it all together. All of it just crumbled.

"I figured the only thing that could save me from all that was something *much* bigger than I am. Much bigger than any person I've ever known—and I've known some powerful people. I finally broke down and prayed for God to either turn my life around or let me die."

I shrugged. "Apparently He still had plans for me."

"And now everything's just magically okay with you?" Tamara asked sarcastically.

"Of course not. You don't get to pray, 'God, please let there be no weeds in my garden when I go outside' and not do any work. If you don't go pull the darn weeds, they'll still be there. What I've come to realize is that God, that faith—your middle name by the way—gives you strength when you can't move a muscle, answers when there are none, and help in places you never would have thought to look. It opens your eyes to the miracles around you. And girl, if your life isn't an example of God saving your butt repeatedly, then I don't know whose is. You've been through worse than I have, with fewer resources, and you're still here. Plus, I swore I'd never talk to you again, yet here I am. You tell me who that was, if not God?"

"It was my bada** momster."

"I only wish I were as strong as you give me credit for. I'm not. I gave up trying to be queen of the universe long ago. Well, maybe not that long ago."

"But I can't even walk into a church without my childhood haunting me," said Tamara, tears in her eyes. "It makes me sick when I think of Dad being a minister."

"I know. I had the same issue for a lot of years. But Dad wasn't God. He was a flawed man. And as flawed as he was, I believe he wanted to be better. He just didn't have the tools. That's not a good excuse for you to give up like he did. Besides, I've come to see God very differently from the angry, judgmental deity that Dad preached about. My relationship with Christ is about peace, love, mercy, forgiveness—especially for myself—and, best of all, salvation. You will develop your own relationship with Him if you give Him a chance. It's *your* relationship, not Dad's. And it's personal."

Tamara looked as if she was letting what she'd heard marinate. "I'm skeptical," she said, "but I'm willing to try."

I nodded my affirmation. The room was quiet.

"I love you," she said. "Hey, my birthday is next week. I know what I want for it."

"What's that?"

"I want you to come to an AA meeting with me." Seeing me roll my eyes, she added, "I went to church with you."

I didn't have an answer for that, so I had to agree.

The meeting I attended with Tamara marked another step in my own healing. I learned more in that ninety-minute session than in the years I'd spent coaching people with addiction. The difference, I realized, was simply *listening*. Not giving advice, not helping. Just hearing their stories. Their fear. Their pain. Their challenges.

My assumptions and judgments deteriorated further. People were not there to make light of their addiction, though humor was frequently used as a way to connect.

As Tamara and I were leaving, a veteran attender stopped me and asked, "Is this your first meeting?"

"Yeah, I came with my sister."

"Ah. You're here as a favor."

"Yeah. And I'm glad I came. It was very helpful to hear the other perspective. I guess I was busy feeling my own anxiety and pain because of what her addiction did to our family."

Looking intensely into my eyes, he said, "If you had to spend ten minutes in Tamara's head, you'd jump out screaming like you were being chased by Freddy Krueger."

Sounded like someone I knew: me, of course.

In that moment I saw that Tamara and I weren't so different. I would never consider myself "cured" of an eating disorder, despite thirteen years without any symptoms. I knew only too well how quickly it could sneak up on me if I wasn't vigilant about focusing on my faith and managing my stress and negative thoughts.

To be healed isn't the same as being cured. But to be healed is to feel mended—whole again after being broken.

"I'm going to make you proud," Tamara said as we exited the building. "I'm not going to let you down."

"That's because you're afraid of me," I said, laughing.

Tamara leaned over and kissed my cheek.

———

Tamara's struggles didn't end there. She relapsed again. Fortunately, I'm the girl who doesn't believe in fairy tales—or fairy-tale endings. So when this story didn't have one, I wasn't surprised. And this time I was much better equipped to handle what happened. I was saddened but not shocked. Angry, but not "done." Hurt but not hopeless.

Just as my life transformation has been messy, painful, and real, my sister's, obviously, has been too. As much as we all love happy endings, the reality is that we are all works in progress, with broken pieces—and hopefully, with repairs.

We win. We lose. We carry on.

We soar. We crash. We pick ourselves up.

Or not. The choice is usually our own. But, sadly, sometimes the disease wins. So Tamara is having to live with the painful truth that no matter what our intentions, our actions have consequences, sometimes harsh ones. Even if we are forgiven, we must deal with the aftermath of our actions.

Fortunately, Tamara has never given up in the face of this sobering reality. She continues learning new skills and growing in her faith and receiving help for her mental health, which had been the missing link for years. Tamara now realizes that her desire to self-medicate comes from the mental anguish she feels when her brain is not balanced. The noise in her head can be deafening. It's not a single or simple issue. At Amen clinics we call these the four circles: biology (genetics, head injuries, diseases, etc.), psychology (how a person thinks), social (who you spend time with), and spiritual (what gives your life meaning). The circles are like four tires on a car. If one goes flat, the car doesn't drive correctly. If more than one malfunctions, the car will probably crash. Tamara finally crashed. But she is still fighting and I believe she will survive and thrive. More importantly, she believes it. As long as she continues to get up and learns from each fall, it's never a failure. My hope is that she develops the skills of a warrior.

———————

One month before the world all but stopped due to the Covid-19 virus, and shortly after Tamara began struggling intensely with mental health issues related to a reaction to psychiatric medication, my nieces came to live with us. Tamara had done the most unselfish thing she could think of for her children. She had asked us to help raise them and create the consistent, predictable environment they needed, until she could do it herself.

"I love them more than anything," Tamara told me, weeping. "But love without stability isn't enough to raise healthy children. I love them too much to keep hurting them. I will never give up, but I need time."

It's that unselfish love that softened me most. In spite of her addiction and mental anguish, Tamara fought when her kids were in foster care. And then, in spite of her own shame, she loved them enough to let them move in with us while she healed. That I could respect.

Do I regret the up-down-up-down struggle to help my sister, knowing that—at least for now—the ending wasn't the fairy tale we'd hoped for? Not in the least. We helped save two scared little girls, which could change their lives and the lives of any children they might bring into the world. And I found something I hadn't even realized I'd lost.

When this episode with Tamara began, I had an overwhelming project. Now, after all the struggle, I had something I'd never expected to find: a sister. Not a saint, but a sister.

Tamara's relapse didn't change that. Nor did it change the fact that the year-long struggle to help Tamara get her children back brought a new dimension of healing to me. After all the years, all the tears, all the trials and tribulations, I had learned it was okay for the warrior to let down her shield to become the "me" she'd been afraid to be. The me that had to look inward, beyond all the scars and battle-ready armor to the vulnerable and broken girl that I hadn't dared confront.

The me with—dare I admit it?—a *heart*.

CHAPTER 18

WARRIOR IN THE GARDEN

A student says to his master, "Master, you teach me to
fight, but you speak of peace. How do you reconcile
the two?" The master replies, "It is better to be a
warrior in a garden than a gardener in a war."

—Unknown

The world was in chaos. Three months of global quarantine—thanks to
Covid-19—was beginning to lift. But that was the stillness before the
storm. The pandemic before the pandemonium. Riots were erupting in major
cities across the country as the world protested the senseless death of a Black
man named George Floyd at the hands of a police officer, Derek Chauvin.

The pain from the past four years, since Daniel and I first got the call
that our nieces had been placed in foster care, had faded like the edges of an
old black-and-white photo—the image visible but no longer crisp. Life had
settled into a comfortable routine in spite of quarantine—or maybe because
of it. Yet there was a shadow over our newfound peace, knowing the world
had gone mad.

"I hate saying this, with everything happening in the world, but I don't mind having to stay home—when home is here," said fifteen-year-old Alize. "I've been through a lot worse than being stuck in a nice house with plenty of food and people I love."

"I'm more than fine with it," said Amelie, now ten. "I feel safe in this house."

"But I'm not sure if I'll ever get used to the quiet here, and I don't mean from quarantine or curfew," Alize said. "It's almost too peaceful. Until we moved here, I'd never had a family gathering without fighting and yelling—or lots of booze."

"I used to feel the same way," I said, hoping to validate her feelings. "After growing up in chaos, it felt wrong when everything was quiet and peaceful. Now I can't imagine my home being any other way."

Chloe appeared and squeezed in between her cousins, and Alize put an arm around her. "I can't imagine what you guys have been through," she said. "The idea of being in foster care is my worst nightmare." Turning to me sheepishly, she said. "I'm just really scared that nothing is ever going to be normal again." Tears welled up in her eyes. "There is so much illness and hatred in the world. So much injustice. I've had a good life. I haven't experienced the things you guys have. But suddenly everything seems so insane—scary. I want to do something, but I feel so . . . helpless."

I was proud of my daughter's ability to reason through her emotions clearly. "Don't ever apologize for *not* being traumatized or for having your feelings," I said.

"How did *you* finally change the cycle?" Alize asked, looking at me.

"Basically, I was tired of feeling like life was always beyond my control. I hated feeling like a victim, so I learned to take responsibility. Metaphorically speaking, I became a warrior instead of a victim or a bystander waiting to be rescued. Proactive instead of reactive."

"Sometimes I feel dirty because of where I came from," said Alize. "I feel like I'm not as good as other people. I'm not sure how to change that."

"I can relate," I said. "Most of my life I was striving to fit in but never quite felt like I was good enough—until I realized that it's the brokenness and imperfections that give me my strength, my unique brand of beauty, even my ability to fight for myself and help others."

"So can I learn to fight?" Amelie grinned. "I want to take karate like you."

I smiled. "You won't get an argument from me, but you're already a fighter, honey. I'd like you to think about becoming a warrior instead. Warriors can fight, but they're able to *avoid* the fight whenever possible—and learn to enjoy the peacefulness."

Standing, I said, "For now I need peaceful young warriors to help me finish organizing the garage. There are dozens of boxes to get ready for donation."

————

"Wait! Not that one," I called as Daniel helped load the last of the donation boxes into the back of the SUV. "That's full of keepsakes, meaningless to anyone but me."

I sat and opened the chipped wooden case filled with mementos, neatly cataloguing forty years of tragedy and triumph: my life.

Daniel leaned over me and removed a note from the top. "I was so proud of you for the work you did with these residents," he said. The note was from Charlie, a recovering addict whom I'd been privileged to help in his journey toward better health. He was among the many folks I had feared when, with great reluctance, I first spoke to the group of addicts at Leslie's rehab center more than eight years ago—people who'd become dear to me in the years since.

With fondness I recalled that day—and another day. In my mind I was back in the cavernous meeting room honoring Charlie and dozens of others who had completed the program.

"I've lost thirty-five pounds," he said, patting his belly. "I finally have a six-pack—but not the kind that will get me arrested!"

Laughter and cheers erupted throughout the audience.

"You rock, Charlie!" I said. And he did.

Thinking of Charlie made me remember Trudy, a woman who had struggled for purpose and significance.

"I hate myself," she had said during a particularly powerful women-only session. "I'm a terrible mother. I lost my kids because of my addiction."

Sitting across from her, I tilted my head in search of answers. Recalling my conversation with Byron Katie years before, I was reminded of a time when I hated myself too. I asked Trudy Katie's questions, and she struggled painfully through them as I had years before. Then we came to the most powerful part: the turnaround, changing a thought to its opposite and crystalizing the truth behind a torturous belief. An hour later her thoughts had been cracked, and new possibilities emerged.

"The only turnaround I can think of is that I was a bad mother to myself," Trudy said. "I didn't discipline my thoughts or my actions, and I didn't get help when I knew I was in trouble."

Bingo! The moment of truth.

A smile slowly warmed her face, the first we'd seen from her.

In the days that followed, Trudy learned how to start disciplining her thoughts. She completely changed her diet, found new confidence, and reconciled with an estranged daughter.

In hindsight I could see how God had used those people and events to heal me and prepare me to work with Tamara. It was in their stories that I'd found purpose and meaning for my own life and hope for my sister and nieces. The stories were also my reward, and Miguel's was among the greatest.

Miguel was the one who scared me most in the beginning, which is why his story had the greatest impact on my own healing. His admission photo showed a hardened, hulking gangster with a perpetual scowl. But his graduation photo looked like a completely different person. In it he held up his old pants, which were large enough to fit two of the new "him." Miguel was proof of God's power. The miracle of healing with kindness and love.

Miguel, I learned, had lost custody of his six children when the LAPD gang unit broke down his door a year before our meeting. "When I started the program, I was depressed, hopeless, gloomy, and overweight," he said. "I had no reason to live. Three times I had tried to pass the GED and three times I'd failed. I thought I was stupid.

"Now, with God's help and a clear mind—now that I know how food has been affecting me—I finally passed my GED. The brain fog is gone. My mind is clearer and sharper. I can focus. And I've lost eighty-five pounds. I never want to go back to where I was. Thank you, Tana, for teaching me about how food affects my mind. And so much more."

I nodded my appreciation, but the credit was all his. I'd only coached him; he'd done the heavy lifting.

I knew all too well that some of these people would stumble on the jagged road to sobriety, just as Tamara had. Sadly, sometimes the disease wins. But the very fact that I was focused on their stories of transformation, rooting for their success, was a testament to my own progress.

Recalling the huge chasm between me and folks like Charlie, Trudy, and Miguel on the day I reluctantly stood on that stage to speak to them, I now realized we were more alike than we were different. For all the help I'd given them, I'd received double the healing. And if I'd become a warrior, so had they.

"Never forget," I'd said to the class on our last day together, "your history is not your destiny."

"Well, look what I found," Daniel said smugly, snapping me out of my reverie. I smiled when I noticed the paper in his hand.

"Don't look so proud of yourself," I said.

He was holding a dog-eared program from a gathering of the American Academy of Anti-Aging Medicine—A4M—at the massive Las Vegas Convention Center. "I *am* proud of myself—for pushing you. But you knocked it out of the park."

"It was pretty surreal, presenting to thousands of doctors from around the world," I said, smiling. "From speaking to addicts to speaking to doctors. Me, the scared little girl. Who would've predicted that?"

I could still hear the applause as I took to the stage in that huge venue and the familiar feeling I carried with me—that I wasn't good enough. That I didn't belong. That I wasn't worthy of this honor. When the e-mail invitation arrived, in fact, I had thought it was a mistake; obviously, they'd meant to send it to Daniel, who was an instructor for their program and a sought-after speaker. I was only a student of A4M.

I had replied to the e-mail, informing them of their mistake and ensuring them that I'd forward it to my husband. A quick reply came, reassuring me that the invite was, indeed, for me. No offense to Daniel, they said, but we want you to speak on our main stage about using food to heal the body and mind.

I was dumbfounded. Me? Speaking to doctors from around the world? What did I have to teach the very people who had taught me much of what I knew? I was flattered to be asked but planned to politely decline, believing myself unqualified.

"Are you kidding?" said Daniel. "The academy isn't in the habit of inviting just anybody to speak for them. They've done their homework. They've seen your bestselling book and know of your medical background. They've watched you on PBS. You absolutely have to do this. It's a huge honor."

So there I was, being introduced as an author, as an expert on food and health, and as someone who was working on her second black belt. I was so jittery I thought I was going to be sick. But as I began to tell my story, passion replaced fear.

"I'm going to tell you a story about a sick little girl who wanted to be a doctor, Bible-believing churches, two gorillas, a group of drug addicts and criminals—and what they have in common," I began.

The inspiration for my presentation, of course, was my life experience—in particular, the work I'd done to help launch the Daniel Plan at Saddleback Church and the work I'd done to help transform the food at the drug rehab center. But I also told the story of Bebac and Mokolo, two gorillas from the Cleveland Metroparks Zoo, who were healed of heart disease and neurotic behaviors by changing their diet from processed biscuits to their natural diet of greens, nuts, seeds, berries, and bamboo.

In each example I gave, food was the primary "medicine."

"We are in a war for our health," I said, "against highly processed, pesticide-sprayed, genetically modified, high-glycemic, low-fiber food."

I went on to tell the audience about being a latchkey kid raised on Frosted

Flakes, Lucky Charms, and Cap'n Crunch. About my murdered uncle, giving my grandmother insulin shots at age eleven, and nearly being raped at fifteen. About my three go-rounds with thyroid cancer and how stress and low-quality food had combined to sabotage my health. I told them about how I'd needed to become my own advocate if I wanted a better life—and to become a warrior for my health.

The presentation was going splendidly. I noted nods of approval, indicating I had my audience's attention. Finally I told of my work with the drug rehab centers and how a group of gangbangers, criminals, and drug addicts had learned the healing power of food and changed their lives.

The screen lit up with the final words that Miguel had shared in his testimonial:

> My life was a mess. Now it's a message.
> I've been tested. Now I have a testimony.
> I was a victim. Now I'm victorious.
> I've been through trials. Now I am triumphant!

I could barely read the words because my eyes filled with tears. I stared at them, trying to regain my composure, feeling weak and small in an arena of accomplished professionals. And then I went off script.

"I have a confession," I said, through tears. "When I started working with this group . . . of addicts . . . I didn't want to do it. I was judgmental. I asked why God would put me there, knowing my past. Was He punishing me?" Taking a breath, I continued with a shaky voice. "But God knew. This has been the most rewarding thing I've ever done."

The applause startled me. Warmed me. Encouraged me. As did the individuals who approached me at the conclusion of my presentation. Dr. Joe Maroon, clinical professor and vice chairman of the Department of Neurological Surgery at the University of Pittsburgh Medical Center—and the team neurosurgeon for the Pittsburgh Steelers— came up to me, beaming.

"Best presentation of the day," he said. "Tears and cheers!"

"I'm a heart surgeon," another doctor told me. "I don't cry. But today you made me cry. And by the way, you may have wanted to be a doctor, but I've always wanted to be a *New York Times* bestselling author. Thank you. You inspired me."

I was walking on air, having just spoken to my second toughest and second favorite audience ever. The first, of course, was the group from the drug rehab center, the people I had nearly backed out on but had ended up embracing—and now had the privilege of honoring in my talk.

In the afterglow I saw my two favorite women, my mother and Chloe, who had flown to Vegas to support me. How blessed I was that my mother and my daughter were two of my best friends. My mother, as always, looked stunning, and Chloe was cute as ever. Both wrapped me in huge hugs. Chloe, a smart but strong-willed nine-year-old, held my hand sweetly.

"Mom?" she said, eyes locked on mine.

"Yes, Chloe?" I asked, beaming with pride.

"You don't know *everything*, you know," she said. "Like, sometimes ice cream is *good* for you." A mischievous smile threatened to emerge.

It was vintage Chloe, her beautiful childlike wisdom capping a spectacular day. I melted into a puddle of pain-seared joy and drew her closer.

"You're right," I said. "I don't know everything. But I do know this: miracles are possible."

I was looking at one. And so was she.

AFTERWORD
God's Golden Repair

The world breaks every one and afterward
many are strong at the broken places.

—ERNEST HEMINGWAY, FROM *A FAREWELL TO ARMS*

I'm not the only one in this story who found transformation and healing. As I write these words, Tamara has struggled but has never given up. She's been sober for more than a year, the longest she's ever gone without substances to numb the pain of sexual abuse, domestic abuse, childhood trauma, and more. And she continues to heal.

Tamara's daughters, Alize and Amelie, live with us now. Both are honor students and thriving. As Alize and Amelie begin to learn new patterns of living, I am confident they will break the cycle of addiction, chaos, and drama for their own children.

Mom's prayers for Joe paid off several months before he died, when he started going to church with Mom and started praying that God would forgive him, especially for some things he'd seen and done in Vietnam. In 2004 Joe said he finally had found peace for the first time. He died only a month later.

Uncle Harold, the reformed playboy, fell head over heels in love, first with a beautiful woman named Pamela and then with God. Pamela refused to go out with him until he changed his partying ways. And he *really* liked her. After reluctantly attending church with a friend, he felt convicted and gave his life to Christ. He told me, "I'm so grateful God pursued me for all those years. His plan for my life was so much better than my own." Harold and Pamela have now been married for thirty-five years.

Daniel, in his quiet strength, has taught me much more by his actions than by his words, wise though they are. When he opened our home to my father and to my sister when they needed shelter from their storms, he affirmed me deeply. In effect he was saying: *Where you came from is where you get your strength. Your past isn't something you need to hide. Your people are my people. They're family. And the healthier they are, the healthier you are.*

Daniel's father, Lou, passed away at age ninety-one, during the writing of this book, shortly after recovering from Covid-19. Holding my husband's hand as he navigated his grief with incredible grace was a bittersweet honor. Louis Amen was an incredible man who will be greatly missed.

My relationship with Chloe is stronger and more amazing than ever. She's now a senior in high school, an honor student, and applying to colleges. She is active at church—or was before the Covid quarantine—and has an incredible heart for service. Seeing her many strengths, I make no apologies for protecting her intensely. Or for the decision to finally stop sheltering her and start preparing her.

Of all the people on my journey, my mother has made the greatest transformation. From a sixteen-year-old runaway and high school dropout, Mom evolved into a shrewd businesswoman—at a time when women had far fewer opportunities than they have now. Now seventy-three, she recently sold her internationally recognized pet-supply manufacturing company and retired a very wealthy woman, helping countless people in need as she went.

Only with the wisdom of age have I come to realize how much Mom sacrificed for me when I was growing up. For all my complaining as a child, I never remember being hungry or not having a warm bed to sleep in or clothing to wear. Most important, I never once doubted her love. I'm eternally grateful to have her as my mother.

Along the way, Mom had a spiritual metamorphosis. Whenever I ask her how she survived, she always says the same thing: "My faith."

I can relate. Both of us were broken. Both of us managed to survive. Both of us learned to thrive.

I liken the process to my favorite form of art, Kintsugi. The name in Japanese means "golden joinery"—more commonly known as "golden repair." It's created by mending broken pottery with liquified gold. The philosophy rests on the premise that the pottery isn't useless because of the cracks and scars, but special for that very reason. The cracks and scars aren't something to hide, but something to display with pride for the unique stories told in each break.

My story. Your story. Each can be eternally shaped—as can the stories of generations to come—with God's golden repair.

ACKNOWLEDGMENTS

The gratitude I feel for the many people I was blessed to learn from along my journey is difficult to put into words. The following people have been instrumental in my personal journey, as well as this story:

Daniel, my amazing husband, for nudging me beyond my comfort zone to take a journey of healing and ultimately to be courageous enough to tell my story.

Mom, for your never-ending strength and unfailing love—and for passing on your tenacity.

Chloe, for the inspiration you've given me to be a better person since the day you were born.

The beneficiaries of the Salvation Army, who became warriors for the health of their bodies and brains.

Greg Johnson, my agent, for believing in this project.

Dr. Lisa Riggs, for helping me believe in myself.

Dr. Curt Rouanzoin, for your ongoing support.

Tamara, for letting me tell your story of transformation and for being my sister.

My nieces Alize and Amelie, for your courage.

Krissy and Tom McCrystal, for loving me when I wasn't very lovable.

Master Bob White, for your ongoing guidance and friendship.

Trisha Williford Heyer, for your early contribution to this project.

And, finally, to the friends who struggled along with me: thank you.

ABOUT THE AUTHOR

Tana Amen is a *New York Times* bestselling author, vice president of the Amen Clinics, a neurosurgical ICU trauma nurse, and a world-renowned health and fitness expert. She has won the hearts of millions with her simple yet effective strategies to help anyone optimize their lifestyle and win the fight for a strong body, mind, and spirit. Tana holds a second-degree black belt in Kenpo Karate and a black belt in Taekwondo. Tana and her husband, Dr. Daniel Amen, have four children and five grandchildren.